8·82

GRAMMATICAL INSIGHTS
INTO
THE NEW TESTAMENT

GRAMMATICAL INSIGHTS
INTO
THE NEW TESTAMENT

by

NIGEL TURNER, Ph.D., M.Th., B.D.

EDINBURGH: T. & T. CLARK, 36 GEORGE STREET

PRINTED IN SCOTLAND BY
CLARK CONSTABLE (1982) LTD, EDINBURGH
FOR
T. & T. CLARK LTD, EDINBURGH

0 567 01017 1

FIRST PRINTED 1965
LATEST IMPRESSION . . . 1983

CONTENTS

4. ST. PAUL'S TEACHING

5. SAINT JOHN

6. OTHER WRITERS

7. THE LANGUAGE OF JESUS AND HIS DISCIPLES 174

PREFACE

I quote from the *New English Bible, New Testament*, copyright 1961, by permission of Oxford and Cambridge University Presses ; from the *Revised Standard Version of the New Testament*, copyrighted 1946 and 1952, by permission of Thomas Nelson and Sons, Ltd., acting on behalf of the National Council of the Churches of Christ in America, the copyright owner ; from J. Moffatt's *New Translation* of the New Testament by permission of Hodder and Stoughton, Ltd. ; from E. V. Rieu's *The Four Gospels* by permission of Penguin Books, Ltd. ; from J. B. Phillips' translation by permission of Geoffrey Bles, Ltd. ; and from the privately circulated *Greek-English Diglot for the Use of Translators*, by permission of the British and Foreign Bible Society.

I should like to record my gratitude to Messrs. T. and T. Clark, for their encouragement to me personally, and for their long-standing enterprise in the cause of Biblical scholarship generally. They share my hope that scholar and student alike will derive a deeper insight and interest in Holy Scripture through accepting the challenge of the problems which are discussed in this study of the language of the New Testament. Our book is published in the sincere belief that the grammarian's toil in the back room should be humbly offered to God in the service of his whole Church.

I am grateful to the printers, Morrison and Gibb, Ltd., for their important and efficient co-operation.

Nigel Turner

Hitchin,
St. James's Day, 1965.

ABBREVIATIONS

A.V.—The Authorized Version of the Bible, 1611 (the King James Version)

Expos. Times—The Expository Times, periodical published by T. & T. Clark, edited by C. L. Mitton.

mg—margin

Moulton-Howard-Turner, *Grammar—A Grammar of New Testament Greek*, T. & T. Clark, vol. I by J. H. Moulton, 1906 ; vol. II (Accidence) by J. H. Moulton and W. F. Howard, 1919–29 ; vol. III (Syntax) by Nigel Turner, 1963.

N.E.B.—*The New English Bible* (*New Testament*), Oxford and Cambridge, 1961.

P.G.—J. P. Migne, *Patrologia Graeca*, Paris, 1857–66.

R.S.V.—The American Revised Standard Version of the New Testament, Nelson, 1946.

R.V.—The Revised Version of the New Testament, 1881.

PRONUNCIATION OF GREEK WORDS

Greek is transliterated for the benefit of the reader who is not a specialist. The following pronunciation is thought to approximate to that which was current in the first century A.D.

a as in hat	u as in put
ā as in father	ai as in aisle
e as in pet	au as in umlaut
ē as in fete	ei as in eight
i as in pin	ou as in through
o as in hot	oi as in oil
ō as in host	

WHY GRAMMAR?

Since it is not common practice to rely much on grammar when it is sought to interpret the Bible, my apology must be that the mechanics of speech provide a delicate and flexible means of communication which is worth scientific study.

Some aspects of grammar are less popular than others. Etymology, now more often known as accidence or *Formenlehre*, which is the study of words in themselves, that is, the conjugation and declension and spelling of each separate word regardless of the rest of the sentence, is the kind of grammar which has given the whole discipline a reputation for pedantry, and it interests no one but the specialist. However, the intelligent reader will appreciate that syntax ought not to share this reputation. Syntax is the way single words are knit together in a phrase or sentence to form ideas, and so it is the accepted means by which one man presents his own mental images to another. It is the study of the way we speak, and only a desert island-castaway would consider this to be academic or antiquarian. Everyone who speaks has his own syntax, as well as his own vocabulary. All the time he is projecting his personality in a way which is satisfying to himself and interesting to others, by means of musical composition or performance, painting, dancing, gardening, dressing, loving, and a thousand other ways, but perhaps the most expressive means of communizing personality is normal conversation. If by chance a man stays to examine the structure of the last sentence he uttered, in that moment he becomes a grammarian, in the special field of syntax, a scientist however modest in the most humane of all investigation. Moreover, that last sentence, examined expertly, might evoke some learned discussion which in turn would illuminate the speaker's idioverse of taste, education, hobbies and even moral fibre.

The study becomes crucial when it begins to take account of the speech-patterns of the different New Testament authors, and supremely of Jesus. It gives aid to the commentator and preacher which is unsurpassed for detail and power of insight. This is a science, not a field for unbridled imagination nor for reading things into an innocent text. All the discipline and patience which men devote to empirical science is demanded and the results are as reliable.

The reader may be disappointed if syntax takes him into the byways

of holy Scripture as well as along the high roads of doctrine and controversies. The research is necessarily microscopic. He may allege
that it fusses too much with adverbs, particles, varieties of subordinate
clauses, moods and tenses. It puts everyone's speech through a vast
number of filters and measures. Nothing is overlooked, not even the
order of words and clauses in the sentence. So, although syntax can
illuminate the large places, perhaps its most valuable contribution for
the careful student will be in sifting out the unobserved revealing
characteristics which distinguish one man from another. It brings
St. John to life and helps the reader to feel his emotional and mental
pulse ; it brings the reader close enough to St. Paul's mind and heart
to understand exactly why he used that very phrase and no other. By
a massive display of detail it makes the Word of God live again.

The first reader I have in mind is trained in other fields, with no
special knowledge of Greek. He will probably be grateful for the
transliteration of Greek and Hebrew words, but will reject over-
simplification. My other reader is the specialist or student who does not
seek a simplification of my Syntax volume in Moulton's *Grammar*,
but rather an expansion of that work in certain directions which were
not feasible in a text-book, where interesting discussions have to be
sacrificed to completeness and breadth of range.* In the present book
we can relax over a few important conclusions of syntax study which
are of interest to the general reader as well as to the scholar, but the
book is not simply a popularization. References are always given in
full and are directed to the primary authorities. I hope that scholars
too will be interested in the conclusions.

Obscure places in biblical interpretation have recently been illumined
by accurate knowledge of the meaning of *single* words. New Testament
"word-books" usually demonstrate that a large proportion of Greek
vocabulary has been consecrated to Christian use and that biblical
words had gained a new meaning which is different from that of secular
Greek. "Biblical theology," which had arisen from this, has recently
been discussed by Dr. James Barr, who mentions the dangers of the
exclusively lexicographical approach in New Testament interpretation
and wisely hints that syntax and style are more likely to be rewarding
than the meaning of individual words (vocabulary) ;† nevertheless
Dr. Barr will find that, in this realm, Semitic influence on Christian
language and the same process of Christian transformation of speech
are even clearer than in vocabulary. Just as a sentence is more

---

* The book is referred to constantly in footnotes, when its contributions to
exegesis are expanded in the present work.
† J. Barr, *The Semantics of Biblical Language*, Oxford, 1961, p. 233. "Theological thought of the type found in the NT has its characteristic linguistic
expression not in the word individually but in the word-combination or sentence."

revealing than a single word, so the examination of a writer's syntax and style is that much more important to a biblical commentator. It is not surprising that fewer books have been written on this subject than on vocabulary, because whereas students of vocabulary can quickly look up lists of words in concordances and indices, in the field of syntax the study is more circuitous. There is no help except in a few selective grammars and monographs, so that the worker really must work his way through all the texts in Greek.

The "biblical theology" which has become characteristic of this century does not necessarily involve a return to fundamentalism, but it does at least assume that the message of the Bible is the supreme authority for Christian faith and the gospel. Then the ways part. Some theologians, no less interested in interpretation but more careful than others to preserve the smallest niceties in representing biblical revelation, are earmarked " Neo-Fundamentalists." Another school of biblical theologians is prone to base its teaching on a vaguer generalization of the Bible text, content with a vernacular translation in place of the original and tending to decry the serious pursuit of Hebrew and Greek. Such an attitude deserves a rebuke. " One who made it his life's work to interpret French literature, but who could only read it in an English translation, would not be taken seriously ; yet it is remarkable how many ministers of religion week by week expound a literature that they are unable to read save in translation ! "*

In the same journal a Toronto teacher indicates the vividness of the Greek language and its importance for New Testament interpretation. "A Greek," he says, " can throw up a word into full emphasis by adding a particle to it, by actually uttering one little sound." That is of course a small measure of the benefit of being literate in Greek and underlines all the more the mischief of the present tendency in the churches. Dr. Ward says that he has been told by ministers that there is no need to "waste time on Greek. It is all in the commentaries."†
However, a little book by a religious of the Community of St. Mary the Virgin, Wantage, encouraging ordinary Christians to learn Hebrew and New Testament Greek, may be a brighter sign of the times.‡

There are those whose way to God is mainly through visual images, material or mental. The images of the Bible speak to both catholics and protestants without the intervention of concepts or the reasoned intellectual argument which belongs to theology. If images alone bring these believers into God's presence and give assurance of his love, they are worthy of minute study, of careful preservation, and accurate understanding. An image marred by dust or scarred by misuse fails

* H. H. Rowley, in *Expos. Times*, LXXIV, 12, Sept., 1963, p. 383.
 † R. A. Ward, *Expos. Times*, LXXI, 9, June, 1960, p. 267.
 ‡ *This is Life*, by a religious of the C.S.M.V., Wantage, S.C.M. Press, 1961.

to convey its message until it is carefully restored and becomes once more a meaningful symbol. Moreover, an image ceases to be a real symbol when it is reproduced in a book of photographs, for nothing can take the place of the symbol itself, in which every line and bright detail is visible and evocative.

The mental images of the Bible are not always faithfully preserved in translation. While the effort of acquiring Greek is beyond the resources of many New Testament readers, the following pages should indicate some of the ways the images are blurred in present translations.

CHAPTER ONE

THE GRAMMAR OF GOD

1. GOD

" God is love " (*I John* 4⁸)

Honest to God has acquainted large numbers of people with the Tillich-Bonhoeffer-Bultmann school of theology, and with the answers which are being given in some intellectual circles to the question, " Does God exist ? "*

It represents a secession from the traditional belief that God " is." Attributes are no longer predicated of him. For instance, on what we thought was excellent authority, we always believed that God " is Love," but accepting the postulates of current existentialist interpretations of Christianity we might be tempted to turn the apostle's dictum inside out and say, " Love is God." Existentialists insist that God is not " out there." The supra-natural realm is a fiction and the term " God " is meaningless outside natural experience. The depths of that experience are God, " the inexhaustible depth and ground of all being." One is urged to forget all that one had learned and " know that God means depth." If love is deep enough, momentous enough, to any person, that depth is God. Love is God. But you cannot turn round and say that God " is love," for that would be to suppose that God has some independent existence.

If one cares to be a little unrigorous over grammar, one may argue that this is precisely what St. John is saying. One has but to ignore the Greek definite article and the phrase can be turned round to mean, " Love is God." But the author of *Honest to God* (p. 52) is prepared to admit that " it is what the Apostle rather carefully refuses to do." St. John inserts the definite article in just the right position to give the sense, " God is love." Otherwise we are presented with an " anti-theistic " idea that God is no more than the relationships which we experience in life, and in spite of everything Bishop Robinson does not want to be driven to this. He seems to prefer the axiom, " Where love is, God is." God is *in* the experience. The axiom is not pushed to the existentialist limit of asserting that God is merely love, although that might be acceptable to those who, more consistent than a bishop would

* J. A. T. Robinson, *Honest to God*, S.C.M. paperback, 1963.

5

like, are nevertheless committed as inextricably as he to the unitary naturalism of modern science and just as anxious to preserve their Christian affiliations.

In view of current controversies it is crucial that St. John should not be quoted for the view that God is a predicate of love, and that human experience can exhaust the Deity. The grammar of the definite article forbids. Nevertheless, in all fairness it should be pointed out that St. John elsewhere does make use of the phrase, " Love is *ek Theou* " (I John 4⁷). Dr. Robinson quotes this (p. 53) but he assumes the normal interpretation of the phrase, which is, " Love is *from* God." It would suit the Christian existentialist better to exploit a legitimate alternative interpretation of the Greek. The preposition *ek* ("from") may be the partitive *ek*, and then the phase becomes the same as "Love is God," or "Love is divine," for the partitive idea involves a partaking of the nature of the object in the genitive case, and St. John would mean that godhead is predicated of Love. Elsewhere he says that " *ek* the crowd " heard Jesus's words, when he means " a crowd " (John 7⁴⁰). He is addicted to the partitive *ek* and uses it frequently when he wishes to express the closest identification, e.g. " If you were *ek* the world (worldly), the world would love its own " (15¹⁹).*

Urging this, I neither share the existentialist thinking nor am impressed by the Tillich-Bonhoeffer quest to follow up the demythologizing of Satan and evil spirits by a further demythologizing of God and good angels. Hardly less satisfactory, however, is the quite recent reaction to this, exemplified in the attempt to distinquish between *evil* as such, which can be safely demythologized, and *God* or *good* as such, which cannot be demythologized, on the ground that good has an essential existence denied to evil. The notion itself is not recent ; it has appeared from time to time in Christian theology among those who were predisposed towards modes of thought characteristic of Idealism. There is some philosophical justification for the distinction. There is no biblical justification, however.

" The only God " or "God alone "? (John 5⁴⁴)

Devotion to grammar is a firm basis for exegesis, but there have been occasions when it has outstripped knowledge. An example is the general renunciation of the A.V. in John 5⁴⁴, where Jesus is represented as saying to the Jews, " How can ye believe, which receive honour one of another, and seek not the honour that cometh from God only ? " The Revisers of 1881 were not satisfied, and all subsequent English versions have followed closely the Greek word-order, correcting what was apparently an oversight in earlier versions. So the R.V. altered

* Moulton-Howard-Turner, *Grammar*, Vol. III, p. 260.

" God only " to " the only God." It appeared to conform to sound principles, because elsewhere in the New Testament when the adjective *monos* is adverbial (e.g. " God only "), it is not found between the article and noun but either before the article (as Luke 5^{21} 6^4, Heb. 9^7) or after the noun (Matt. 4^4 12^4 17^8) ; in consequence, in John 5^{44}, *monos* occurring between the article and noun ought to be taken closely with the noun and interpreted as " unique," " lonely," " sole existing." That is reasonable, but one instance outside the New Testament presents a different picture. In the Septuagint version of Susanna (verse 15) *monos* occurs and, although it is not between an article and the noun, it is in a position where it must be taken closely with a noun from the grammatical point of view. Yet the *sense* of the passage makes a close connection quite impossible, and we are warned against making word-order decisive for the meaning of *monos*. Susanna " went in with *two only* maids " must mean that she took with her *only two* maids, not that the maids which she took were unique or lonely! Grammatically one expects the word " only " to occur as near as possible to any word which it may qualify ; one feels the strangeness of its position between " two " and " maids." All the more careful then must one be with John 5^{44} where the context demands the rendering of A.V., for one must rule out any suggestion that the Jews would accept glory from many gods as opposed to one ; and so to speak of " the only God " in this context is unsuitable. On the contrary, the spiritual danger facing the Jewish people was, according to Jesus, that they were accepting glory from other sources as well as God. He reminded them that glory should be sought *only* from him.

Grammarians must feel uneasy about this, because there are no other instances where *monos* with the adverbial meaning occurs between article and noun. However, the history of the text of this particular verse proves to be instructive. One very ancient and important variant leaves out the word " God " and reads simply " from the Only One."* Although it is supported by the Bodmer papyrus no. 2, dating from the second or third century, the variant cannot be correct ; it must reflect a very early mistake in scribal copying, for it is a clear instance of *homoioteleuton*.† A sight of the Greek will reveal how easily the mistake might have arisen.

* Before the discovery of the Bodmer papyri was known to the world of scholarship this reading was attributed to only the following : Codex Vaticanus, the Washington Codex (called the Freer Gospels), two Old Latin manuscripts of the fourth century, a Coptic version (not very ancient), Armenian manuscripts, and a quotation by Origen as early as about A.D. 200, with one by Eusebius about a century later.

† I.e. the mistake of omitting a word which has the like ending to a word coming before it, so that the scribe's eye travels back from his copy to this second word which, because of its like ending, he thinks he has already copied.

ΠΑΡΑ ΤΟΥ (ΘΕΟΥ) ΜΟΝΟΥ ΟΥ ΖΗΤΕΙΤΕ. The mistakenly omitted word is in brackets, in the position in which I think it should go ; the like endings of *ΤΟΥ* and *ΘΕΟΥ* are apparent. The mistake had been made so early and had become so widespread that when it was eventually noticed, the correction may at first have been tentatively recorded in the margin. Later, when it became part of the text, it may have been carelessly inserted in the wrong place : that is, after *ΜΟΝΟΥ* instead of before it, especially as this was equally possible grammatically. The original position of *ΜΟΝΟΥ* may well have been just before the verb " seek not," and the meaning therefore was, " The glory that comes only from God you seek not."

By this supposition we return to the A.V.

Truth and the Truth

In the Johannine epistles, as in the fourth gospel, *alētheia* ("truth") is a key word, and one may ponder whether its interpretation is affected by the presence or absence of the definite article. Since the article occurs when Jesus is reported as saying, " I am the Truth " (John 14[6]), one assumes that when *alētheia* is preceded by the definite article it will normally be personalized, have a capital letter, and be synonymous with Jesus himself. Subject to certain conditions, that is likely to be true in biblical Greek, because often the article will transform an abstract noun into something more concrete. " Omission of the article tends to emphasize the inherent qualities of abstract nouns while the article makes them more concrete, unified and individual."[*] Inevitably there is something delicate about this distinction. Why else would articular and anarthrous *alētheia* occur together in the same sentence ? St. John discriminated, but at the same time an underlying connection was contrived by the use of the same word. One might render into English both the personalized articular *alētheia* and also the word-play, in John 8[44], like this : " Your father the Devil was a murderer from the beginning and has no standing whatever in (Christ) the *Truth*, because there is no *true sincerity* in him," reproducing *alētheia* in its two distinct senses. Another verse where they both occur together is III John 3 and here too the distinction has never been observed, since it is generally understood that the first *alētheia* (in spite of being articular) refers to an abstract characteristic of Gaius, his " sincerity " or " truthfulness," and it has escaped notice that this more intelligibly refers to Christ as the Truth. So the A.V. has : " the brethren came and testified of the *truth* that is in thee, even as thou walkest in the *truth*." The N.E.B. of 1961 also avoids the word-play and treats *alētheia* uniformly without regard to the definite article : " friends came and

---

[*] Moulton-Howard-Turner, *Grammar*, vol. III, p. 176.

told me how *true* you have been ; indeed you are *true* in your whole life." The difficulty in taking the first truth as a reference to Christ the Truth arises because it is not appreciated that *sou* need not be a personal possessive pronoun ; it is not "*thy* truth." The verb " to testify " (*marturein*) often has an indirect object in the genitive case. That is how *sou* (genitive of *su*) will comply with this construction : " the brethren came and testified *about* you *to* (Christ) the Truth." The latter noun is in the dative, signifying the person *to* whom the testimony is made. The construction is exactly paralleled by Josephus in his *Antiquities of the Jews** where he records how king Demetrius, grateful for the help given by certain Jews in quelling sedition, sent these Jews to the high priest in Jerusalem " and testified *to him* (dative case) *about* their assistance (genitive case)." There need be no clearer parallel. So much then for the first mention of *alētheia* in the verse : it is Christ the Truth. But in its second mention, when it is anarthrous, it has the abstract meaning : " even as you walk in *sincerity* (i.e. sincerely)."

It would be too naïve to suppose that because *alētheia* with the article is usually Christ the Truth it necessarily follows that without the article it is always " sincerity." Such over-simplification excludes a setting where an article which would normally be present is absent when its noun occurs as a predicate and at the same time its position in the sentence is before that of the verb. Hence it must not be presumed that there are two distinct meanings of the word *alētheia* in John 17[17]: " Sanctify them in the Truth ; thy Logos is the Truth." It is an instance of the predicate occurring before the verb " to be " and losing its definite article in consequence.[†]

Johannine teaching about truth and the Truth really amounts to this. If the word is not personalized, St. John means something like our word " sincerity." Christ is full of grace and sincerity (John 1[14]), and later he states that Jesus Christ is the origin of that same grace and sincerity (hence the need for the definite article because of ana-phora[‡]—the writer must draw attention to the recent mention of these words) : John 1[17]. True believers will worship God in a sincere and spiritual manner (4[23f.]). To the uninitiated Roman procurator there was apparently no difference between the articular and anarthrous *alētheia*, and yet the evangelist himself knew the difference, for the two are placed together in outstanding juxtaposition (John 18[38]).

---

* Refer to Benedict Niese's editio minor, vol. III, p. 143, line 23 ; i.e. Antiqu. Iud. XIII 142.

† The Greek word-order is : " Thy Logos Truth is." It is an instance of Colwell's rule. For this, see C. F. D. Moule, *An Idiom Book of New Testament Greek*, Cambridge, 1963, p. 112. Moulton-Howard-Turner, vol. III, pp. 183–4.

‡ Moulton-Howard-Turner, *Grammar*, vol. III, p. 173.

The Lord's words to Pilate refer to the Truth, not in the typically Greek or philosophical sense as an abstraction, but personalized and conceived as an attribute of God which in certain contexts is virtually equated with himself. " I was born that I should bear witness unto *the* Truth (articular). Everyone who belongs to *the* Truth (articular) hears my voice." To this Pilate replied, " What is truth?" (no article). St. John exhorted Christian believers to love one another *sincerely* (i.e. " in truth " : I John 3[18] ; so too II John 1), and he loved Gaius *sincerely* (III John 1). An adverbial phrase of this kind is *sincerely and lovingly* (i.e. " in truth and in love " : II John 3). St. John rejoiced when he found Christians who behaved *sincerely* (i.e. " in truth " : II John 4).

Indeed the phrase, " to behave in truth," is used several times and the writer does not insert the definite article except in III John 4, and that is not an exception, for it refers back to a previous mention of the word (grammatical anaphora), and it gives the meaning, " with that *same* sincerity."

The heritage of the word Truth in its background of Hebrew thought was " reliability," " stability," " faithfulness," " spoken truth," " religious knowledge." But, besides all this, *'emeth* was a principle of reality and justice which to the Hebrews had its seat in God himself. Truth to a Greek was something close to nature and reality ; it was the reverse of mere appearance or falsehood : an event, as opposed to a dream. In the context of human behaviour the Greek looked upon Truth as sincere living, not in relation to a transcendent norm but a quality which the generality of men would describe as " truthfulness." I am convinced that the Christian Church borrowed a large part of its vocabulary from Hebrew roots, and in particular that it added much that was new to the Greek word for " truth " (*alētheia*), notably the qualities of reliability, stability, faithfulness, and especially conformity to a transcendent and supernatural pattern which is nothing less than God himself. The word *alētheia* has been born again. It is normally St. John's practice to use the definite article before this word when it has the new and Christian sense. This being so, when it is said that John the Baptist bears witness to the Truth, John the Baptist is bearing witness to Christ. The Truth is said to be known by Christians, and the Truth (that is, Christ) gives them liberty (John 8[32]). Then both Christ and the Logos are equated with the truth (John 14[6] 17[17]) and so is the Spirit (I John 5[6]) ; but this association of the Truth with the Spirit in phrases such as " the Spirit of the Truth " (John 14[17] 15[26] 16[13], I John 4[6]) probably assumes the close relationship of Christ with the Spirit and especially his promise to send the Holy Spirit to believers and by this Agency to guide them into the fulness of himself, the Truth (John 16[13]). On the other hand, the witness of Christ on earth is to the Truth (18^{37}) and he utters the Truth ($8^{40, \ 45, \ 46}$, 16^7) as if it were extrinsic to himself. Nevertheless in the Johannine epistles we discover the additional idea that the Truth dwells in us (I John 1^8, II John 2) and we in the Truth (I John 2^4), and this is what St. John in the gospel says about our relationship with Christ : " Abide in me, and I in you " ($15^{4f.}$). The privilege of knowing Christ, which is fundamental in his gospel, has its direct counterpart in the phrase which St. John uses in the epistles—" knowing the Truth " (I John 2^{21}, II John 1).

One or two other phrases present some difficulty, especially the " doing " of the Truth (John 3^{21}, I John 1^6). Here the definite article is found and there is no reason for its insertion (whether because of anaphora or the presence of a preposition) except that which has guided us so far in this chapter. The article is intended to be a personalization. In this connection it is the verb " doing " (*poiein*) which is the difficulty. However, it is worth questioning the usual assumption that the phrase means " behaving (or living) truthfully (or sincerely)." There is of course such a phrase in Hebrew, but it should be observed that the Septuagint translators regularly omit the definite article when they have to render this expression. Their practice, it seems to me, lessens the probability that the phrase in St. John with the article means the same thing. For St. John the verb *poiein* may have some specialized religious significance, like " to worship " or " to be a disciple of." " The man who is *a disciple of* the Truth comes to the light so that it may be clearly seen that God is in all he does." " If we say that we have fellowship with him and walk in darkness, we lie and are not *disciples of* the Truth " (John 3^{21}, I John 1^6).*

Divine causality in St. Paul's epistles

To what extent does an intellectually honest and professionally trained teacher discard the theological concepts of his youth when he experiences sudden conversion ?

Saul, a Pharisee versed in rabbinical orthodoxy, might subconsciously have retained the traditional Jewish view of divine causality long after becoming a Christian. That view was that all phenomena derive from God, whose will in some sense lies behind each event in the world and behind every deed of men. We find ideas of predestination and fatalism as little to our taste as the Christian Jews of the first century would find our reverent agnosticism.

We must not press St. Paul's predestination too far. The idea has

* Another phrase which presents difficulty because of the presence of the article is " to speak the truth," which is stereotyped ; it is doubtful whether any personalization is intended here.

become closely associated with his name, but it seems to me that there is a grammatical explanation for much of the feeling of finality and fatalism so often produced by constructions in which the preposition *eis* is involved.

Xenophon and some later writers placed this preposition before the articular infinitive to form a purpose-clause on comparatively rare occasions, but it is in biblical Greek (the Greek Old Testament) that the construction commonly occurs in contexts of firm causality in the Hebrew and is an incontestable purpose-clause. Thence it became a fairly frequent means of expressing purpose in post-classical Greek. Nevertheless, the biblical student has need of circumspection and must remember that the *eis to*-with-infinitive construction owes its origin, as far as biblical Greek is concerned, to a literal translation of the Hebrew *infinitive construct*, which is preceded by the preposition *le* (which tends to be translated into Greek as *eis* in all contexts). Now this particular instance of Hebrew syntax has a much wider use than that of a final clause. Indeed, rather than purpose, it may be said to express the *direction* of the action of the main verb on which it depends and to differ but little from a bare infinitive (i.e., without preposition or article). For instance, it may be no more than a peri-phrastic future tense, when " Yahweh to (*le*) save me " means "Yahweh *is ready to* save me." Again it may be a gerundive. " What to (*le*) do more for my vineyard?" means " What *ought I to* do more . . .?" And, " Not to (*le*) mention Yahweh's name," means " Yahweh's name *must* not be mentioned."

Remembering that *eis-to*-with-infinitive in biblical Greek is a literal rendering of this rather comprehensive Hebrew construction, we shall readily appreciate that the apparent rigidity of divine causation in some places where St. Paul uses this construction will have to be substantially reduced. I have in mind several passages in the epistle to the Romans. The way that most English versions take these passages runs something like this :

" I may impart to you some spiritual gift, *in order that* you may be edified (1[11]). . . . God's creation has been made visible to the heathen, *in order that* they may have no excuse (1[20]). . . . God's righteousness was declared, *in order that* he might be just and might justify the believer (3[26]). . . . Abraham was circumcised *in order that* he might become the father of believers (4[11]). . . . God displays his grace, *in order that* his promise might be sure to all the seed of Abraham (4[16]). . . . Abraham against hope believed in hope, *in order that* he should become the father of many nations (4[18]). . . . You became dead to the Law *in order that* you might be joined to someone else (7[4]). . . . The elect of God are conformed to the image of his Son, *in order that* he should be the First-born among many brothers (8[29])."

It is plain that if there is any causality in, for instance, that last sentence, it is quite the reverse of that supposed to be expressed by St. Paul in Greek. The sentence must be turned round, to get the priority of causation right : Christ became man's first-born Brother in order that man might be conformed to Christ's image.

Our strong suspicion therefore is that *eis to*-with-infinitive is a construction which does not necessarily express the result of strict causality in the theme of the epistle to the Romans. It may be translated, " and so."

It is agreeable to confirm by modern study conclusions reached on other grounds by biblical scholars of other days. Bishop Westcott was without the advantage of that very close study of Septuagint language which enables us to assess the Greek Bible as a whole. He was guided by a sure instinct when he distinguished *hina*-clauses from *eis-to*-with-infinitive, holding that the latter construction marks the remoter aim and a looser connection with the governing verb, whereas *hina* is often more definitely causal.

2. JESUS IS GOD

> *Jesus is God ; let sorrow come,*
> *And pain, and every ill,*
> *All are worth while, for all are means*
> *His glory to fulfil ;*
> *Worth while a thousand years of woe*
> *To speak one little word,*
> *If by that " I believe " we own*
> *The Godhead of our Lord.*

Such was the assurance of a Victorian convert to Rome.

The same absolute reply to the abiding question, " Who is Jesus ? " is implicit in the ancient title of St. Mary which has been current among Eastern churchmen from early days. *Theotokos* means Mother of God. Not even Mother of the Son of God. He is God, who was born of Mary and God. Nicely balanced and judicious theologians avoid using the title, but it has rarely been an embarrassment for the Catholic churches, Greek and Roman, whose devotion it assists, although the Church of England both in formulary and prayer avoids a statement as unqualified as " Jesus is God." One would have thought it well enough grounded, for it emerges directly from the Nicene Creed, a momentous part of Holy Communion by which worshippers affirm their belief " in one Lord Jesus Christ, the only-begotten Son of God, begotten of his Father before all worlds, *God of God*."

A recent development in the controversy about the godhead of Jesus has involved the World Council of Churches. Article 1 of the Basis, set forth in 1961, states : " The World Council of Churches is a fellowship of Churches which confess the Lord Jesus Christ as God and Saviour according to the Scriptures and therefore seek to fulfil together their common calling to the glory of one God, Father, Son, and Holy Spirit."

The heresy, according to Dr. Nels Ferré,* is that of docetism. The stark statement of the World Council, he feels, commits its subscribers to believe that the whole godhead was incarnate in Jesus. The statement makes no reference to his humanity, and Ferré insists that " Jesus is not God, but the Son of God." Jesus is God incarnate, not " God in himself," and the World Council would have done better to choose the words, " We worship the eternal God, as he was in Christ, reconciling the world to himself." Others who fear that Article 1 will stick in the throat of intelligent people, who worship God and seek a universal faith, endorse the sentiment.

In his appeal to the great unchurched, the author of a recent paperback† criticized a popular kind of devotion because it pushed the Chalcedonian definition to one of its extremes. The extreme of believing that God himself has become incarnate, clothing and veiling himself in humanity. The writer finds heresy here and says it is the extreme of docetism *and* monophysitism.

The heterodoxy of the World Council's statement is unlikely to worry the average Christian, for he will find more relevance in what the earliest Christians believed and what the New Testament reveals.

The dying proto-martyr, St. Stephen, addressed Jesus as if he were God. A pious Hellenistic Jew would not pray to one less than God. It may not be so generally appreciated that St. Paul slipped naturally and casually into the affirmation that he who shed his blood upon the cross was God. The reference is to Acts 20[28], where St. Paul at Miletus spoke to the Christian elders about " the church of *God* which he bought for himself by *his own* blood." The blood of God! Some aberrant manuscripts have the inoffensive reading, " the church of the Lord " —implying the Lord Jesus. But they must be rejected on the ground that the more startling or difficult reading is the one likely to be correct ; scribes would not invent a conception of such unexpected originality as " the blood of God." We are left with the original and plain statement of St. Paul that Jesus is God, and it worries those scholars who think that it represents a Christology too advanced for the New Testament period. There is only one way out, the grammatical expedient whereby " his own " is understood as a noun (" his own One "),

* *Expos. Times*, LXXIII, no. 12, Dec., 1962.

† J. A. T. Robinson, *Honest to God*, S.C.M., 1963, p. 70.

rather than a possessive adjective. In consequence, standing as it does in the genitive case, one may place before it the word " of " : i.e. " of his Own." The expedient lowers the Christology drastically and reduces St. Paul's affirmation to something like this : " The church of God which he bought for himself by the blood *of* his Own "—as in the margin of the N.E.B. It is a theological expedient, foisting imaginary distinctions into a spontaneous affirmation, and is not the natural way to take the Greek. It is unlikely to have been the meaning envisaged either by St. Paul or the writer of the narrative. The easy thing would be for them to add the word " Son," if that was intended.

Besides, this is not an isolated occasion for St. Paul. In Rom. 9⁵ Jesus the Messiah is described as " God, blessed for ever." This is where the margins of the R.S.V. and the N.E.B. seem to me to be correct as against their texts. The text of the N.E.B. simply closes the sentence at " Messiah " and begins anew with an exclamation. " May God, supreme above all, be blessed for ever ! " So it avoids assigning the quality of godhead to Jesus Christ, but it introduces asyndeton and there is no grammatical reason why a participle agreeing with " Messiah " should first be divorced from it and then be given the force of a wish, receiving a different person as its subject. It would in fact be unnatural to divorce it from its antecedent. It is better to follow the margin and read, " sprang the Messiah, supreme above all, God blessed for ever." That the interpretation is the natural one and ought not to be relegated to the margin, can be seen by comparing the same construction in II Cor. 11³¹ where again the participle of the verb " to be " occurs in close conjunction with this adjective, " blessed." No one would submit that the participle in this context was a wish or exclamation, or that it introduced an entirely new person. No one would deny that it refers back to the previous subject, and that surely is the correct way to view the same construction in Rom. 9⁵. The Messiah is God.

Happily in Heb. 1⁸ the N.E.B. no longer hesitates to accept into its text the statement that Jesus is God. " Thy throne, O God, is for ever and ever." It consigns to the margin the grotesque interpretation which obscures the godhead of Jesus (" God is thy throne for ever and ever ").

Another controversial passage is Tit. 2¹³, where in its text the N.E.B. happily adopts the entirely natural translation, " our great God and Saviour Jesus Christ." This way of reading the Greek has the support of most of the early Greek fathers as well as great names in more recent times : Ellicott, Bernard Weiss, Christopher Wordsworth, and R.V. (text). The celebrated Greek father, St. John Damascene, for instance, discussing the title Theotokos, explains that to give Jesus the title of God is by no means to ignore his humanity. Anyone born of Mary must be a man. But what the title involves is simply and starkly the *deification* of humanity. At that moment, a man becomes God.* What says the writer to Titus? According to the A.V., which follows the Vulgate closely, he does not say that Christ is God. He distinguishes them. Grammatically it might all seem to depend on the Greek definite article. There is only one article, and that is at the beginning of the phrase " God and Saviour " ; it seems thus to join the two nouns closely together and to exclude the possibility of a distinction such as " God and *the* Saviour." Unfortunately, at this period of Greek we cannot be sure that such a rule is really decisive. Sometimes the definite article is repeated even where there is clearly a separation in idea. " The repetition of the article was not strictly necessary to ensure that the items be considered separately."† Nevertheless, if there be ambiguity, as there is here, correct grammatical principles ought to be decisive. Moreover, there are other considerations besides the grammatical. " God and Saviour " was in fact a phrase in use at this period and applied to the Roman emperors. What more natural than that Christians should have appropriated it on behalf of their own Lord Jesus, their only potentate, their lord of lords, their king of kings?

The same grammatical principle affects the phrase in II Peter 1[1] where there is but one definite article linking the two parts of a single phrase, " Our God even Jesus Christ." The distinction between God and Christ in the next verse may be against this, as Mayor remarks, but Mayor also had to point to many examples of " God " applied to Jesus Christ in the New Testament and early Fathers—not to mention the exclamation of the apostle Thomas, " My lord and God !" Moreover, the next verse has a shorter textual variant with much in its favour, and this would render Mayor's observation regarding this verse nugatory. Grammatically too it is relevant to note this author's practice of linking very closely similar ideas in one phrase with one definite article, thus " our lord and Saviour," repeatedly.

And what then of II Thess. 1[12] ? " Our lord and God Jesus Christ " would be the correct rendering. We must also seriously consider the possibility of departing from all our English versions by translating Eph. 5[5], " in the kingdom of Christ who is God."

It is a far-reaching consideration, affecting many passages, and the simple grammarian may be forgiven for suspecting that special pleading has contributed to the debilitation of tremendous affirmations in the New Testament.

Dr. Moffatt, in a version which is now more generally recognized as

---

* *De fide orthod.* III 12. Similarly the Athanasian Creed states that Christ's person is one, " not by conversion of the Godhead into flesh : but by taking of the Manhood into God."

† Moulton-Howard-Turner, *Grammar*, vol. III, p. 181. The reference is to Tit. 2[13].

brilliant paraphrase than as skilful translation, set a fashion in this kind of thing when he changed St. John's proclamation that " the Word was God " into an ambiguous assertion that " the Logos was divine " (John 1¹). The implication is that even human persons may be called divine, in a sense. Dr. Moffatt considered that he had Greek grammar on his side. The word for God, *theos*, does not have the definite article ; therefore *theos* is not a noun but a kind of adjective ; therefore it must be translated " divine " and not " God." The fallacy of this has been exposed since Dr. Moffatt's time, but he has never lacked a following. The one he would doubtless be most anxious to disown is the utterly unsuitable translation of a German ex-Roman priest, " the Word was a god."* Understandably, unitarians find difficult the apparent contradiction that in the first verse of the gospel " God " appears to mean the Father, while it is predicated of the Word in the same verse. Christians may be illogical, but they find no difficulty in thinking that this verse refers to God the Son.

The claim of unitarians to be logical should of course be respected, but the grammarian will resist their attempts to impress grammatical principles in the service of their cause in a way which is not legitimate. The fact that *theos* has no article does not transform the word into an adjective. It is a predicate noun, of which the subject is *Logos*, and it is a fairly universal rule in New Testament Greek that when a predicate noun precedes a verb it lacks the definite article ; grammatical considerations therefore require that " there need be no doctrinal significance in the dropping of the article, for it is simply a matter of word-order."†

Once again dilution of the high Christology of a New Testament author is seen to be based on a fallacious appeal to unfounded grammatical principles.

3. A Holy Spirit and the Holy Ghost

To explore the relationship of God the Holy Ghost to the world of spirits in general is to invite disaster from any number of hidden rocks and currents. Simply in the hope that grammatical study may throw light on a difficult problem, I will pursue a narrow course in a very wide sea.

The question is whether every mention of *pneuma* (spirit) in the New Testament ought to be understood as a reference to the Holy Spirit, co-equal and co-eternal with the Father and the Son. Many writers assume that this is so, except in the case of unclean spirits,

---

* *The New Testament—A New Translation and Explanation Based on the Oldest Manuscripts*, by Johannes Greber, English Tr., 1937.

† Moulton-Howard-Turner, *Grammar*, vol. III, p. 183.

but in the epistle to the Romans, for instance, it is incredible that St. Paul's mention of spirit is not so much a person as an aspect of human nature which is to be contrasted with flesh. Moreover, if the New Testament authors took " spirit " into their vocabulary for an *unclean* demon, equally probably they had a demon in mind when they referred to *holy* spirit.

If then a distinction between a spirit and the Spirit is feasible within the writings of the New Testament, on what grounds is the distinction to be made ?

At once, one will suspect that the Greek definite article has some influence. As its name implies, its usual function is to make an object more definite by pointing to it, broadly as in English except that the principles guiding its use in Greek are different from ours. The study of the article is so complex, so preoccupied with many baffling exceptions to all the precepts which have been advanced, that it daunts the student. Whatever grammatical text-book is consulted, a system of rules for every conceivable kind of noun is followed by a mass of exceptions in the literature ; and in biblical Greek the influence of a Hebrew construct-state complicates the matter further.

Progress is difficult, but one need not despair ; and although some grammatical conclusions will have a negative implication, others are theologically important.

Enquiry might usefully begin by collecting the indubitable references to the Holy Spirit. These are found conspicuously in the narrative of the day of Pentecost. The way the definite article is employed in these references will perplex at first, because in Acts 2[4] Holy Spirit is without the article, and in Acts 2[33, 38], etc., *the* Holy Spirit is preceded by it. However, that is no problem, for a well-known principle is involved, the use of the definite article with proper names. St. Luke regarded " Holy Spirit " (in the context of Pentecost) as the name of a divine person ; that is, " Holy " is not thought of as an adjective. In classical and Hellenistic Greek the practice tends to be that if proper names have no adjectival attribute and no phrase in apposition to them they are written without the article *at their first mention*. The article is apparently unnecessary with a proper name and serves only as a base on which to build qualifying words and phrases. But this concerns only the first mention in any context. After that, the definite article assumes the function of demonstrative pronoun, pointing a finger at someone who had already been introduced. That is the grammatical explanation of the absence of the article in Acts 2[4], for this is the introduction of the Holy Spirit into the narrative of Pentecost, although he had of course been previously mentioned even as early as 1[2].

St. Luke may be a touchstone for the rest of the New Testament.

This, I suggest, is his practice : as a general rule, and subject to conditions, whenever the Holy Spirit has the definite article the reference
is to the third person of the Trinity (expressed either as *to Pneuma to
Hagion* or as *to Hagion Pneuma*), but when the article is absent the
reference is to *a* holy spirit, a divine influence possessing men. A
complication supervenes, inasmuch as the definite article may be
absent from the name in some circumstances without impairing the
reference to the Holy Spirit. One circumstance, as we have seen, is
the initial mention of the Holy Spirit in a book, or even a narrative
or speech within the book. But in the following circumstances also the
article may be dispensed with : when " the Holy Spirit " forms part
of a prepositional expression and in other situations where the influence
of the Hebrew construct-state can be plainly detected, that is to say,
when " Holy Spirit " precedes another noun in the genitive case,
forming an expression like " the Holy Spirit of God." Hebrew syntax
waives the definite article before the first noun in such connections,
and biblical Greek adopts the procedure in sympathy. But in the
absence of these circumstances, and only then, it is fairly safe to say
that omission of the article is an indication that the reference is not to
the Holy Spirit but to a holy spirit.

This residuum of anarthrous references to a holy spirit repays
scrutiny, at least as far as the writings of St. Luke are concerned.
Adoption of our rule implies that neither John the Baptist nor his
mother and father were inspired directly by the Holy Spirit, but that
they were guided by a vaguer and less personal divine spirit (Luke $1^{15.}$
$^{41.}$ ^{67}). Moreover, it was not the third person of the Trinity that
overshadowed St. Mary and empowered her to conceive the Messiah ;
it was this indefinable and holy power of God, which strengthened
human beings in a supernatural way as it had done to the heroes of
Israel in Old Testament times (Matt. 1^{20}, Luke 1^{35}). We can tell from
the absence of the article in Luke 2^{25} that the aged Simeon was subject
to the same influence.* John the Baptist announced that the One
coming after him would baptize with a holy spirit and with fire (Luke
3^{16}), but when the dove descended upon Jesus St. Luke probably
intended to convey that this was the Holy Spirit, as the definite article
appears in 3^{22}. However, this may be due to anaphora, in spite of the
fact that verse 16 is some distance away. It seems probable that the
Holy Spirit did not lead Jesus into the wilderness, since the articular
en tō pneumati of Luke 4^1 is clearly an anaphoric reference to the
previous line of the narrative : " Jesus, full of holy spirit, . . . was led
by the same spirit. . . ." Moreover, the " good gift " which God the
Father offers to those who ask him is not likely to be God the Holy

* The presence of the article in verses 26 and 27 is due to anaphora, referring
back to the immediately preceding reference in verse 25.

Spirit, as it is anarthrous (Luke 11[13]); it is that powerful spiritual unction with which Jesus himself was anointed and which enabled him to counter the activities of evil spirits (Acts 10[38]).

The question of the inspiration of Scripture is bound to be raised. It was noted that Zacharias, Elisabeth, John and Simeon, though spiritually inspired, are not said to be filled with the third person of the Trinity. That is true of Scripture too, for in Acts 4[25] the Psalms are said to have been spoken by God through David's lips by means of a holy inspiration (literally "holy spirit"). St. Timothy was reminded by the apostle that Scripture is inspired by *God* (II Tim. 3[16]). But under that comprehensive name the Holy Spirit must be included, for St. Peter deliberately said as much in his speech at Pentecost (Acts 1[16]).*

This is not to suggest that the third person of the Trinity was thought to have been inoperative before Pentecost. On the contrary, the forebears of those whom St. Peter addressed had resisted the Holy Spirit all through their history (Acts 7[51]).

Stephen and Barnabas incidentally are said to be filled with spiritual inspiration (Acts 6[5] 7[55] 11[24]) and the believers in Samaria received the same spirit by the laying on of the hands of the apostles Peter and John (Acts 8[15, 17, 19]). The strange appearance of *to pneuma* (with article) among several references to anarthrous *pneuma* (verse 18) can be interpreted only as an instance of anaphoric usage. The author wished to add some emphasis : " Simon was aware that through the laying on of the apostles' hands *this same* spirit was bestowed. . . ." Later, the situation arose again in Ephesus on St. Paul's third journey, where he found certain " disciples " who had not received the spiritual unction and who told him that they had not even heard that anyone else had received it (Acts 19[2]). This I take to be the better form of the text ;† but, according to the usual form, the disciples must be understood to deny knowledge of any holy spirit ; presumably they knew only of evil spirits. Then St. Luke brings back the definite article anaphorically, saying, " When Paul laid on his hands, *that very* holy spirit came upon them " (19[6]).

These results fall far short of infallibility, because one does not always know whether the definite article is inserted theologically (i.e. to indicate the Holy Spirit) or whether it is due to the grammatical device of anaphora. Sometimes there can hardly be doubt, as when the article appears and yet there has been no previous mention of the word, for here the article must have doctrinal significance. When St. Peter accused Ananias of hypocrisy he specified that he lied to the

---

* See also Acts 25[28].

† It is vouched for by the Michigan papyrus, by Codex Bezae, the Sahidic version, and the margin of the Harklean Syriac version.

Holy Spirit, that is, to God himself. The article is there, and it is certainly not anaphoric, occurring at the beginning of the story (5^3). We know our test to be valid in this instance at least, because in verse 4 St. Peter actually says, " You lied . . . to *God*." There is no doubt either about the significance of the definite article when, in certain contexts where anaphora does not arise, St. Peter and the apostles told the sanhedrin that they were witnesses of the resurrection, and added, " So also is *the* Holy Spirit " (Acts 16^{32}) ; and St. Stephen made accusation against the sanhedrin that " you always resist *the* Holy Spirit " (Acts 7^{51}) ; and *the* Holy Spirit spoke to St. Peter immediately after his vision (Acts 10^{19}), and later on (11^{12}).

Important for Christian history and theology is the statement in Acts 11^{15}. The use of the article cannot be anaphoric, unless the reference is in any case to the Holy Spirit in verse 12. We may safely conclude that what came to the assembled company of Cornelius's relatives and friends at Caesarea was no mere divine afflatus, but the Holy Spirit himself, he who came to the apostles on the day of Pentecost (2^4). This is remarkable, because in every other instance except Pentecost it is not the (articular) Holy Spirit who comes upon converts, e.g. the Samaritans on whom Peter and John laid hands, and who received a divine spirit only. What is the special significance of the outpouring at Caesarea ? St. Peter opened the Christian Church to the Gentiles. Surely, this is the second Pentecost, the Gentiles' Whitsuntide, a new and very significant outpouring of the Holy Spirit, a second fulfilment of Joel's prophecy. Here for the first time an official Church leader in obedience to a vision breaks down the barriers in the new Israel of God, affording a precedent which was quoted with effect at the Council of Jerusalem. St. Peter granted that St. Paul's converts in Galatia had received *the* Holy Spirit (Acts 15^8).

Christian prophecy was a gift of the Holy Spirit himself, and Agabus spoke directly from God (11^{28} 21^{11}) ; the prophets at Antioch too spoke by the Holy Spirit (13^2). The latter statement occurs at the opening of a narrative (chapter 13) and the whole chapter which pre- ɔdes has no reference to *pneuma*, so that the question of anaphora does not arise, and the article therefore is doctrinal. However, verse 9 has an anarthrous mention of *pneuma*, which suggests that when St. Paul rebuked Elymas in Cyprus he was in the same state as Stephen, " full of *a* holy spirit."

Fairly substantial support of this articular theory arrives when some of the anarthrous occurrences of *pneuma*, like this concerning St. Paul in Acts 13^9, are seen to be capable of only one interpretation and the complicating question of anaphora does not obtrude. Concerning Barnabas, for instance, it is said that " he was a good man, full of *holy spirit* (no article) and of wisdom " (Acts 11^{24}). It cannot be thought that this is anarthrous because it is the first mention of the word in the narrative ; it has already occurred three times in the chapter.   So there is no ambiguity, as there is in some instances.   If then Barnabas received not the Holy Spirit but *holy spirit*, we are on sure ground in supposing that the same is true of Stephen.

In some ways the conclusions are limited and negative, because of the complicating anaphora and construct-state, and because other writers than St. Luke need investigation.   But the positive results appear to be reliable.   In many instances we can feel certain whether St. Luke refers to a holy spirit or to the Holy Ghost himself.

CHAPTER TWO

JESUS OF NAZARETH

1. The Census before the Census (*Luke* 2^2)

When was Jesus born ?

The chronology of the New Testament is affected by an apparently minor point of grammar, and the alleged lack of care in St. Luke's dating of the birth calls for re-examination in its light.

St. Luke appears to state that Jesus was born in the time of Quirinius and during " the first census," but it has been long disputed whether he intends the first census *that was ever taken* in Palestine by the Romans or the first census *that Quirinius took* in his term of office as legate of Syria. The N.E.B. has the first suggestion in its text and relegates the latter to a footnote which reads, " This census was the former of the two which Quirinius held while he was governor of Syria."

One's first impression is that St. Luke was confused about the date of Quirinius. The earliest census which this official could have conducted was that which was held in A.D. 6. Quirinius never officiated as legate during the reign of king Herod, in which, St. Matthew says, Jesus was born.

St. Luke should not be convicted before we have considered that small point of grammar. Greek at this period was as relaxed as any modern language in observing the correct distinction between comparative and superlative with regard to " former " and " first." There was in Hellenistic Greek, as there is in English to-day, a preference for " first " when in fact " former " or " prior " is more grammatical. Strictly, " first " means number one among at least three, while " former " is the word which compares only two. St. Luke was professional, but many use " first " where the meticulous prefer " former."

A Roman Catholic scholar, Lagrange, offered a solution which completely vindicates St. Luke's accuracy. " First census " must be taken in its Hellenistic connotation as the first of two, and then we must expand the clause a little. " This census was *before the census* which Quirinius, governor of Syria, made." Lagrange was not the first (or " former!") to offer the suggestion. It was known to the grammarian, G. B. Winer, whose survey of the New Testament language appeared in its first edition in 1822, and who scorned the suggestion as " ungrammatical." The phrase is compressed, but it is no more ungrammatical than the phrase in John 5[36], " I have a testimony greater than (scil., the testimony of) John," or the highly compressed I Cor. 1[25], " the foolishness of God is wiser than (scil., the wisdom of) men." The words in parenthesis are absent from the Greek and yet must be supplied. There is no grammatical reason for not as readily supplying the necessary words in the sentence of St. Luke. " This census was *prior to* (the census) of Quirinius."

St. Luke then does not say that Jesus was born during the regime of Quirinius. The evangelist is referring to a census, of which we know nothing, held before that of Quirinius in A.D. 6, and there is the additional difficulty of believing that an emperor who was a paragon of wisdom would have taken the census in a dependent king's dominion. At least there would have been resistance, and of this too we hear nothing in contemporary records. However, we have St. Luke's own testimony to the census and he should be accounted an authority. On the analogy of what happened later, the census was probably held fourteen years earlier than that of Quirinius. If so, St. Luke's dating of the birth was 8 B.C., which is very reasonable. Herod died in 4 B.C. Jesus was just under two when they escaped to Egypt, or so Herod thought, and having stayed in Egypt for two years he would be a child of four when Herod died and the holy family moved to Nazareth.

2. A GRAMMARIAN'S MEDITATION ON THE BIRTH OF JESUS

Mary and Joseph were betrothed when Mary was found to be pregnant. The *Aktionsart** of the aorist tense makes it clear, if not emphatic, that this occurred *before ever* they came together. There is no possibility that the pregnancy took place within marriage. Some would like to assume this, by translating the Greek : " Before they began to live together regularly. . . ." But St. Luke's careful use of tenses forbids it. Such an interpretation would demand the present tense, the tense of continuity, which alone could change " coming together " into " living together."

After his perplexing discovery, Joseph was told by the angel not to be afraid. Mary had received the same encouragement at the annunciation, but the different tenses which were used on each occasion indicate that a different message was intended. The negative imperative in the angel's message to Mary is in the present tense and therefore means, " Stop being frightened!" A present imperative is no general command, touching some future contingency, but it indicates that

* Tenses in Greek indicate the *kind* of action, rather than the *time* of the action. Hence grammarians in Germany coined this technical term, which has now become universally accepted.

Mary was already afraid and must cease to be so. The angel's syntax was different when he addressed Joseph. Joseph had been puzzled by the condition of his betrothed, and was pondering his next move. The angel did not accuse him of being afraid to marry Mary, for he used the aorist subjunctive in place of the present imperative. " Never at any time in the future be afraid to take her to wife." That was the importance of the tense in the dream-message, and it proves that Joseph's hesitation in marrying was not activated by motives of fear, so far. Gossip and social pressures might soon make him afraid, and the angel warned him.

In that dream the angel mentioned Mary's " unborn baby." That is the way to render the neuter participle into English. Classical and Hellenistic writers often used a neuter participle although a person was intended, and as it is the *present* participle here, it is correct to render it by a plain noun, by " baby " rather than by " that which is conceived in her." The latter is the pedantic translation of the A.V., followed unnecessarily by the R.V. and the R.S.V.

Then the angel added, concerning this unborn baby, " It is he *and no other* " (such a rendering is not pedantic, for the pronoun *autos* is most emphatic) " that shall save his People from their sins."

Many months afterwards, the Magi visited the holy family and, in the hallowed words of the Christmas story, they came " from the east " (Matt. 2^1).

St. Matthew wrote the word in the plural, and *anatolē* undoubtedly does mean " east " when used in this way. However, there is the interesting point that in modern Greek the plural of *Anatolē* is a proper name signifying " various parts of Asia Minor [i.e., *Anatolia*]," just as if we used *Londons* for " the various districts which make up the metropolitan area." In some parts of Greece they use the plural of Eudelos in this way : *pamen kata tous Eudēlous* means " we went into the neighbourhood of Eudelos."* If the idiom goes back to the days of the evangelist, then these districts of Anatolia are the country from which the Magi travelled. They were " wise men from the west." Grammatically speaking, geography apart, the idea of wise men from the west is feasible when the Septuagint is consulted. This is a Greek version of the Old Testament, used by St. Matthew, and there in Gen. 11^2 and 13^{11} this very phrase, " from *Anatolē* " (plural), translates a Hebrew word which is more likely to mean " eastwards " than " from the east,"† for Lot must have travelled " eastward " in order to occupy the Jordan valley (13^{11}). Even if St. Matthew cannot be understood

---

* A. Thumb, *Handbook of the Modern Greek Vernacular*, tr. by S. Angus, T. & T. Clark, 1912, p. 31.

† F. Brown, S. R. Driver, C. A. Briggs, *A Hebrew and English Lexicon of the Old Testament*, Oxford, 1906, under the word קֶדֶם 1. b.

to mean that they came from various parts of Anatolia, there is still the possibility that he thought they travelled " eastwards," since he would know how the Septuagint had rendered the Hebrew word.

If they saw this star " in the east " (Matt. $2^{2.9}$), it is again more probable that the Magi were travelling eastwards from some western land like Asia Minor, than westwards from Persia or the East. True, *anatolē* is here singular, by contrast with the plural in the wise men's journey (2^1). The Greek language generally reserved the plural for the compass-point and the singular for the literal meaning of the word, viz. " rising," and some have urged that the Magi saw the star " at its rising," that is, " when it first shone." This point cannot be pressed. The singular is sometimes used in biblical Greek for the directions, north, south, east, and west, as in the true text of Rev. 7^2 16^{12} 21^{13}. The scribes or editors responsible for our oldest manuscripts felt that the plural of *anatolē* was correct when " east " is intended by the author ; and so in Rev. 7^2 16^{12} Codex Alexandrinus displays the plural by way of correction, and in Rev. 21^{13} an important tenth-century uncial manuscript reflects the same early correction.

Wherever they came from, and whatever the direction of the star, there is no doubt about their question to king Herod. " Where is the new-born king of the Jews? " They did not ask, " Where is he that is born to be king of the Jews? " as is suggested by nearly all the English versions, uncritically following the Vulgate. Goodspeed and Moffatt are honourable exceptions. This point I sought to establish when I examined the construction in St. Matthew's language,[*] i.e. the participle used attributively between an article and noun. It is characteristic of those parts of Matthew which are peculiar to the evangelist and it is intended as an adjectival and not a substantival participle. This is not merely a matter of the niceties of grammar. The usual rendering (" he that is born king ") is wrong in its emphasis, because what the Magi were seeking was that great one who had just been born, and it was not so much a concern to them *who* he was as *where* he was. They were thinking not of the destiny of the baby but of his birth. An appreciative letter arrived from the Rev. E. F. F. Bishop. He wrote, " I am glad to have read your comment in the E.T., on the Feast of the Epiphany and Orthodox Christmas. I am sure you are right in stressing the *where* and not *who* in the question of the Magi. This is the Semitic way—which leads to the question whether *king of the Jews* may not be a circumstantial clause, as it seems in Arabic, especially with the absence of the article, which would not have been present in Aramaic."

The Magi's question prompted the king to seek information from his own advisers on the precise place of birth. His request was not

* *Expos. Times*, LXVIII, no. 4, Jan., 1957, p. 122.

peremptory. Surprisingly the verb "enquired" is in the imperfect tense (Matt. 2⁴), which means that he scarce expected his demand to be implemented. Tentative requests are often described in that tense. King Herod suspected all around of plotting against him, especially those nearest his throne, and his suspicion comes out in St. Matthew's report. "Where? But I expect you will not tell me."

The holy family returned to Palestine, for Joseph received certain tidings (Matt. 2²⁹). He heard, "They are dead" (plural in Greek). Joseph knew that the meaning was, "*He* is dead." The enemy was Herod the Great. There was a kind of vogue in post-classical Greek for the plural where the singular was clearly intended.* It should not be reproduced in English.

The family went to Nazareth, and like many another incident in the gospel, St. Matthew saw it as the fulfilment of the Old Testament. Here too comes the same idiom of plural for singular, for although the Greek has "prophets," only one prophet is involved, and the words should be referred back to the prophecy in 2¹⁵, "Out of Egypt shall I call my son." "He shall be called a Nazarene" (2²³) is not in fact part of any prophecy and may even be a scribal gloss or a comment by the evangelist.

3. JOHN THE BAPTIST

"The beginning of the gospel was John" (Mark 1¹)

Primarily the Anglo-Saxon word "gospel" means good tidings, like the Greek which it translates, but in a secondary sense it has become the technical term for a book dealing with Jesus's life.

At the outset St. Mark introduces the word "gospel" into what has generally been regarded as a title or subtitle for the whole book: "The beginning of the gospel of Jesus Christ." Absence of a verb has promoted the suggestion that the phrase is a title rather than an integral part of the book. But usually in Greek the copula verb "to be" tends to be omitted whenever possible, and on this assumption some have doubted whether it was St. Mark's intention to make verse 1 the title of the book after all. May he not rather have intended it to be the subject of a sentence of which verse 2 is the predicate? By supplying "is" or "was" they arrive at a new version of his opening words. The gist is that the "beginning of the gospel" is Isaiah's prophecy concerning the messenger, John the Baptist. The suggestion is good because everyone will agree that the roots of the Christian

---

* Another instance of the post-classical allusive plural is seen in Matt. 14⁹ = Mark 6²⁶, where Antipas promised with an oath to give his step-daughter whatever she asked, and because of the oath was bound to execute John the Baptist. The Greek has "oaths," but the A.V. and N.E.B. avoid the pedantry of the R.V. and R.S.V. and use the singular.

gospel do in fact lie deep in history. You might go further still and
find the ultimate " beginning of the gospel " in the promise of God
that Eve's descendant would bruise Satan's head (Gen. 3[15]). Nevertheless, in spite of the theological impeccability of the suggestion, there
is a real stylistic difficulty about supplying " is " or " was " in any
sentence written by St. Mark. In many writers of Greek, even biblical
Greek, it would be easy enough. They regarded the copula verb as
at best an encumbrance in a simple subject-predicate sentence, and in
fact they went even further than this and sometimes omitted " is "
or " was " when its meaning was stronger than a mere copula. St.
Mark is a notable exception. He was inclined to insert these words
where more literary authors ignored them as weak copulas. St. Mark
indeed confined the ellipse to fixed phrases like " if possible " (for " if
it is possible ") and " all things possible " (for " all things are possible ").
Sometimes he omitted the copula in exclamations like " Whose
image is this! " Yet even here, four times out of five he inserted it.
This is a feature of his style and for that reason the grammarian must
feel considerable doubt about the interpretation, " The beginning of
the gospel *is* or *was* as it is written in Isaiah." A pity, when the suggestion is theologically acceptable.

But we need not revert to the suggestion of a title. An alternative
is the punctuation adopted by Bishop Rawlinson in his Westminster
commentary on the gospel, depending on the fact that St. Mark is very
fond of parenthesis—the device of introducing material which has no
syntactical connection with the rest of the sentence. Bind together
verses 1 and 4, and regard the intervening matter as parenthesis. It
will read like this. " John the Baptist, baptizing . . . and preaching . . . ,
was the beginning of the gospel of Jesus Christ." This simple and clear
statement was in the evangelist's mind as he took his pen, but a complicating parenthesis occurred to him as he began to write. Somewhere
we must insert : " As it is written in the prophets, Behold I send my
messenger before thy face who shall prepare thy way ; the voice of
one crying in the wilderness, Make ready the way of the Lord, make his
paths straight." One might almost class it as a footnote.

Such an interpretation puts the claims of John very high. He
announces the Messiah. More ; he is part of the gospel itself. It is
an exalted image, which may have assumed dangerous proportions,
and the statements in chapter 1 of St. John's gospel look very like an
attempt to revise the depiction.

" *Jesus of Nazareth in Galilee came* " (*Mark* 1[9])

" Jesus came from Nazareth in Galilee " to be baptized by John in
the river Jordan. So the sentence is usually construed, but it would

be more correct to say that " Jesus of Nazareth in Galilee " came and was baptized by John in Jordan.

The title, " Jesus of Nazareth," sounds strange here at the beginning of Mark. The writer evidently intended it, for he has omitted the definite article before " Jesus " and the importance is that it is his almost invariable rule to omit the article before this sacred name only when an appositional phrase is introduced.* We must therefore understand the phrase, " of Nazareth in Galilee," as appositional to " Jesus."

Was Jesus baptized by immersion ? This may be so, according to St. Mark. However, in the later tradition reflected by St. Matthew Jesus seems to have been baptized by a method which did not involve actually going into the water. I base the supposition on a difference in the prepositions used by each evangelist. St. Mark reports that Jesus went up " out of " (*ek*) the water, while St. Matthew says that he went up (the bank ?) " away from " (*apo*) the water. Strictly, *ek* implies motion from within a place or object while *apo* implies motion away from the outside. There is much doubt whether there was a significant difference in meaning between them at this period, especially in biblical Greek. One can only point out that the change from *ek* to *apo* by St. Matthew is notable and may indicate a development in the gospel tradition concerning the method of the baptism. Certainly in some other respects, such as the increasing emphasis which is laid on the public aspect of the vision, the four gospels betray signs of a developing tradition in the baptism narrative.

4. GRAMMAR IN THE GREAT SERMON

The supreme example of Christ's teaching, the sermon on the Mount, is conspicuous for its commands and prohibitions, but the generality of our English versions display little appreciation of the significant difference between the present and aorist tenses in commands and their negatives.

For Greeks of all periods, a present imperative was an order to do something constantly or to continue. Examining carefully the kind of action (linguists everywhere follow the Germans in calling it *Aktionsart*), grammarians have analysed it as either *durative* (lasting) or *iterative* (repeating) in all moods of the present tense. The *Aktionsart* of the present must be clearly distinguished from that of the aorist, which is not durative or iterative and expresses no more than one specific instance of the action of the verb, involving usually a single moment of time. One will readily appreciate that an aorist command does not

---

* For a development of the grammatical argument, see Moulton-Howard-Turner, *Grammar*, vol. III, pp. 166f.

envisage a general precept but is concerned with conduct in specific instances. Indeed, it often involves the initiation of action that has not yet begun, as when Jesus enjoined his disciples to " consider the lilies of this field."* They were walking in the countryside but had not observed the tiny flowers until he drew their attention to them. His exclamation on this particular occasion was meant for that occasion only. " Look ! You have not yet noticed the lilies in this field ! Consider them now !"

The same principle holds in negative commands. If the tense is the present, prohibition will be against continuing an action which has already begun. If it is aorist, prohibition is against beginning it. Although there are some passages where a change of tense apparently has no significance other than a desire for variety in style, intentional distinctions in the Greek have proved too subtle for modern interpreters.

Precepts of our Lord spring vividly to life under this rule of grammar. He says that a spirit of forgiveness is a prerequisite to acceptable worship. " First be reconciled once and for all (aorist) to your brother, and then come and offer as many gifts as you like (present) " : Matt. 5^{24}.

Jesus's teaching becomes at once impressive and meaningful when the difference in the tenses is observed. We are to *stop* laying up treasures on earth (Matt. 6^{19}). He knows that his disciples have begun to do this, and the tense is present.

How would all this be affected by the assumption that Jesus most probably spoke the words in Aramaic, not in Greek ?† The assumption is not universally upheld, and there is no denying that the written record in Greek aims at preserving his meaning very carefully. His next injunction to his disciples is not to be anxious (6^{25}), and the tense makes it clear. The disciples are already anxious, and he says, " Stop this ! " It calls for the present imperative. Then why change to the aorist tense in verse 34 ? Because there he brings this particular discussion to a close, and his words refer to the future. By now his presence and his discourse may have calmed their fears, and he says that they must not let this occur in future. " Do not ever begin to be anxious again. To-morrow will look after itself."

As to our tendency to criticize, Jesus had some stern precepts. He used the present tense. We must stop judging others, and then we shall not ourselves be judged (7^1). More than a precept, his words were indirect accusation. On the other hand, his teaching about the taking of oaths involved no accusation. He used the aorist tense to prohibit swearing by heaven, by earth, by Jerusalem, by the head, or any other

---

* Why " this " field ? The Greek is explicit. When *agros* occurs without the definite article it is usually to be taken of the countryside generally. Christ used the article apparently redundantly, making it mildly demonstrative.

† For discussion on this question, see the final chapter of this book.

way. For some reason, his listeners may already have renounced oath-swearing and his commandment was that they should never in future resume the practice (5^{34-36}). This they had already learned from John the Baptist, whose disciples they may have been before they transferred allegiance to Jesus, especially as we learn from Josephus that the people called Essenes, whom John resembled in many ways, denied themselves the use of oaths.* The tone of our Lord's precept is in marked contrast with that of his own kinsman when he wrote his epistle at some later date, by which time Jewish members of the Christian Church stood in need of rebuke for perpetuating the practice of oath-swearing. St. James put his prohibition in the present tense, bidding his readers refrain at once from the practice (James 5^{12}).

As to prohibitions concerning fasting, Jesus used the present tense to forbid his disciples to continue to assume the dismal looks and long faces which were customary. Their Essene or similar background might have ruled out oaths but it would not discourage asceticism ; indeed, the Baptist's disciples were said to be strict about fasts. Now they are told to desist.

In some commandments of the sermon we see a change of tense which is too relevant to be accidental. One of them concerns self-denial, cross-bearing and discipleship. Self-denial and cross-bearing are covered by the aorist and so they involve a decision once and for all ; but discipleship is indicated by the present tense and must be a general command, durative and iterative. " He must once and for all deny himself and seize his cross ; then let him follow me as a continuous discipline " (Luke 9^{23}).

Incidentally the same principle of grammar resolves a textual problem in this verse. The addition of " daily," which has excellent manuscript authority, is impossible with the aorist imperative, for it makes the command durative. It has the support of the original hand of Codex Sinaiticus, together with Vaticanus and Alexandrinus, and the omission has been widely condemned as a scribal harmonization with the parallels in Matthew and Mark. However, grammatical evidence about the significance of tenses in the imperative must make us acclaim the testimony of Codices Bezae and Ephraemi, with the Old Latin and Syriac versions.

Some commandments seem to be applicable only until the second Advent and the reason why they have the aorist tense may be that they do not constitute general or permanent legislation. " Turn the

---

* *De Bello Iudaico* II viii, 6 : " That which needs a divine oath to accredit it is condemned already." Like some Pharisees, they enjoyed exemption from the oath of loyalty to Herod (*Antiquitatum Iudaicarum* XV x, 4). But there is some inconsistency, since the Essenes compelled novices to take tremendous oaths *before* becoming full members of the community.

other cheek!" "Enter your chamber and shut the door when you pray." These are for the time being. The apostle temporarily commands Timothy, "Keep this commandment until the appearing of our Lord Jesus Christ," and, "Them that sin rebuke before all" (I Tim. 6[14. 20]).

Whenever a petition is made to God in prayer it is nearly always in the aorist tense. So in the Lord's prayer we are taught to say (according to St. Matthew), "Give us *this moment* our daily bread!" It is peremptory and St. Luke appears, by a change of tense, to have moderated it : "Continue to give us bread day after day." But other equally peremptory clauses follow. "Thy name be hallowed *now!*" "Thy will be done *now!*" "Forgive us now *once and for all.*" The explanation of the petitioning aorist may be that such demands are always pressing and urgent to the petitioner. At the same time, feelings of reverence probably dictated that God should not not be invited to commit himself to permanent concessions on our behalf. So it is from day to day that we must not only live, but pray, and every prayer must be *ad hoc*, with no attempt to seek long-term agreements. Contemporary pagans had realized this, for the tense is found in some of the Greek papyrus fragments which were recovered from Egypt.

Imposing too are the categorical prohibitions of the great sermon when one evaluates the truth about the tenses. "Do not think *for one moment* that I have come in order to destroy the Law" (Matt. 5[17]). "*On no account* sound a trumpet before you when you do alms" (Matt. 6[2]). "*On no account* give that which is holy to the dogs" (Matt. 7[6]). "*Never for a moment* take thought for the morrow" (Matt. 6[34]).

A feature of style known as *chiasmus*, whereby two or more concepts are presented together and afterwards repeated in the reverse order, marks the great sermon. Sometimes recognition of *chiasmus* furthers the true interpretation of the Scriptures, for it appears to be often employed. The well-known A.B.B.A. pattern occurs in the sermon on the Mount, and seems to determine the sense of Jesus's saying about economy in the presentation of truth : "Give not that which is holy to the dogs (A), neither cast your pearls before swine (B), lest the swine trample them under foot (B), and the dogs turn and rend you (A)." In the usual interpretation the swine turn and do the rending. The interpretation demanded by *chiasmus* makes much better sense.

5. SOME HEALINGS OF JESUS

The significance of tense

The importance of tenses is by no means confined to the great sermon. When Jesus spoke to the haemorrhage victim about her present health, he used the perfect tense deliberately (Matt. 9²²). He was saying in effect, " You have received healing and *are now* in perfect health. Your faith has accomplished this." After that, the tense becomes aorist as the evangelist looks back upon the event and records it historically. " At that very moment the woman *did* receive healing."

Tense-wise, the woman's aside is also worthy of note (Matt. 9²¹). She employed a form of conditional sentence which refers to the future : " If I touch his garment I shall receive healing." The interesting point is that the syntax is unexpected. The protasis of this future conditional sentence is usually expressed by the particle *ean* with the verb in the subjunctive mood of the present tense, but the woman uses *ean* with the verb in the subjunctive mood of the aorist tense.

The explanation must be that the woman was visualizing a definite event occurring only once in the future (" if I just touch ") and taking place before the time of the action of the main verb (" once I have touched, then . . ."). This kind of conditional clause has almost a temporal meaning (" when " for "if") and represents rather more than mere probability. There was no doubt in the woman's mind. She said to herself, "After I have touched that garment, I shall receive my healing."

The expression, " receive healing," is preferable to " be saved," although that seems to be the more literal rendering of the Greek verb. The meaning, " to be saved," is carried by the present stem of *sōzesthai*, but we are not concerned with that tense. Here are the aorist and perfect tenses ; and the aorist of verbs which in their present stem express a state (e.g. the state of being saved) is known to grammarians as the " inceptive aorist " because its *Aktionsart** expresses a single act which represents entrance into that state. In the instance before us, the inceptive action of the state " to be saved " is most naturally expressed in English by the words " to receive healing." The reason is fairly clear. " Saved " in this context refers exclusively to physical health, having nothing to do with theology. Its perfect tense implies that the effect of the inceptive action still remains at the time of speaking. This is not grammatical sophistry, for there is abundant evidence that to New Testament writers the aorist of this verb did not mean " to be saved." As soon as the ink was dry, New Testament books were translated into Syriac to support the Gospel's advance eastwards and north-eastwards, resulting in versions which are called the Old Syriac. Let us see how these contemporary translators understood the aorist of *sōzesthai*. They employ the Syriac verb which means " to get new life " or " begin to live," wherever the evidence of these versions survives. Almost certainly the ancient Syriac translators had in mind the Old Testament conception of Yahweh as the Fountain of Life and interpreted the Greek aorist accordingly. They

* See p. 24.

confirm in this way the testimony of St. John's gospel where this verb
is wholly avoided and the author constantly uses a different phrase to
express the meaning "to have everlasting life." St. John's usage
therefore is further evidence for a very early interpretation of the
meaning of the synoptists when they choose the aorist tense of *sōzesthai*.

The same accurate discrimination of tenses is discovered in the
remarks made to him whose name was Legion. "Go home," said
Jesus, "and show your family the kind of man the Lord has made of
you." The *perfect* tense indicates the abiding result of what God had
done for the demented sufferer.* When Jesus spoke again, he used
the *aorist* tense : "and tell them God has given you a touch of his
love" (Mark 5[19]).

It may be true that Jesus was not primarily a worker of miracles.
Nevertheless, there is a mistranslation in our English versions which
beclouds the fact that the miracles recorded in the canonical gospels
are only a smatter of the total number of his mighty works. It is
misleading to render the elative superlative as "*most* of his mighty
works" (Matt. 11[20]). The elative of "many" is "very many."
Jesus is upbraiding the cities in which "his very many mighty works"
were performed.

"Whenever they saw him" (Mark 3[11])

Another feature of grammar vouches for the strenuous nature of
Jesus's healing ministry.

The use of an augment-indicative (i.e., either imperfect or aorist)
in association with the particle *an*, is one of the best established prac-
tices in New Testament and Koine syntax for a certain type of subordinate clause. It is a serious departure from classical Greek, in
which the optative mood was employed. The clause is iterative, which
means that a repetitive act is envisaged, best expressed in English by
"Whenever (as often as) he came."

Acquaintance with this new principle in the later Greek affects our
understanding of the gospel narrative. At the beginning of his ministry
Jesus spent a strenuous period in Capernaum and adjacent districts
of Galilee, and concerning that time we read, "Whenever (*hotan* with
imperfect indicative) the unclean spirits saw him, they used to (imperfect indicative) fall down before him and cry out. . . . Then he
would habitually charge them (imperfect indicative) not to make him
known" (Mark 3[11]).

The description, therefore, concerns not a definite occasion but something that happened again and again. This is significant in Mark 11[19]

---

* Some MSS have aorist, which I take to be an early attempt to standardize the
style of St. Mark.

where the imperfect indicative and (except in Codices Alexandrinus and Bezae) the particle *hotan* occur. The meaning must be " whenever it was evening " or " every evening," and not " when it was the evening " of that day. The R.V., although it has been challenged, was correct. The picture is that of Jesus leaving Jerusalem *every* evening. Then the next verse will begin, " *One* morning, they saw the fig-tree. . . ."

6. His Gracious Words

" Despairing of no man " (Luke 6³⁵)

The phrase appears in the strange context of lending money. Our Lord exhorted his disciples to lend. According to the text of the N.E.B. he amplified as follows : " Lend, without expecting any return." The precept is difficult, and yet it accords well enough with the high standards of self-denial he set for all his disciples. But as a translation there is also something difficult about it, and the footnotes of the N.E.B. present us with the alternative, " Lend, without ever giving up hope." Unfortunately the meaning is not too clear, unless one has opportunity to look at the Greek, where there is a variant in the text which prompted the N.E.B. footnote. But what is the " hope " which is not to be given up? Is it the hope of ever having the loan returned? That would be an unworthy motive for a disciple, however apposite for a money-lender. Or does it mean that we must not give up hope concerning the borrower's welfare? If so, to avoid ambiguity, we could surely translate, " Lend, without despairing of any man."

In this dilemma we must look more closely at the alternatives in the Greek text. First, we will take the best-known reading, the form of text which is followed by the N.E.B. in the body of its translation. In the phrase, " expecting nothing in return," the significant word in Greek is *mēden* (" nothing "), attested by some of the best manuscripts.* It is the text which is accepted by the majority of modern editors, Alford, Tregelles, Bernhard Weiss, Lachmann, Westcott and Hort, the R.V. of 1881, von Soden, Vogels, Lagrange, Merk, Bover. An impressive array! Nevertheless, in order to make sense of *mēden* it is essential to adopt a meaning for the accompanying verb for which there is very little support. It is required to mean " to expect in return," or " to hope to receive back." In the twelfth century, Euthymius Zigabenus accepted this meaning in his comment, " expecting nothing from them." Still further back, it will be found that the

* Not least by Codex Vaticanus (the oldest complete Greek Bible in the world), Codex Alexandrinus (a fifth-century manuscript in the British Museum, presented by the patriarch of Constantinople to Charles the First), Codex Regius (in Paris), and Codex Sangallensis (a ninth-century manuscript in the library at St. Gall).

Church fathers, St. Gregory of Nyssa and St. Chrysostom, paraphrase the verb as if it meant " to hope to receive back."* Moreover, the list of those who accept this meaning of *apelpizontes* is so impresive it is small wonder that Rudolf Bultmann supposes Luke 6³⁵ to mean, " Lend out without the expectation of being repaid," or, if the thought of usury is in the Lord's mind, " without expecting any interest upon it."† Bultmann provides no evidence, except the analogy of the parallel compound verb *apaitein* (" to ask back ") with the supposition that *apelpizontes* (" to hope back ") is an abbreviation of *apolambanein elpizontes* (" to hope to receive back "), like the German *zuruckerwarten*. The Vulgate version supports this, with its *nihil inde sperantes* (" hoping for nothing therefrom "). It may further be argued that this rendering of *apelpizontes* agrees with the context, which says. " If ye lend to those of whom ye hope to receive, what thank have ye? " (verse 34).

So much for the context, and yet suitability to the context is not necessarily decisive against more definite proof of the general usage of a word. If *mēden* is retained, the translation will have to be the ambiguous "nothing despairing," and so it is worth exploring the possibilities of the variant reading, *mēdena*,‡ which is accepted by a few modern editors, notably Tischendorf, and is put by Westcott and Hort in the margin (hence also in the margin of the R.V.). The word is masculine (" no one "), whereas *mēden* (" nothing ") was neuter, and it presents two possibilities for translating the verb *apelpizontes*. (a) In modern Greek the verb means " to render desperate," and this is the interesting way in which the ancient Syriac versions of the Gospels translate the phrase : " Lend, and make no man desperate." (b) But the meaning which has the best authority in both secular and biblical Greek is " to despair." In the Greek rendering of Isaiah 29¹⁹, " the poor among men " is translated by the perfect participle passive of this verb, in a way that literally means " the despaired of." So too in the Apocrypha (Judith 9¹¹) and in the first epistle of St. Clement (59³) God is said to be the Saviour of " those who are despaired of." It is deeply significant, and there is a moving petition in a prayer in the *Martyrium* of St. Theodotus,§ in which the perfect participle passive

---

* G. W. H. Lampe, *A Patristic Greek Lexicon*, Oxford, 1961, fasc. I, p. 181.

† Ed. G. Kittel, *Theologisches Wörterbuch zum Neuen Testament*, II, p. 531.

‡ In Codex Sinaiticus (the rival to Vaticanus in age and purity of text, purchased by Britain from the Bolshevists for £100,000, now in the British Museum), the Washington Codex (a valuable gospel manuscript of the fourth or fifth century), Codex Zacynthius (a palmipsest manuscript of no more than parts of Luke 1–11, but dating from the eighth century, and now in the British and Foreign Bible Society library), Codex Petropolitanus (fragmentary and ninth-century, but significant), Codex Monacensis (ninth or tenth century), and in less important authorities.

§ Edited by F. de Cavalieri, *Studi e Testi*, 6, Rome, 1901, p. 74.

is used : " O Christ, who art the Hope of those who are despaired of."
In spite of the paraphrase by St. Chrysostom, mentioned above, the
father nevertheless has a phrase very like that in Luke 6[35] when he
says, " Let us despair of nobody " (*mēdena apelpisōmen*).*

Besides having the support of ancient authority this meaning matches
the meek spirit of our Lord and particularly that tenderness to the
outcast and despaired of, which St. Luke is careful to indicate in his
gospel.

" Despairing of no man " is the kind of slogan which is characteristic
of St. Luke, alongside others like " seeking and saving."

The reading of *mēdena* is the more convincing since it enables one to
understand how the alternative reading might have arisen. A scribe
had the letter alpha twice in the original from which he was making his
copy. The first alpha ended one word and the second began the next ;
he made the easy error of reproducing only one alpha in his copy.
What in fact he did was to transform *ΜΗΔΕΝΑ ΑΠΕΛΠΙΖΟΝΤΕΣ*
into *ΜΗΔΕΝ ΑΠΕΛΠΙΖΟΝΤΕΣ*.† It is an explicable mistake, and
one which had far-reaching consequences in textual transmission.

Forgiven because she loved ? Or loving because forgiven ? (*Luke 7*[47])

In the absorbing incident concerning the woman in Simon's house
there is a point which has some significance in current discussions, and
it is important we should see the matter aright.

It is the place of love in Christian life. Do the personality and
sacrifice of Christ provoke love in us, or does our love for him provoke
the forgiveness of God? Both propositions may be true, but which of
them was Jesus affirming to the world by the pronouncement he made
in Simon's house?

The notable Pharisee had rudely omitted the usual civilities of
welcoming his guest, and Jesus took his place at the table without
comment. Then something remarkable occurred. A prostitute, knowing that he was there, entered and washed his feet with her tears,
wiped them on her hair, kissed them, and anointed them with ointment
from an alabaster box which she had with her.

The host, scandalized, said nothing.

" Simon," said Jesus, reading his thought, " I have something to
say to you."

" Teacher, say on!"

" There was," said Jesus, " a creditor who had two debtors, one

---

* Homilies on the Epistle to the Hebrews, 10[4] (F. Field, *Johannis Chrysostomi
interpretatio omnium epistularum Paulinarum*, vol. 7, Oxford, 1862, 12.110 B).

† In English characters : *mēdena apelpizontes* into *mēden apelpizontes*.

owing five hundred pence, the other fifty. He forgave them both, as neither could pay. Then tell me, which of them will love him most?"

" He, I suppose, to whom he forgave the most."

" Your opinion is right." Jesus addressed Simon, but turned to the prostitute. " See this woman ? When I arrived, although you provided no water to wash my feet, she washed them with her tears and wiped them with her hair. You gave me no greeting at all, but this woman has not ceased kissing my feet since I arrived. You provided no oil for my head, but this woman has poured ointment on my feet. Therefore, I tell you, *her many sins are forgiven, because she has loved greatly.* One who has had little forgiven loves little."

" Your sins are forgiven," he said to the woman. " Your faith has saved you. Go in peace."

Students have challenged the translation, " Her many sins are forgiven because she has loved greatly." It is said to be a dangerous doctrine. Simply as a reward for falling in love the woman's whole past is blotted out. The implication is that prostitution involved no love, no genuine emotion, simply a mechanical travesty of it, but now she has at last come into the sunlight of sincerity. Did Jesus mean to assert that as a direct result of her real emotion she had received God's forgiveness for everything? Can it be true that love, in itself, covers all sins? An interpretation like this lends support to those who are thinking their way towards a new morality. " Love will find the way," is a phrase which is applied to morals in books like *Honest to God*, with the similar aphorism, " Love has a built-in moral compass." Lest his position " be greeted as licence to laxity," the author instanced a young man whose true love for a girl will keep him moral, because love involves a respect too deep to use her for his own ends. Bishop Robinson's point is that *nothing else* but love " makes a thing right or wrong."*

Objections to the naïve illustration will spring readily to mind. The important point in our present discussion is that Bishop Robinson's dictum that nothing is prescribed except love for " man come of age," which he accepts from Tillich, is likely to appeal to the comparatively young. In a chapter contributed to a slight work recently produced by divinity teachers at Cambridge,† under the heading, " Psychological Objections to Christian Belief," Mr. H. A. Williams actually mentions the incident in Simon's house and rejects outright any translation which fails to give to Jesus's words the plain meaning that the woman's great love is the ground of her forgiveness. The Cambridge teacher has the impression that this is the sole legitimate rendering of the Greek

---

* *Honest to God*, pp. 118 f.
† *Objections to Christian Belief*, Cambridge, 1963.

and, claiming the authority of the late Dr. R. P. Casey, he presents no
linguistic evidence.

No one will deny that, literally rendered into English, the Greek
words are as follows : " Therefore I tell you, her many sins are forgiven,
because she has loved greatly." However, it is a nice point whether the
grammarian ought to interpret the words in the sense that love is all
that is required for winning divine pardon.

This would be to concede that Jesus was quite confused in his mind.
He had related to Simon a parable, the whole point of which was that a
man loves much *because he is forgiven*. To the question, " Which of
them will love him most ? " the Pharisee had answered, " He, I
suppose, to whom he forgave the most." It would have been impossible at the end of such a parable to argue that a woman was forgiven
because she loved much ; one avoids the absurdity by making a
scape-goat of the evangelist. Has St. Luke confused two stories? In
all fairness, let us look at the grammar of the Lord's remark to Simon.
It is legitimate, both in Greek and English, to understand the words
in the following way : " Because she has fallen in love, *this proves
that* her sins have been forgiven." The word *hoti* (" because ") may
convey either the proof of a proposition or the reason for stating it,
and between the two only the context can decide, together with any
other relevant circumstances, such as St. Luke's literary style in
similar situations. An example in English will make the point clear ;
it involves " because " used in a context where that word gives the
proof of the proposition rather than the reason for it. " Because he is
free, that man has been acquitted." His freedom *proves* his acquittal,
and it is quite wrong to say that he was acquitted *on the grounds that*
he was free. It may be just as wrong to say, " Her sins are forgiven
on the ground that she loves much."

In fact this is a feature of Lucan style. In Luke 1[22] " they perceived
that Zacharias had seen a vision in the temple, because (*hoti*) he
beckoned to them and remained speechless." Obviously, *hoti* refers
back to the first verb (" perceived "), just as in Jesus's remark to Simon
it refers back to the verb " I tell you." Jesus is saying, " I can tell
you she is forgiven, and I can tell you because she loves." The same
style lies behind Luke 6[21], where Jesus says, " Blessed are ye that
hunger now ; (this I know) because ye shall be filled." It cannot be
interpreted as, " Ye hunger now because ye shall be filled."

In the words of Jesus to Simon the Pharisee, renowned commentators
like Bengel, Alford, Godet, and H. A. W. Meyer, were aware of this
linguistic characteristic and had no doubt about the meaning. The
prostitute's love was understood to be the proof, not the cause, of her
forgiveness. In fact the argument of Jesus is *a posteriori* and its force
is this : " You would not have seen so great love as that, if this woman

were not already forgiven and if she did not know that she was." The *knowledge* of forgiveness is the really important element in what our Lord had to say. He himself actually used the word *faith* in order to describe the certainty in the mind of the forgiven woman. " Your faith has saved you," he said. And that faith had led to love.

Emotional speech

So heavy a veil is drawn over the less important details in our Lord's earthly life, over the frowns and smiles and laughter which are part of our humanity, that every attempt to pierce the reserve of the evangelists' prose is acceptable. It is a field where the grammarian's minute investigation could be helpful.

An instance of such research is the exclamation *O*! Its use as a vocative before a proper name is now obsolete in English and it was nearly so in contemporary Hellenistic. It was characteristic of abnormally emotional speech and for that reason it is worth observing its use in the New Testament.

One occasion was when Jesus was addressing the Syrophoenician woman. She had approached him about the illness of her daughter and he had observed her great faith with genuine astonishment. Emotion is betrayed in the exclamation, "Your faith is great indeed," for the unusual position of the word " great " lends feeling and emphasis to his appreciation of her attitude, and this is further underlined by the vocative exclamation, " O woman!" (Matt. 15[28]).

On other occasions when he used the word " woman " as a vocative, the absence of *O* reduces the emotion. Even on the cross, where emotion was likely to be in evidence, it was in a matter-of-fact manner that Jesus commended his mother to the care of St. John. " Woman, behold thy son " (John 19[26]). It is like the provision of an elder son for a mother's needs and recalls the same absence of emotion when the wine failed at the wedding in Cana. " Woman, leave this to me "* (John 4[2]).

By contrast, when Jesus came down from the mount of Transfiguration and heard that the inadequate faith of his disciples had failed to heal the dumb boy, he used the exclamation *O* as a sort of groan. " O faithless generation!" (Mark 9[19]).

Emotion was in the words of the risen Lord when he joined Cleopas and his friend on the road to Emmaus. He was surprised at their failure to understand the significance of Old Testament prophecy and exclaimed, " O foolish ones, and slow of heart!" (Luke 24[25]).

* For the basis of this translation, see pp. 43–47.

" We tried to discourage him." " Stop trying !" (Mark 9³⁸, *Luke* 9⁴⁹)

At a certain point in his ministry, the disciples, led by John the son of Zebedee, reported to Jesus that they had discovered a man exorcising evil spirits in his name. They had repeatedly discouraged this man, not being their Master's disciple, without complete success. Due account must be taken of the imperfect tense which is read in the better text of the gospels, both in St. Mark's version of the incident and in St. Luke's. The Byzantine text, which gradually became authoritative throughout the middle ages and formed the basis of Erasmus's text and the received text until the nineteenth century, has the aorist tense in both gospels ; it must be a correction.

The imperfect is conative or desiderative, representing an action which was never completed, perhaps was never adequately and wholeheartedly attempted or was too strongly frustrated. A good translation will reproduce this, as do Rieu's and the N.E.B.: " We tried to stop him." The point strangely escaped the scholarship of Moffatt, Goodspeed, the R.S.V., and J. B. Phillips. Monsignor Knox, of course, followed the aorist (Latin perfect, as opposed to imperfect) of the Vulgate.

A further test of good translation follows immediately in the reply of Jesus to his stormy disciple. Using a prohibition in the present tense, he said, " *Stop* discouraging him!" It was not a general prohibition, never to discourage the man, for that would be aorist. The disciples must change their course of action immediately. There are accents in his voice saying, " Change your attitude. Go at once to this man. Shake hands with him."

Does any English translation pass this test?

" Be in a state of having been " (Luke 12³⁵ᶠ·)

An American Quaker writes interestingly about the perfect imperative in the gospels.* He explains it as the apparently illogical command to be already in a certain state. Certainly that is grammatically the meaning of the perfect tense in general, and therefore inclusively of the perfect imperative. " Let your loins be girt " (Luke 12³⁵ᶠ·) will then be more precisely rendered, " Let your loins be already girt." To put this in the second person will be to bring the point out even more clearly ; it is not, " Gird up your loins," but " Be the kind of person who never needs to be told to gird them up, because he will always live in this condition."

* H. J. Cadbury, *Jesus*, 1962, pp. 90–91.

Cadbury describes it as the achieving of a spiritual maturity, like that which Jesus himself possessed, and he aptly quotes a friend who wrote to him in time of stress, " I have discovered that one cannot become a Christian in times like this. One must have been a Christian " (p. 90).

It is not so obvious how appropriate this grammatical nicety can be when Jesus used the perfect imperative to rebuke the elements on the lake of Galilee (Mark 4³⁹). What is the point of bidding the rough waves, " Be in a state of having been rendered harmless"? There must be some point, for already the same verb had been used in the aorist imperative (Mark 1²⁵) when an unclean spirit was commanded to " be harmless," i.e. " become harmless." Jesus is lord over the wild elements as well as over evil powers in the spiritual realm.

The visible kingdom of God (Mark 9¹)

This could be the place to discuss the force of the perfect participle, in a phrase like that in Mark 9¹, where Jesus said, " Some that stand here shall not taste of death till they have seen the kingdom of God *come* with power." The translation does no justice to the tense of the word in italics. Giving the perfect tense its due force we should read, " till they see the kingdom of God already established with power." St. Matthew and St. Luke found the grammar difficult and each in his own way altered it, but St. Mark was often subtle in spite of his generally rough style. Evidently something remarkable about the Lord's diction needed to be preserved. His words appear to be spoken immediately before the Transfiguration and that is where the significance lies. Either the Transfiguration itself was " the kingdom already established " or it provides the clue to it. As the Lawgiver and the Prophet discussed the crucifixion, one supposes that the death of Christ would mark the establishing of the kingdom.

Grammatically it is legitimate to see the Lord's phrase in a different light : " Till they know *that* the kingdom of God *has come* with power." In fact, the kingdom has come and no one realizes it yet, but some of those present would soon do so. It involves substituting " know " for " see," but both Greek verbs have the same form in this tense. Against this suggestion, used by Dr. C. H. Dodd to support a theory about Realized Eschatology, it must be said while such a construction is good classical Greek, nevertheless in biblical Greek " this kind of participle (especially in the perfect) is more plainly separated from the object of the main verb, and becomes in effect a distinctive complement, leaving the object and its main verb still very closely linked together."*
In other words, it would be more in accord with St. Mark's style to

* Moulton-Howard-Turner, *Grammar*, vol. III, p. 161.

translate our phrase, " till they see the kingdom of God, which has already come with power." Better still, and more in keeping with its context of the Transfiguration, " till they see the kingdom of God in power, which has already come (*scil.* without power)." The meekness of Jesus on the mount and the incomprehension of three disciples reflect the powerlessness of the kingdom at present ; but the brightness of the vision looks ahead to the time when " the kingdom in power " will be plainly seen.

" Madam, leave this to me " (*John* 2⁴)

At the Cana wedding, Jesus is reported as saying to his mother, " What have I to do with thee ? " (A.V., R.V., R.S.V.). If this is intended as a mild rebuke, it is strange that Mary proceeds to give confident directions to the servants, and Jesus lost no time in working the miracle.

The curious phrase, *ti emoi kai soi*, is literally, " What to me and to you ? " but grammatical discussion has led to no widely accepted meaning. Some have felt acutely the Hebraic sound of the words, but the phrase actually occurs in classical Greek as well as several times in the New Testament and in the Greek version of the Old Testament.

(1) Matt. 8²⁹ (= Mark 5⁷, Luke 8²⁸). Two demoniacs, who emerged from tombs in the Gadarene country as Jesus came along, cried, " O Son of God, *what to us and to you ?* Have you come to torment us before the time ? " The context demands a meaning like " Why are you troubling us ? "

(2) Mark 1²⁴ (= Luke 4³⁴). A man possessed with an unclean spirit cried in the Capernaum synagogue, " Jesus of Nazareth, *what to us and to you ?* Have you come to destroy us ? " Again, the meaning seems to be, " Leave us alone ! "

(3) John 2⁴. When at the Cana wedding the mother of Jesus reported that the wine was exhausted, he replied with the phrase in question. The evangelist has probably not recorded everything that was said between mother and son, nor how much the mother already knew about the son's powers. His reply is puzzling. " Woman, *what to me and to you ?* My hour has not yet come." One is tempted to transform the statement into an interrogative and to read, " Has not my hour come yet ? " Even so, the doubt about the meaning of " What to me and to you ? " is unresolved.

It is possible that the language of the evangelists or even of Jesus himself betrays the influence of Hebraistic construction behind a Greek façade. The phrase is used by the Greek version, the Septuagint, to translate the Hebrew idiom *mah-llī wālāk*, which is explained by

Brown-Driver-Briggs* as " What is there (common) to me and to thee ? i.e. what have I to do with thee ? " The insertion of " common " is gratuitous, but we may as well see how well such a translation meets the needs of the contexts.

(4) Judges 11¹². The phrase occurs in Jephthah's message which he sent to the Ammonites who had declared war against Israel. Jephthah said, " *What to me and to you*, that you have come to me to fight against my country ? " The sense required by this context is hardly that of Brown-Driver-Briggs, although it is corroborated by A. B. Davidson,† and the meaning which is most suitable would be, " What quarrel is there between us ? " Nevertheless, equally possible is the interpretation, " Why are you meddling in my affairs ? "—an interpretation which actually follows from the other.‡

(5) II Samuel 16¹⁰. King David's fortunes were at a low ebb during the revolt of Absolom, when he was dramatically cursed by Shimei near Bahurim. This member of Saul's displaced house cried, " Begone, you man of blood. Yahweh has avenged on you all the blood of the house of Saul," and he threw stones at the king as he travelled. One courtier, Abishai, son of Zeruiah, angrily exclaimed, " Why should this dog curse my lord ? Allow me to go and take off his head." Abishai in turn was rebuked by David, who used our formula : " You sons of Zeruiah, *what to me and to you?* Why should I challenge the man if Yahweh has told him to curse ? Let him alone. Let him curse."

David's meaning is clear. To those who sought to give advice he replied, " Leave me alone ! " The circumstances are similar to those at Cana, for St. Mary may have been seeking to give advice when she said, " They have no wine."

(6) II Samuel 19²² ⁽²³⁾. When later the revolt was crushed and David had returned to Jerusalem, Shimei grovelled for his life. Abishai was present and demanded Shimei's death as soon as he saw him. Again David rejected the advice. " You sons of Zeruiah, *what to me and to you*, that to-day you should be like an enemy to me ? to-day no one in Israel shall die. I am conscious of being king over Israel." The meaning of the phrase is as before. *Do not meddle* !

(7) I Kings 17¹⁸. Elijah found hospitality in the widow's house at Zarephath until the death of her son, when she approached the prophet with the idiom used by Jephthah and David. " Man of God, *what to me and to you ?* You have come to record my sin and cause my son to

---

* Francis Brown, S. R. Driver, C. A. Briggs, *Hebrew and English Lexicon of the Old Testament*, Oxford, 1906, see under מה.

† A. B. Davidson, *Hebrew Syntax*, T. & T. Clark, 3rd. ed., 1901, p. 8 : *what have I to do with thee ?*

‡ G. F. Moore, *Judges* (International Critical Commentary), T. & T. Clark, 1908, p. 290 : " What is there between us to justify this war ? "

die ! " The meaning may be, " What have you against me ? " (R.S.V.)
—which was possible also in Jephthah's remark—but as likely is the
meaning, " Why are you meddling in my affairs ? " It suits all the
contexts examined so far.

Montgomery* regarded it as a characteristic expression of ancient
religion, the *Scheu vor Heiligkeit* (shrinking before the Holy), the woman's
finding a divine person in her house gives her an instinctive desire to
escape or to be left alone, as when St. Peter discovered the Lord's
divinity and said, " Depart from me " (Luke 5⁸), and when the centurion's similar discovery led to a desire that Jesus would not enter
his house (Matt. 8⁸).

(8) II Kings 3¹³. Elijah's mantle had fallen on Elisha, and in Samaria
the bad Jehoram had made preparations to quell a rising of the Moabites
with the help of Jehoshaphat of Judah and the king of Edom. Their
armies faced a dangerous situation on the way to Moab when water
supplies failed. They consulted Elisha. Addressing his words to the
king of Israel, who was disloyal to the religion of Yahweh, Elisha said,
" *What to me and to you?* Go to the prophets of your father and the
prophets of your mother ! " What did Elisha mean ? It is unlikely
that he asked, " What have we in common ? " His question is surely
an ironical rebuke, an invitation to turn to someone more suitable for
this particular task. Ahab and Jezebel had introduced foreign priests
and prophets into Israel. The meaning is, once again, " Why are
you troubling me ? "

(9) II Chronicles 35²¹. Josiah of Judah met his death in a foolish
action against Pharaoh Neco on the plain of Megiddo which preceded
the famous battle of Carchemish. It was provoked by the king of
Judah, although before the battle Pharaoh had sent envoys assuring
him that the quarrel was not against Judah but against the Babylonian
empire, and Josiah was requested to remove himself from business
which did not concern him. Pharaoh used the same idiom : " King
of Judah, *what to me and to you?* I am not attacking you but the house
with which I am at war." Again the meaning is, " Do not meddle in
my affairs."

In each instance, the Greek Bible of the earliest Christians translates
mah-llī wālāk by the same formula as is used by the evangelists.

Apart from the Hebraic background of the idiom, what was the
position in the earlier stages of the Greek language itself ? In the
dramatists the two parts of the phrase are used separately. *Ti moi*
means "What is it to me?" (simple ellipse of the verb " to be ") ; and
ti soi means " What is it to you?" The implication is that the matter
is no concern of the person mentioned and that he should not meddle

* J. A. Montgomery and H. S. Gehman, *The Books of Kings* (International
Critical Commentary), T. & T. Clark, 1951, p. 295.

with it—a meaning which coincides precisely with what is demanded in the Old Testament contexts. " Do not meddle ! " Where the phrase is not so simple but includes two datives, it appears that the first person mentioned is the one in danger of being troubled. For instance : " Why should these matters concern you ? " (Herodotus V. 33 : *soi* occurs first).* It is reminiscent of the Hebrew idiom which the Septuagint renders by *ti soi kai eirēnē* " what to you and peace? ") in II Kings 9¹⁸, where Jehu sends a message in reply to the king's anxious query, " Is it peace? " Jehu replies, " Why are *you* concerned about peace? " for he knows that Joram is prepared to attack. On the whole, however, the Hebraic idiom is not quite in accordance with classical Greek idiom where *ti estin emoi kai soi* is authoritatively said to mean, " What have you and I in common? "† and the element of interference and concern is not always present. Thus, Demosthenes says, *Ti tō nomō kai tē basanō ?* (literally, " What to the Law and to torture ? ") in a context which implies not " The Law is not concerned with torture," but " The Law and torture have nothing in common " (so Kühner-Gerth).‡ In biblical Greek, however, the idea of concern is usually very much to the fore, and this is seen especially in the message which Pilate received from his wife urging him not to interfere with his prisoner. " *Let there be nothing to you and that innocent man* ! " (Matt. 27¹⁹).

It is therefore proposed that in the New Testament instances of the idiom the idea of meddling is prominent and should be brought out in the translation. It is all the more gratifying to discover that this has been done in the privately circulated editions of *Matthew* and *Mark* published by the Bible Society to assist the work of native churches in producing their own versions of the Bible.§ " Why are you interfering with us ? " It is a welcome departure from such authorities as H. B. Swete (" What have we in common with Thee? "),‖ who take it to imply repudiation of fellowship. The commentary of Dr. Vincent Taylor correctly reviews the position. " In Cl. Gk. the question . . . would mean ' What have we in common ? ', but here it probably corresponds to the Heb. . . . with the meaning ' Why dost thou meddle with us? ' "¶

The makers of the N.E.B. have presented two quite different translations of the same idiom. They give us "What do you want with me/

---

* See also Demosthenes 29. 36.

† " Was hab' ich mit dir gemein ? "   R. Kühner, *Ausführliche Grammatik der griechischen Sprache*, besorgt v. B. Gerth, Hanover, 1898, i, p. 417.

‡ Demosthenes 29. 36.

§ *Mark : a Greek-English Diglot for the use of Translators*, British & Foreign Bible Society, 146 Queen Victoria Street, London, 1958. *Matthew* followed in 1959. See Mark 1²⁴ 5⁷, Matt. 8²⁹.

‖ H. B. Swete, *The Gospel according to St. Mark*, Macmillan, 1902, pp. 19, 94.

¶ V. Taylor, *The Gospel according to St. Mark*, Macmillan, 1955, p. 174.

us?" in the synoptic gospels, and "Your concern is not mine" for Jesus's remark to his mother at Cana, in the fourth gospel.

The remark of Jesus to his mother appears to be a polite request to refrain from interference and to leave the whole matter to him. Perhaps that is why she thought that he had a definite plan in mind and asked the servants to be ready for any orders.

7. WHY JESUS USED PARABLES (Mark 4¹²)

The fourth chapter of Mark provides the reason why Jesus chose the parabolic method of teaching.

His disciples had come to him privately and asked him about "the parables." The plural does not make very good sense, since they asked him only concerning the Sower, and not surprisingly a whole manuscript tradition, including that followed by the A.V., changed this plural into a singular. St. Mark has adopted a mannerism, of which St. Matthew is more characteristically fond, the *pluralis categoriae*, and in English the translation of the A.V. is incidentally correct in spite of its poor textual foundation.

His explanation was given because the disciples asked him to interpret one specific parable, the Sower. He replied, "You yourselves are allowed to know the secret about the kingdom of God, as distinct from those who do not belong to your circle and have to be content with parables." This was "*in order that* they may see indeed and not know ; and that they should not at any time repent and their sins be forgiven them" (Mark 4¹¹· ¹²). That is a fair translation, but not the only possible one. As an explanation of parabolic teaching it is fatalistic enough to repel much Christian taste and feeling, and other meanings have been proposed for " in order that " (representing the Greek words *hina* and, negatively, *mēpote*). Loth to ascribe the sentiment to Jesus himself, some endeavour to reconstruct the original Aramaic, confident that St. Mark's report in Greek is a distorted version of what he really said.

As the words stand they seem to represent a purpose-clause stating that Jesus has deliberately chosen to teach in parables *in order that* the majority of his hearers might not understand and might thereby lose their chance of salvation. Dr. T. W. Manson felt the difficulty acutely and visualized the underlying Aramaic, in which he suggested that an ambiguous particle (*dᵉ*) might have caused the confusion since it has several functions. If *dᵉ* were used by Jesus as a relative pronoun the sense of the whole passage would no longer scandalize us. It was the Greek translator who thoughtlessly read it as a particle carrying a purposive meaning. Dr. Manson then explained the second conjunction, *mēpote*, as having the meaning " perhaps." So an innocuous sense was obtained. The connection is not that of causation but is entirely accidental. Dr. Manson argued that the quotation from Isaiah—that is, the clause beginning with the first " in order that "—conforms to the Aramaic paraphrase (Targum) of Isaiah which was read in the synagogues. The Targum differs from both the Hebrew text and the Septuagint, and Manson believed that St. Mark misunderstood it by taking the ambiguous particle d^e in the wrong sense. The difficulty is that Manson assumes that Jesus taught in Aramaic rather than Greek, and there are good reasons why serious consideration should be given to the view that there was a biblical or Jewish kind of Greek spoken in Palestine during the first century.* It would be the language of Jesus as well as of Mark and Luke and John. If the proposition is sound it makes translation hypotheses untenable. Although Aramaic constructions would influence this kind of Greek, they would not transform *hina* into a relative pronoun.

Apart from this, Dr. Manson's suggestion makes the explanation of Jesus a poor answer to those who sought the meaning of the parable of the Sower. The words, " who see indeed but do not know," are an accurate description of the disciples themselves who have heard the parable and seen his works, and yet who come to him in self-confessed ignorance. What distinction can there be, on those grounds, between them and the outsiders?

But *hina* need not be purposive. While there is no evidence for *hina* meaning " who," there is evidence for its imperatival use. Nevertheless this too must be rejected if we are to avoid an interpretation which repels the moral sense. We could legitimately regard *hina* as consecutive (" so that "), which would be inoffensive enough since it would express merely the result. The second conjunction, *mēpote*, will then be taken in the sense of " perhaps." There is precedent enough for both of these in Hellenistic Greek. However, yet another explanation has been offered by Dr. H. G. Meecham,† that this *hina* might foreshadow the later and rarer meaning " because." He noted that the Chester Beatty papyrus in Rev. 14¹³ actually reads *hoti* (" because ") for the generally accepted *hina*, and this better suits the context in Rev. 14¹³, as indeed it would also in Rev. 22¹⁴. But in both those contexts the better known imperatival *hina* would be even more suitable : " May they rest from their labours ! " (14¹³) and, " May they have right to the tree of life ! " (22¹⁴).

It is evidence of the embarrassment which Christian commentators have found in these words of Jesus that yet another suggestion has been put forward. Dr. William Manson has suggested that the Greek

---

* See the last chapter of this book.
† Reviewing Canon C. F. D. Moule's *Idiom Book*, in *New Testament Studies*, vol. I, no. 1, pp. 62–65.

word *kai* ("and") rendered a Semitic subordinating particle which had the nuance "although."* Dr. W. Manson allowed *hina* to retain its purposive force, but it then becomes inoffensive because of the prior force of "although." "In order that they may see indeed *although* they do not perceive ; and hear *although* they do not understand." To soften the ensuing *mēpote* Dr. W. Manson resorts to the explanation once again that this is the particle of cautious assertion ("perhaps").

The reader may be tempted to cut the Gordian knot and return to the traditional translation in which *hina* has its classical meaning "in order that." It is a point of view not without exponents, who believe that the quotation from Isaiah reflects the early Church's concern to explain the lack of response to their Messiah on the part of the Jews. Primitive Christians found the solution by supposing that the identity of Jesus was deliberately kept secret by Jesus himself. It was God's plan to withhold enlightenment from the ordinary people of Israel and to allow them to hear the parables without discovering their significance. This may have been because they would have drawn a wrong conclusion about his Messiahship, had they been aware of it.

In two articles† Mr. T. A. Burkill has shown that St. Mark's view about the Messianic "secret" agrees with a similar view in the writings of St. Paul, especially in Rom, 11$^{5-8}$, and also with the presupposition of St. John throughout his gospel. St. Paul saw the secret as due to God's deliberate act, but in his view it was achieved not so much by the parabolic method as by a process of making dull the spiritual faculties of the Jews. St. John's picture is a little different : there was no deliberately withheld Messianic secret, for Jesus was proclaimed from the first by many signs, and the reason why men heard without perceiving was because they were blinded by the nature of the Light itself and because they deliberately chose darkness.

This approach seems to me to accord better than any other with the tenor of the quotation in its original context in the sixth chapter of Isaiah. Although it is not introduced by the first "in order that," nevertheless the second conjunction is there under the form of *pen* in the Hebrew, with its undoubted meaning, "lest." The prophet saw the darkening of the national mind as part of God's inscrutable providence and it looks as if St. Mark, and indeed Jesus, did so too. Jesus took pains, according to the synoptic gospels, to hide his true identity from most of the Jews throughout his ministry.

It may be helpful to collate the suggestions of various interpreters.

---

* *Expos. Times*, LXVIII, no. 5, p. 134.
† *Theologische Zeitschrift*, XII, 1956, pp. 585ff ; *Novum Testamentum*, I, fasc. 4, Oct., 1956, pp. 261f.

	Traditional	C. F. D. Moule	H. G. Meecham	T. W. Manson	W. Manson
hina	" in order that "	" so that "	" because "	" who "	" in order that "
mēpote	" in order that . . . not "	" perhaps "	" perhaps "	" perhaps "	" perhaps "

Translation	" To you is given the secret of the kingdom of God ; but all things are impossible to those outside,

IN ORDER THAT they may see indeed and not know, and IN ORDER THAT they may hear indeed and not understand : IN ORDER THAT they should not repent and receive for giveness."	SO THAT they see indeed but do not know, and hear indeed but do not understand.	BECAUSE they see indeed but do not know, and hear indeed but do not understand.	WHO see indeed but do not know, and hear, indeed but do not understand.	IN ORDER THAT they may see indeed, ALTHOUGH they do not know, and IN ORDER THAT they may hear indeed ALTHOUGH they do not understand.
	PERHAPS they will repent and receive forgiveness."			

8. THE COURTESY OF JESUS

To a centurion (Matt. 8[5–13])

A centurion who was stationed at Capernaum begged Jesus in the early days of his ministry to heal his paralytic son—or was it his servant ? The Greek is ambiguous.

At once Jesus said he would come and heal him. So all our English translations render it, but the Greek may have the aorist subjunctive rather than the future indicative. At this point the centurion made his protest. He was not worthy that Jesus should come into his house.

The whole conversation was, I think, more subtle than this, and Jesus was more sensitive to the feelings of the centurion and desirous to avoid embarrassment. Our usual versions miss all this. In the wretched centurion's hour of sorrow it is incredible that Jesus would state his intention of provoking comment and criticism. He would have known in what an awkward situation he, as a Jew, was placing the officer. The Gentile would feel in all politeness he ought to refuse and would resent being forced into a position where he had caused a Jew to offend against the precepts of his own religion. Yet how could he refuse the demand of this healer to open his house to him ?

It is an unthinkable situation, and indeed the Greek grammar conveys no such thought. What Jesus really said was, " *Am* I to come and heal him ? " Grammarians call it a deliberative question. Alike in classical Greek and Hellenistic (including the New Testament) the future tense is used like this. The scribes who made the earliest Bible manuscripts wasted little effort on punctuation and the absence of a question-mark in the printed editions means nothing at all.

It may be assumed that Jesus asked the officer whether he really wanted him to come down to his house and perform the healing. It was a very tentative offer on Jesus's part to break the divine Law in order to perform a work of mercy. " Is that what you want *me* to do ? " he asks. " Me, that am a Jew ? "*

There was nothing irreverent about the tentative question. Rather, it anticipated the shock which the man would feel, by adopting the form of a deliberative question, and this reveals that Jesus fully expected a strong protest from the Gentile soldier. What he did not apparently anticipate was the man's unique affirmation of faith. It was overwhelming and Jesus rewarded it at once. A faith so great made it possible for him to perform the miraculous work of healing there and then. No need to go to his home. No need to upset the local Pharisees and other good people. No need to hurt a soldier's sense of social decorum.

This story is told by St. Matthew. St. Luke's version is different in several important details and may not refer to the same incident (Luke 7).

To disciples (Luke 17⁵)

When his disciples said to him, " Give us more faith,"† our Lord's reply is notable for its grammar, since it contains that scourge of

---

* The *egō* in the Greek is not necessary and its gratuitous insertion is probably emphatic ; at least this would be so in the classical language, although more latitude was allowed in biblical Greek as well as in the contemporary papyri.

† I believe this to be the true meaning of Luke 17⁵, rather than " Add faith to us " (i.e. to our other virtues), because the literal expression, " Add faith to us," is Hebraic, like that in Isaiah 2¹⁹ (" The meek shall increase their joy ") and 26¹⁵ (" Thou hast increased the nation "), and involves increasing the substance rather than adding a new substance.

beginners in Greek, an unfulfilled conditional clause, and this particular instance breaks all rules. It is unfulfilled in the present time, and the protasis (the clause containing " if ") ought to have its verb in the imperfect indicative mood, and the apodosis (main clause) should have it in the imperfect with the addition of *an*.

Jesus is reported as using the present indicative in the protasis. Among the texts of the Ptolemaic papyri, the only precedent I know is part of an illiterate letter written in 153 B.C. I would not infer that Jesus habitually used uncultured Greek, but unless he resorted to it deliberately the construction is not such as would occur even to a moderately literate person. If Jesus regularly spoke Aramaic,* these would not of course be his actual words, and the evangelist will have deliberately made use of the grammatical anacoluthon in order to translate into Greek something significant that was conveyed to his disciples in Aramaic.

Could this have been a subtle politeness ? A grammarian would complain that the present indicative in the protasis in place of the correct imperfect had changed the clause from an *unreal* to a *real* condition. It means that the supposition introduced by " if " is no longer a vague one but is a real situation. It means that Jesus was not saying, " *If* you had faith " (implying that they had not), but " If you *have* faith " (leaving the matter open, but implying that they have). The disciples had little enough, but it was comparable in potentiality to a grain of mustard seed. Besides, the disciples themselves had claimed to have some faith. This was implicit in their request to have it increased. Jesus was charitable enough to let this go unchallenged. To have preserved correct grammar and to have said, " if you had faith," might have taken them aback and have appeared like a snub. His ungrammatical words are expressive.

The feature of syntax opens our eyes to the gentleness of this answer to his disciples' request : " Since you have some faith, small as it may be, you could say to this sycamine tree, Be plucked up by the root. . . ."

To his enemies (*John* 8[39])

Our third example depends upon a highly probable variant reading in the manuscripts, and is an instance of the same rare conditional construction that we have already observed in Luke 17[5].

The Jews in their controversy with Jesus had claimed, " Abraham is our father." The dialogue was doubtless acrimonious, but it appears exceptionally so if the accepted version of Jesus's reply is followed. The rendering of the English versions is along these lines : " If you were (*ēte*) Abraham's children, you would do (*epoieite*) the works of

* But see the discussion in the last chapter of this book.

Abraham." However, a glance at the margins of the R.V. and of the N.E.B. will reveal that it is possible to follow a quite different text : " If you are (*este*) Abraham's children, do as Abraham did (*poieite*)." The tense of the verb in the protasis is now present, and the mood of the apodosis is no longer indicative, but imperative. This form of text harmonizes better with the context, but is suspect on those very grounds, for it reads like an alteration carried out by editors or scribes in order to make things easier. A little before this (verse 37), Jesus had admitted, " I know that you are Abraham's seed," and he was making use of their own claim in order to further his argument. "Abraham is our father," and he offered the rejoinder, " Yes. Then do what Abraham would do. You are seeking to kill a man who speaks the truth."

The same construction occurs in John 7[4], a conditional sentence consisting of *ei* with the present indicative, followed by an imperative in the apodosis. There is therefore some precedent for it in this gospel.

However, in 8[39], the reading which involves this construction may not be the correct one. It fits the context a little too perfectly, and there is a third textual possibility. Some manuscripts have a version of Jesus's reply which is grammatically difficult and therefore the most likely of the three variants to have given rise to the others, by a process of simplification : " If you are (*este*) Abraham's children, you would do (*epoieite*) the works of Abraham." This kind of conditional sentence sounds equally incongruous in Greek or English. " If you were," would be the usual form, and one is prompted to ask precisely what the conspicuous change to the indicative mood involves. This might be a condensed construction, capable of expansion into, " If you were justified in claiming that you are Abraham's children. . . ." On the other hand, it may well be a further instance of the phenomenon in Luke 17[5]. It will be recalled that Jesus used the present indicative in the " if "-clause of a conditional sentence in the interests of courtesy. " If you were Abraham's children " sounds too definite an implication that they are failing in their claim, and it makes the wording of the assumption less discourteously definite when it is phrased, " If you are Abraham's children." The innuendo has gone. It is tantamount to an admission, virtually the equivalent of the previous reading, " If you are the children of Abraham, you ought to do the works of Abraham." So the large number of textual authorities, headed by Codex Vaticanus, which reflect this departure from what I believe to be the true text, are in fact carefully interpreting it, although they make the grammar more acceptable in the process.

The celebrated editor, Tischendorf, advocated it, but the reading is supported by Codex Sinaiticus which this scholar discovered in exciting circumstances and for which in consequence he often paid too much regard.

The following table sets out the three textual possibilities and presents the chief authorities in support of each.

TEXTUAL AUTHORITY		ENGLISH TRANSLATION	
Ancient	Modern	Protasis	Apodosis
Codex Ephraemi 5th cent. Codex Sangallensis 9th cent. Koridethi MS. 9th cent. Egyptian Versions (Sahidic and Bohairic) 3rd cent.?	Textus Receptus A.V. R.S.V. N.E.B.	" If you were (*ēte*) Abraham's children,	". . . you would do (*epoieite*) the works of Abraham (or ' what Abraham did ')." (+ *an* in Greek : some authorities)
Bodmer papyrus 2nd–3rd cent. Codex Vaticanus (original scribe) 4th cent. Old Latin Version (Codex Corbeiensis II) 5th cent. Vulgate Latin	Westcott and Hort Nestle R.V. (mg.) N.E.B. (mg.)	" If you are (*este*) Abraham's children,	". . . do (*poieite*) the works of Abraham." (R.V. (mg.) " ye do ")
Codex Sinaiticus (original scribe) 4th cent. Codex Bezae 5th cent. Codex Vaticanus (very early correction) Codex Regius 8th cent.	Westcott and Hort (mg.) Alford Tischendorf Bover	" If you are (*este*) Abraham's children,	". . . you would do (*epoieite*) the works of Abraham." (+ *an* : corrector of Codex Sinaiticus)

9. GROWING OPPOSITION TO JESUS

Who devoured widows' houses ? (*Mark* 12³⁸⁻⁴⁰)

Why Jesus denounced the scribes and Pharisees so scathingly has often been a matter for wonder and sometimes for criticism. They were the respectable and pious people of the time.

It may ease the difficulty a little to find that grammar demands a re-wording of one of these direct attacks in our English versions.

Mark 12³⁸⁻⁴⁰ is the case in point. It accuses the scribes of inordinate fondness for greetings in market-places, chief seats in synagogues, and the best places at banquets. This much is undeniable and cannot be altered, but what follows is dubious. The scribes " devour widows' houses, and for a pretence make long prayers : these shall receive greater damnation."

It is a matter of grammar whether the relative pronoun which precedes this piece of information ought to be construed as " who " or " those who." In the second alternative, the relative pronoun will mark the beginning of a new sentence and will make it a general one, not necessarily referring to the scribes. It would be anyone who devours widows' houses. The idea is at least as old as the eighteenth century and was suggested by Dr. J. A. Bengel whose acutely perceptive comments on Scripture come down from 1750, and he was supported by the nineteenth-century commentator, Dr. H. A. W. Meyer. Moreover, the punctuation which is presupposed is advocated in the critical Greek editions of C. Lachmann (1842–50), Tischendorf (8th. edition, 1865–72), S. P. Tregelles (1857–71), Westcott and Hort (1881), Nestle (1898 onwards), and Bover (4th. edition, 1959). These editors considered that a new sentence began at verse 40, and that the reference was more general than the scribes. " Those who devour widows' houses, and for a pretence make long prayers, shall receive greater damnation."

The R.V. depends upon this exposition of the Greek, marking a departure from the A.V.

Two important considerations weigh against it. First, St. Luke knew St. Mark's gospel and he made it clear that he thought verse 40 referred to the scribes who had previously been mentioned ; he used the relative pronoun and present indicative at the beginning of the verse in place of St. Mark's definite article with the participle. Secondly, the logical sequence is impaired. After a detailed condemnation of the scribes' hypocrisy, a repetition in merely general terms comes as an anticlimax. It is perhaps for this reason that the R.S.V. and the N.E.B. revert to the interpretation of the A.V. On the other hand, grammatical evidence is conclusive against these two considerations and supports the nearly unanimous opinion of textual editors. The evidence is three-fold. In the first place, " those who devour " (a phrase in the nominative case) cannot be associated very closely with " the scribes " (which is actually the genitive case), and most probably indicates a new set of people entirely. Secondly, it is characteristic of St. Mark's style to begin a sentence with a participle and to follow it up later with a resumptive " this " or " that," which makes it the more probable that verse 40 is an independent sentence. Thirdly, St. Mark liked to use an articular participle in place of a noun. He does of course sometimes use it in place of a relative clause (as A.V., R.S.V., and N.E.B. take it here), but then the articular participle has a position very close to its antecedent noun, which is not so in our passage.

Who thought Jesus was mad ? (Mark 3²¹)

St. Mark appears to imply that Jesus's family considered him to be mad, but the implication is only apparent, as close scrutiny of the grammar will disclose.

Dr. C. H. Turner, who made his best contributions to biblical scholarship in the realm of language, reminded scholars as long ago as 1924 in articles in the *Journal of Theological Studies* that the plural in Mark may be impersonal. Largely it concerns the phrase, " they said," which occurs in an important context, like, " They said, ' Not on the feast day.' " It was not the scribes and chief priests who said it, but rumour or people in general. A context of even greater significance is 3²¹, where the majority of our versions (the Bible Society's Diglot* and the N.E.B. being honourable exceptions) imply that the mother and kinsmen of Jesus considered him mad. It was rumour, not his own family, that spread the doubts of his sanity. The family was anxious, having heard he had taken no food, and they wished to have a quiet word with him, especially when they heard the rumours.

Greek is a language which possesses no convenient indeterminate subject to serve in an impersonal phrase. English has " one," French has *on*, and German has *man*. Greek must have recourse to the third person plural of a verb. Moreover, in biblical Greek, which sometimes shows the influence of Aramaic idiom, the third person plural of an active verb serves the purpose of the passive voice of the same verb— with, of course, a change of subject. The reason for this is that Aramaic tends to avoid the passive voice, with " They kill," instead of " They are killed." St. Luke can write (in 12²⁰), concerning the soul which " is required," that " they require it."

Many instances occur in St. Mark's gospel. " They (i.e. " people ")

* See above, p. 46.

came to see what had happened " (5¹⁴). " They took up twelve baskets "
(i.e. " twelve baskets were taken up ") (6⁴³). " They (i.e. " people ")
recognized him " (6⁵⁴).

Jesus and the Pharisees (Luke 11⁴¹)

Jesus's accusations against the Pharisees were serious, and some
critics have suggested that they were not altogether justified. According to St. Luke, many were delivered on the occasion of a dinner to
which Jesus had been invited by a Pharisee. To the Pharisee's com-
plaint that he had not ritually washed his hands, Jesus replied, " You
Pharisees clean the outside and leave the inside full of wickedness ! "
He explained that God made both inside and outside, but his next
remark (11⁴¹) is very puzzling. " Give alms of such things as ye have ;
and behold, all things are clean unto you." This rendering of the A.V.
is merely a way out of a difficulty, as the Revisers appreciated when
they gave us the awkward substitute, " Give for alms those things
which are within ; and behold, all things are clean unto you "—with
a marginal alternative, " Give for alms those things which ye can."
It is all an anticlimax, compared with St. Matthew's version (23²⁶) :
" Cleanse first that which is within the cup and platter, that the outside of them may be clean also."

Accordingly it has been suggested that Jesus gave the teaching in
Aramaic, using the word *dakki* (" cleanse "), which was mistaken for
zakki (" give alms ") by the Greek translator. The theory goes back
to Wellhausen,* but although he claimed that he found *zakki* with the
meaning " give alms " in the Palestinian Talmud, it is by no means
clear, and Jastrow's dictionary gives no hint of that meaning. Indeed,
zakki and *dakki* both mean " cleanse." It is possible, without assistance
from Aramaic, to assess the meaning, if we regard the phrase *ta enonta*
(" the inward things ") as adverbial accusative, meaning " inwardly."
So Jesus exhorts, " Give alms from the heart (sincerely)." He has in
mind the Pharisees, who parade almsgiving before the public gaze.
Generosity must be genuinely felt. Adverbial accusatives are common
enough in the New Testament.†

Pharisees and the market (Mark 7⁴)

The approach to a problem in the gospels often depends on the
student's opinion of the original language of Jesus. Greek or Aramaic ?

In Mark 7⁴, most English versions, following a good rule of classical
and later Greek (that *apo* may sometimes mean " after " in a temporal

* But is often revived, e.g. in Moulton-Howard, *Grammar*, vol. II, p. 471.
† Moulton-Howard-Turner, *Grammar*, vol. III, p. 247.

G.I.—3

sense), render Jesus's saying accordingly : " *When they come from (apo)* the market-place the Pharisees do not eat, unless they wash themselves " (A.V., R.V., R.S.V., Rieu, N.E.B.). It is true that *ek*, not *apo*, is more commonly used in classical Greek with the meaning " after," but *apo* is quite common in the New Testament,* e.g. " after the days of John " (Matt. 11[12]), " after that time " (Matt. 16[21] 26[16], Luke 16[16]), " after weakness " (Heb. 11[34]).

A deviation from this position was first seen in the versions of Goodspeed and Moffatt. " They will not eat anything *from (apo)* the market without first purifying it by sprinkling it " (Goodspeed). " They decline to eat what comes *from (apo)* the market, till they have washed it " (Moffatt). However, this translation is grammatically insecure, quite apart from the word *apo* ; Goodspeed and Moffatt assume that the verb " wash " or " sprinkle," in the middle voice, can be interpreted in the transitive sense. The Diglot edition of Mark, privately circulated by the British and Foreign Bible Society (1958), takes this point, but unfortunately confirms Goodspeed and Moffatt in their rendering of *apo*. " They do not eat anything from the market-place unless they wash themselves."

Goodspeed, Moffatt, and the Diglot probably base their rendering of " *apo* the market-place " on the grammatical point that *apo* with a noun is a literal version in Greek of the Semitic idiom for the partitive expression " some of."† This would be reasonable, assuming that Jesus uttered the saying in a Semitic tongue. But is it logical to accept *apo* as partitive and then to translate " something *from* the market-place ? " If *apo* is partitive, the meaning must be " a part of the market-place "—which is unacceptable.

The expression ought to be taken in the Hellenistic Greek sense, " after the market-place." It appears to suit the context less well, for there is a suggestion in the context that the apostles were eating food from the market-place, but it should be remembered that the disciples had been in the market-place and ought to have washed their hands after contamination with the mixed crowds.‡ That is what the Greek must mean.

" *Out into darkest darkness* " (*Matt.* 8[12])

One is accustomed to the phrase, " outer darkness," but may wonder precisely what Jesus meant by it. Whereas in classical Greek the comparative degree of an adjective is fairly strictly used, in Hellenistic it is found to be at times no more than a positive adjective, whilst

---

* *Ibid.* p. 259.
† M. Black, *An Aramaic Approach to the Gospels and Acts*, 2nd. ed. Oxford, 1954, p. 37.
‡ H. B. Swete, *The Gospel according to St. Mark*, Macmillan, 2nd. ed., 1902, p. 144.

at other times the degree of comparison is often increased to that of superlative.

In such a situation, one may doubt whether Jesus was using " outer " in its strictly comparative sense when he spoke of the kind of darkness into which sinners may be sent. One may doubt whether Jesus distinguished between an inner and an outer darkness. More likely that he envisaged an ever-increasing intensity of it as the sinner moves further from God's presence, and that he was warning the Jews of the danger facing them—the outermost darkness of all, the nemesis of blind refusal to believe. Few translators or commentators have made the point, but the committee responsible for the N.E.B. were at least aware of the easy use of comparatives in Hellenistic Greek. They have, however, understood the comparative as purely positive, whereas the superlative would have been better in this context.

There are many ways in which the lax use of the comparative degree affects interpretation in the New Testament ; and that Jesus used " greater " when " greatest " was intended is not really open to doubt. He used *meizōn* (" greater ") in Matt. 18$^{1.\ 4}$ and Mark 9^{34}, where the contexts make it clear that in classical Greek *megistos* (" greatest " or " very great ") would be required. It is not a matter of opinion, for the true comparative would be an impossible meaning.

Similarly, Jesus said " smaller " when he meant " smallest " in Matt. 11^{11}, Luke 7^{28} 9^{48}. Again the contexts prove that the comparative is used as a superlative.

Among New Testament writers, only the author of II Peter retained the classical *megistos* for " greatest," and he belonged, or aspired, to the new school of Atticistic authors who revived in the Hellenistic age the canons of the classical style of Attic Greek. Such literary pretensions are foreign to most New Testament authors, and even St. Paul was capable of referring to the *least* honourable parts of the body by means of the comparative degree (I Cor. 12^{23}).

Attacks on the kingdom of God (Matt. 11^{12})

The teaching of Jesus on the kingdom has been widely discussed. Not the least of the difficulties about it is his assessment of John the Baptist and the Baptist's place in the kingdom. Having said that he was the greatest of men and yet less than the least in the kingdom, Jesus proceeded to the remark, " From the days of John the Baptist until now the kingdom of heaven . . .," and here follows a deponent verb. Such verbs are passive in form but active in meaning, and one would suppose that Jesus meant, " The kingdom has been forcing its way forward," or perhaps that the kingdom comes with violence. That interpretation is placed in the margin (not the text) of the R.S.V. and

N.E.B. However, most versions take the verb as truly passive, e.g. suffereth violence " (A.V.). Knowing the verb to be deponent, commentators have been dissatisfied with the grammatical assumptions of the A.V. rendering, and puzzled too about the way the kingdom might be subjected to violence.

Dissatisfaction increases when it is seen that St. Luke in the parallel passage clearly used the verb in its active sense as a true deponent.

The consideration which has most influenced translators and commentators towards the passive is the tone of the sentence which follows. " The violent take it by force." Grammatically too they are right. Notwithstanding that the verb is usually deponent, it nevertheless belongs to a group of transitive deponent verbs which in both classical and later Greek might also be used in a passive sense.*

The words of Jesus are still puzzling but we need have no doubt that St. Matthew understood him to mean that the kingdom was now facing opposition.

The sign is Jonah (*Matt.* 12³⁹ff., *Luke* 11²⁹)

Although Jesus refused to satisfy the demand of his countrymen for a sign, he did make the exception of stating that " the sign of the prophet Jonah " was granted to this generation.

The Old Testament story of Jonah may be searched in vain for trace of " a sign " of Jonah, and there has been much debate on this. Surely, grammar is again the way to the answer. The genitive, " of Jonah," is a well-known construction, the epexegetical genitive. It has little to do with possession ; it explains, expands, defines. The " sign " which Jesus promised to his generation was Jonah himself—not the sign *of* Jonah, but the sign *which is* Jonah.

Jesus therefore is represented as both Jonah and "more than Jonah " (not " greater than," in view of the neuter gender). He is the prophet to the Gentiles, but without the lack of sympathy which curtailed Jonah's usefulness.

10. MARRIAGE AND DIVORCE (Mark 10⁹, Matt. 19³, Luke 16¹⁸)

In order to resist the conclusion that Jesus forbade divorce absolutely, some have argued that he merely forbade either party to a marriage to dissolve it unilaterally.

In support of this, I have seen it pleaded that the words, " Let no *man* put asunder " (Mark 10⁹), really mean " Let not *a husband* put asunder " (scil. his own marriage). This, however, is to overlook that whereas in verse 2 the word *anēr* (" husband ") is used, our Lord

---

* Thucydides indeed used this very verb in that sense. III 21, 2.

changed to the word *anthrōpos* when he said, " Let no man put asunder "
in verse 9, and *anthrōpos* means a member of the human species, but
never " a husband."

The Pharisees certainly thought that his prohibition was absolute.
It is essential to understand rightly the nature of the question with
which they approached Jesus (Matt. 19³). " Is it permissible to divorce
a wife for *any* cause ? " According to the A.V. they asked, " Is it
lawful for a man to put away his wife for *every* cause ? " This is interpreted more fully and clearly by the N.E.B. " Is it lawful for a man
to divorce his wife *on any and every ground* ? " One has to be careful
about the use of the Greek word translated " every." Before an
anarthrous noun it has the meaning " every," but in biblical Greek
(perhaps under Semitic influence) the word *pas* in these circumstances
is often made to carry the sense of " any." The grammatical arguments
concerning *pas* without the definite article, as distinct from *hekastos*
(" each "), are given in Moulton-Howard-Turner (vol. III, p. 199).
The point really is that *pas* does not involve every individual—like the
English word " each " and the Greek *hekastos*—but rather " any you
please to mention."

Now the Law of Moses lists several causes for divorce and the
Pharisees were asking whether Jesus agreed with *any* of the grounds
allowed by Moses. Doubtless they suspected that he was idealistic
enough to condemn the practice altogether, and to allow no exceptive
clause. The A.V.'s " every " spoils the point of this, for it presupposes
that the Pharisees were seeking his opinion on the varying merits of
each Mosaic ground for divorce. Did he accept all the grounds, or
were there some which he would like to reject ? But this is a very
different question. The margin of the N.E.B. is more correct than its
text : " Is there *any* ground on which it is lawful for a man to divorce
his wife ? " Jesus's strict ideas on the indissolubility of marriage were
well known. The Pharisees were not attempting to inveigle him into
taking sides in a rabbinical dispute so much as betraying surprise that
he was stricter even than the school of Shammai.

This view of the question in St. Matthew's gospel agrees with the
form of the parallel question in St. Mark's : " Is it lawful for a man to
put away his wife ? " Inability to appreciate the true meaning of the
Greek word *pas* in this situation has caused many commentators to
assume that the question in Matthew has a different meaning from that
in Mark—which is improbable.

11. WHERE IS THE KINGDOM OF GOD ? (Luke 17²¹)

Exponents of theological Liberalism were prone to quote Jesus as
saying, " The kingdom of God is *within* you," intending to convey the

idea of a spiritual kingdom within the heart. In the present reaction against this, there is no longer a tendency to interpret *entos* as " within."* For long it has been assumed that the old idea was out of harmony with Jesus's teaching on the kingdom, too subjective, too individualized, not corporate enough.

Nevertheless, it seemed to accord with the teaching of St. Paul, especially if for " kingdom " we substitute " Spirit." The Spirit of God and of Christ dwells within the individual. A basis for the identification of the kingdom and Spirit in this respect is provided by St. Paul's own words in Rom. 14[17] : " The kingdom of God is righteousness, peace and joy in the Holy Spirit."

It is frequently said that, in our Lord's teaching, the kingdom is represented as already come, or to some extent " realized." He declared that it had come upon us (Luke 11[20]) ; that the finger of God was casting out Beelzebub here and now. The kingdom is among us or in our midst. However, C. S. Carpenter pointed out some time ago,† that if St. Luke had meant to say " among you " he would have avoided the preposition *entos* and made use of some other expression like *en mesō* (" in the midst "), which already occurs in Luke seven times in addition to four times in the Acts of the Apostles.

Carpenter drew our attention particularly to Luke 22[27] and quoted one of the apocryphal sayings of Jesus‡ : " The kingdom of heaven is *entos* you, and whosoever shall know himself shall find it."§ He was of course addressing the Pharisees, whom he often accused of paying too much attention to the externals of religion. On this occasion, he was paying them the compliment of allowing that within their hearts too the Spirit and the kingdom were at work.

There is a suggestion, based on the use of *entos* in the contemporary non-literary papyri, that St. Luke understood its meaning to be " within your grasp."‖ The kingdom was an opportunity, a challenge, which the Pharisees were allowing to slip away. Interesting as that may be, the contemporary evidence favours the meaning " within," whether of time (e.g. " *within* the period ") or of space (e.g. " storechamber *within* a dining-room "). One contemporary usage is " within " the

---

* But Canon C. F. D. Moule is disposed " to be still so old-fashioned as even to entertain the possibility " that the word means " within." *Journal of Theological Studies*, N.S., vol. XV, April, 1964, p. 11.

† *Christianity according to St. Luke*, S.P.C.K., 1919, p. 103.

‡ B. P. Grenfell and A. S. Hunt, *New Sayings of Jesus*, 1904 ; *The Oxyrhynchus Papyri*, vol. IV, London, 1898 ff., 654[16].

§ The saying is fragmentary, but any probable reconstruction supports the inwardness of the kingdom. Moulton and Milligan comment : " the context favours the translation ' within you '." *Vocabulary of the Greek Testament*, Hodder, 1930, p. 218.

‖ C. H. Roberts, *Harvard Theological Review*, XLI, 1948, 1.

human body (physically), as shown by a medical receipt dating from the beginning of the first Christian century : it describes a remedy for nose-bleeding, consisting of a mixture of incense and onion juice, applied *entos* the nose.* On the other hand, a much later papyrus (third century) refers to a person under twenty-one as being *entos* the Laetonian law ; it means " within the jurisdiction of," or perhaps— since safeguarding against fraud was the object of the law—" within the protection of."†

The wide variety of contexts in the contemporary use of *entos* increases the difficulty in Luke 17²¹. " Within you " is a possibility, no less than " under your control." But I see little evidence for the common interpretation, " in your midst " (adopted in the margin of the R.V., in the R.S.V., by Moffatt, by Knox in the margin, and by the N.E.B. in the text).

Is there sufficient reason then for rejecting the phrase of the A.V., followed by Goodspeed and Rieu, " the kingdom of God is within you " ?

On this background, the story of the Rich Man and Lazarus is misplaced on the lips of Jesus. The strong spatial conception of the bliss of the saints appears to be foreign to the foregoing interpretation, " the kingdom of God is within you." There is a textual problem which may to some extent mitigate the spatial element in the bliss of Abraham's bosom (Luke 16²⁵), and on the textual problem grammar sheds its light.

Not rarely grammatical study enlightens problems of text. The rare thing is when it supports a reading of the Textus Receptus,‡ on which the A.V. was based and which was superseded by the Revisers' text and others before 1881. "But now he is comforted and thou art tormented " (Luke 16²⁵) was replaced by the R.V.'s " But now *here* he is comforted," endorsed by the R.S.V. and N.E.B. The point should be decided by grammatical considerations which may be simplified as follows.§ The Textus Receptus has the Greek word *hode* (short *o*), which means " this man " (" he ") and forms a satisfactory balance to *su* (" thou ") in the following clause : " this man . . . but thou. . . ." It may be assumed that Christian scribes of a very early period fell into the same error as when they copied the Greek Old Testament, the Septuagint : they thought that *hode* was a Hellenistic form of the similar word *hōde* (long *o*), meaning " here," and so these New

---

* J. H. Moulton and G. Milligan, *op. cit.*, p. 219, quoting B. P. Grenfell and A. S. Hunt, *op. cit.*, vol. VIII, 1088³³.

† Moulton and Milligan, *op. cit.*, p. 219 ; Grenfell and Hunt, *op. cit.*, vol. X, 1274¹³.

‡ The text of Stephanus and Elzevir which held sway in Protestant scholarship from the mid-16th. to the mid-19th. century.

§ Moulton-Howard-Turner, *Grammar*, vol. III, p. 44.

Testament and Septuagint scribes made the necessary correction. In the Septuagint, a parallel error occurred when scribes came across *hoide*. It is evident therefore that the reading of the great uncials is inferior and the better reading is preserved only in late Byzantine manuscripts and a few belonging to the much earlier and more valuable Caesarean family of textual authorities, besides having the support of the second-century heretic Marcion.

Although the spatial element of heaven and hell is already implicit in the parable, the text which inserts " here " without justification gives the impression that the comfort has some necessary connection with the *place* as such. The places, heaven and hell, are introduced only as details to help the narration of the story. One may still believe in heaven and hell as states or conditions, not localities. The kingdom (of God or Satan) is still " within " you.

12. Opinions About Jesus

" A prophet like one of the prophets " : parenthesis and " nonsense "
in Mark (6[15])

Most writers indulge in certain mannerisms. On rare occasions, St. Mark's particular habit of inserting parentheses may be effective, since it takes the reader cosily aside into the writer's confidence, but more often the device is clumsy and confusing.

Often it helps exegesis if the parenthesis is removed altogether and then re-inserted at a different point, so that the additional information makes all things intelligible. Few exegetes have essayed to do this, although C. H. Turner and Maximilian Zerwick have set an example.*

Sometimes parenthesis involves the interjection of a whole sentence—not a word or two—into the heart of another sentence. It is characteristic of speakers rather than writers—a writer has more opportunity to revise his work and smooth out avoidable interjections —and we observe that St. Paul fell into the habit, perhaps because he made a practice of dictating letters to a scribe.† If St. Paul did this, why not St. Peter ? The parenthesis in Mark then originated in St.

---

* C. H. Turner, *Journal of Theological Studies*, XXVI, 1925, pp. 145-156 ; M. Zerwick, S.J., *Untersuchungen zum Markus-stil*, Rome, 1937, pp. 130-138. M. E. Thrall discusses the possibility of altering the order of some phrases in Mark ; cf. *Greek Particles in the New Testament*, Brill, 1962, pp. 41-50. E. V. Rieu's translation indicates some of St. Mark's digressions in a footnote (on 3[4.19] 3[14b]), but this is not the same as re-inserting the parenthesis at a different point in the narrative.
† Instances of parenthesis in his letters : Rom. 3[5] 7[1], II Cor. 6[13] 12[2], Eph. 2[5], Col. 4[10], II Thess. 1[6-10a].

Peter's habit of dictating his reminiscences to his scribe in Rome, St. Mark.*

Besides the example at the very beginning of his gospel, already considered, other examples in Mark come readily to mind. The parenthesis in the story of the healing of the paralytic is taken over by St. Matthew and St. Luke : " He saith to the sick of the palsy " (Mark 2^{10}). Hardly less obvious is the parenthesis of " that is to say, a gift " in the Qorban saying ; for this also has no real grammatical integration in the sentence (Mark 7^{11}). Another well-known instance is the Abomination saying (13^{14}), where the parenthesis, " Let the reader understand," is also taken over by St. Matthew. On the other hand, the long explanation about the Pharisees and unwashed hands ($7^{3f.}$) is digression, not parenthesis ; it interrupts neither the flow of thought nor the syntax.

An important feature about St. Mark's use of parenthesis is that often, in order to make good sense, the parenthesis has to be brought forward from its present position to one which better suits the context. For instance, in 2^{15}, " for they were many " refers not to the disciples but to the crowd of tax-collectors and sinners. We ought to read the words in the following order to make the right sense : " While he was dining at home many publicans and sinners—there were many such who followed him—came and joined Jesus and his disciples. (Here place a full-stop.)† There followed him also the scribes of the Pharisees." The conclusion is that in Mark we are concerned not merely with parentheses but with sense-displacements which must either be Marcan idiosyncrasy or, more likely, reproduce St. Peter's actual words. There occurs to us the picture of an impulsive ex-fisherman, late of Galilee, now in Rome, relating his stories about Jesus, forgetting a detail here and there, then inserting the information a moment later when he recalled it, but inserting it at a less suitable position in the sentence. As we shall see, this must have happened very often in his breathless re-telling of the resurrection episodes, where excitement was at its height and most likely to interrupt the narrative, for St. Mark has given us three instances of misplaced parenthesis in the resurrection story ($16^{3f.7.8}$).

The question of the use of parenthesis by St. Mark involves his use of *gar* (the connecting particle meaning " for "). Readers of the gospel have often felt that his use of *gar* is inconsequential and, far from being explanatory, is actually a means of conveying further information.

---

* I am indebted to Mr. George Rust for the suggestion that St. Peter need not have dictated anything to St. Mark. Old men have the habit of always telling their stories in the same words, and John Mark, knowing St. Peter's version of the stories by heart, may have written after the apostle's death.

† This is based on St. Mark's style. I owe this point to Dr. G. D. Kilpatrick.

Mark 5⁴² is an apparent instance. The daughter of Jairus, taken by the hand and told to rise, immediately got to her feet and began to walk. Then St. Mark adds the inconsequential statement, " For (*gar*) she was twelve years old." The phrase is not explanatory in the context. No one ever suspected that the child was too young to walk. Yet *gar* is explanatory in at least ninety percent of its occurrences. The only satisfactory explanation is to resort to our opinion that St. Mark is engaged in the practice of misplacing his parentheses—or was it St. Peter's ? In fact, it goes back to his statement that Jesus in Aramaic referred to her as a *talitha* or " tender lamb " and used the sexless (not feminine) imperative *qûm* (not feminine *qûmî*). For (*gar*) she was (only) twelve years old.

Now we are equipped to consider a major difficulty, the apparent ineptitude of the phrase, " a prophet like one of the prophets " (6¹⁵). The accepted rendering of the verse is, " Some said that he was Elijah, and others that he was a prophet, like one of the prophets." Some translators, conscious of the ineptitude, adorn it gratuitously to make it meaningful, e.g. " a prophet like one of the *old* prophets."

Without the unwarranted addition of " old," the phrase is a mere platitude, and, despite appearances, St. Mark is not abnormally given to pleonasm.* It is another of those delayed parentheses and the logical sequence is, " John the Baptist is risen and therefore mighty powers are at work in him, *like one of the prophets*. Some said that he was Elijah and others that he was a prophet." That arrangement offers a reasonable sequence, because the great prophets Elijah and Elisha were miracle-workers.

No emendation or re-arrangement of the text is under discussion. It is simply a question of the author's (or St. Peter's) idiosyncratic style which requires in intelligible English or Greek a different arrangement for correct understanding.

What the chief priests and scribes thought (Mark 14¹ᶠ·)

While the woman was anointing Jesus in Simon's house at Bethany on the Wednesday of Holy Week, there was a meeting in Jerusalem to discuss ways of arresting and disposing of him secretly.

St. Mark's wording in the first two verses of chapter 14 needs careful construing. Until comparatively recently, and particularly before

---

* The student should not think I have forgotten the needless insertion of such words as the verb " to be," for these are in keeping with contemporary literary trends. Moreover, certain pleonastic idioms, like " he answered and said ", are rarer in St. Mark than in other New Testament writers. The frequent " saying " is equivalent to inverted commas. Neither St. Matthew nor St. Luke thought good to alter " he took and . . ." (6⁴¹ 14²²ᶠ·), or " he rose and . . ." (2¹⁴), or " he answered and said " (3³³ 8²⁹ 9¹⁹).

C. H. Turner, St. Mark's stylistic features attracted little attention, and it was normally assumed that the chief priests and scribes in Jerusalem became more desperate as the week wore on and discussed methods of arresting him quietly prior to securing his death ; the day of Passover had to be avoided for the alleged reason that the Jewish people were likely to riot in Jerusalem if a public personage were arrested among vast crowds.

Two points, both linguistic, are against the assumption. First, St. Mark was fond of parenthesis. Secondly, he was addicted to the vague " they." St. Mark was intending to convey that the chief priests and scribes discussed methods of arresting Jesus by stealth, in their anxiety to avoid a clash with Jewish crowds, but I suggest that the motives for suspecting the clash are not those which are normally given. These motives are not so much the unwisdom of making an arrest among the Passover crowds, as secret information which they had received, through gossip or through their own spies, that public opinion (" they ") would not tolerate any defilement of the solemn Passover day. They (people) said, " Not on the feast ! " It is one of St. Mark's parentheses, and the whole passage must be read as follows :
" The chief priests and the scribes sought how they might take him by craft and put him to death, to avoid an uproar of the people (for the people said, ' Not on the feast day ! ') "

It should be added that " for " is the correct reading (verse 2), rather than " but," as " but " seems to have originated in a scribal harmonization from Matthew.

13. THE GREAT MIRACLE

They kept coming back for more (Mark 6⁴¹)

Only one miracle of Jesus is described in all four gospels.

When Jesus fed the multitude which included five thousand men, as reported in Mark 6⁴¹ (Luke 9¹⁶), the tenses which describe the critical moment of miracle are noteworthy. As already explained,* the aorist tense is that of punctiliar action while the present represents linear action. So we read first that Jesus " gave thanks " (aorist) ; that was a completed action. He then " broke the loaves " (aorist again) ; a completed action. But then followed an action which was not finished for a long time. It went on and on, and is therefore expressed by the imperfect tense. " He kept on distributing to the disciples." The disciples came to Jesus repeatedly for more food, and they handed it to the people. Then there is a return to the aorist tense when St. Mark writes, " He divided the two fish among them all." The aorist does no more than describe the action as a whole, without considering any of

* See pp. 29f.

the three parts individually—the blessing, the breaking, the distri-
bution.

It is an interesting point that, when St. Luke described the scene at
Emmaus after the resurrection, he preserved the same sequence :
aorist—aorist—imperfect. Here also there was a blessing of bread.
Before Jesus was recognized by Cleopas and the other disciple, he
" gave thanks, blessed, and *kept on* distributing " the bread to them.

It is not very likely that these two disciples were at the Last Supper.
It is more probable that they had witnessed the miraculous feeding,
for in the description of the Last Supper the tenses do not follow this
pattern. The point is interesting but it may not be significant.

" Why did we bring no bread ? " (Matt. 16⁷)

Having fed and dismissed the four thousand, Jesus took a boat and
sailed into the district of Magdala. Some Pharisess and Sadducees
who found him here demanded a " sign " of his authority. After that
he dismissed the crowd, rejoined the disciples, and sailed back across
lake Genassaret. The disciples discovered that they had forgotten to
bring loaves of bread with them. Jesus used the occasion to remark,
"Take heed and beware of the leaven of the Pharisees and of the
Sadducees."

According to the A.V., the disciples took this as a rebuke for their
forgetfulness. They said, " It is because we have taken no bread."
But did Jesus rebuke them ? There are sufficient grammatical grounds
to make us pause. Doubt on the part of the Revisers of 1881 is reflected in the wording of the R.V., the sense of which is followed in the
N.E.B. : " We took no bread." And there is still a further possibility.
At this period of Greek the relative and interrogative pronouns were
often confused, and it would make better sense in the context if the
statement of the disciples was transposed into a question by the
assumption that *hoti* (short for *ti estin hoti* : "why is it that ? ") is an
interrogative pronoun with the meaning " why ? " The assumption
is at least as probable as that of taking *hoti* either as recitative, introducing direct speech, like our inverted commas, or as a conjunction
meaning " because."

The Lord was not scolding them, therefore, but the disciples were
scolding one another. " *Why* did we bring no bread ? "

14. Events in Holy Week

Palm Sunday

St. Matthew makes the point that a prophecy was fulfilled when,
on the Sunday of Holy Week, Jesus sent his disciples into a village

near the Mount of Olives to bring back an ass and its colt. " Thy king cometh unto thee, meek and sitting upon an ass, and a colt the foal of an ass." He describes the placing of garments upon both animals and apparently states that Jesus was mounted upon both (21⁷).

St. Matthew was not so obsessed by the fulfilment of prophecy that he interpreted Zachariah's imagery literally.

" Sitting upon an ass *and* a colt," said the prophet, meaning, of course, *even* a colt. There is no need to think that the evangelist was misled by this double function of the Hebrew " and." The *pluralis categoriae* has already been observed as a feature of his style* and, just as concerning Herod he said, " *They* are dead," so here of one animal he says, " Upon *them.*" Such a view renders much critical exegesis and scribal correction superfluous.

" Friend, what have you come for ? " (Matt. 26⁵⁰)

Having instituted the holy Supper, Jesus accompanied his disciples to the garden of Gethsemane where he was swept with a wave of sorrow. Returning to his disciples three times after praying, he found them asleep. " Sleep on now," he said, on the third occasion, " and take your rest : behold, the hour is at hand, and the Son of Man is betrayed into the hands of sinners. Rise, let us be going : behold, he is at hand that doth betray me."

Judas immediately appeared, with a posse of people who were armed. He kissed Jesus, with the greeting, " Hail, Master ! " Already he had bargained with the chief priests and elders, and agreed on a way of identifying his Master in the dusk. But Jesus addressed Judas first. The A.V. quotes him : " Friend, wherefore art thou come ? " (*Hetaire, eph' ho parei ?*)

In all ages, Bible translators found the Greek phrase difficult. Our classical English Bible frankly translates the Latin Vulgate rather than the Greek, and the Vulgate (in one form) has *ad quid*, which can be taken most naturally to mean " for what purpose ? " This is understanding *quid* as an interrogative pronoun, but the difficulty is that the Greek *ho* is not an interrogative, but a relative pronoun, and so the phrase *eph' ho* (" that for which ") cannot really stand on its own without the supply of some suitable verb (" do ") to go with it. We must suppose that Jesus meant, " *Do* that for which you have come." The suggestion was made by Dean Alford and Bishop Lightfoot ; later it was adopted in the R.V. Equally correctly the exclamation " behold " (French *voici*) might be supplied instead of " do " or " say." " Here is that for which you have come ! " A self-surrender on the part of Jesus.

* See p. 47.

Others suggest improvements on the translation by supplying a different variety of missing phrase. For instance, " Friend, (you give me a kiss) *for which* you have come." Or : " Friend, (by this kiss you achieve the purpose) *for which* you have come." Or it may be turned into a question : " Friend, (is the kiss the reason) *for which* you have come ? "

No one is happy to have to supply what is in the brackets ; it is too much. At the same time, the kiss of Judas must have been prominent in Jesus's mind as he spoke. Linguistically it is one of the most difficult passages in the New Testament, and the suggestion that the words were inscribed on the drinking cup at the Last Supper is neither helpful nor probable. In such instances there is a temptation to turn away from all manuscripts and early versions of the Bible and, assuming that they have at this point departed from the true text, invent for oneself a suitable emendation by the ingenious device of altering as few letters as possible. The learned Friedrich Blass, at first a classical scholar and then a New Testament grammarian, did just that in the present instance. It was apparent to him that four letters had dropped out of all existing manuscripts, by the scribal error which is technically called haplography (writing once what should be written twice). These are letters which occur in the word for " friend," and they should occur again immediately after it. So instead of *HETAIRE, EPH' HO PAREI* we ought to insert the four letters and read : *HETAIRE, AIRE EPH' HO PAREI.*

Emendations, however plausible, are a last resort in New Testament criticism, for a wealth of textual material has been handed down from very early times. One must suppose that somewhere among the mass of evidence the true reading in each instance is to be found. In the classical studies, with which Blass had been familiar, nothing like the same quantity of textual evidence is available, and emendation is forced upon us. Moreover, our present knowledge of biblical and ecclesiastical Greek syntax is more advanced than it was in the days of Blass and Lightfoot, and it is no longer necessary to resort to emendation in Matt. 26[50]. Indeed, there need be no supplying of missing words either. It is known that it was usual in some writers of Hellenistic Greek to confuse relative and indirect-interrogative pronouns. By no means all writers do this, but it is probably the clue in the passage before us. On this point, St. Luke appears to correct St. Matthew several times. Nearly always it is the *indirect*-interrogative which is confused with the relative, but there seems to be no reason why in this passage it should not be that rarer confusion of *direct* interrogative with the relative pronoun. In that way the Vulgate translation would be explicable and there is some evidence from the Septuagint and from ecclesiatical Greek of a later period for this startling transformation of a relative pronoun into a direct interrogative pronoun.* For instance, the abbot Arsenius (A.D. 354–450) who was tutor to the emperor Arcadius and is immortalized in Kingsley's *Hermits*, uses the relative pronoun *ho* in the combination *di' ho* (" for what ? ", i.e. " why ? "). It is virtually the same phrase which Jesus used in his question to Judas. His question therefore amounts to " *Why* have you come ? "

Other instances are found in ecclesiastical Greek, and in the Septuagint *hoti* (a relative pronoun compounded of *ho*) very often means " why ? " Moreover, it can be interpreted in this way in the New Testament.†

St. Peter's denial (*Mark* 14⁷²)

St. Peter heard the cock crow twice after denying his Master, and " when he thought thereon " he wept. " From the first," writes Dr. Vincent Taylor (his commentary, p. 576), the phrase " has proved difficult." There is no object for the intransitive verb *epibalōn* (" when he applied "). Most translators supply an object, and the A.V. supplies " mind " (" When he applied his mind," i.e. " when he thought thereon ").

The R.V. has an alternative in the margin, " he began to weep." " Begin " is a possible translation of *epibalōn*. Indeed, a few manuscripts have the Greek word which undoubtedly means " begin," showing how some scribes were trying to solve the meaning of the difficult *epibalōn*. This is true too of the makers of the early Syriac versions. The Latin Vulgate followed the same idea. There are still further alternatives, and in the contemporary papyri from Egypt the verb means " to set to work." One might say, " Peter set to, and wept." The suggestion came from J. H. Moulton,‡ but I scarcely think it convincing in our context.

Dr. Field of Norwich, a scholarly critic of the Revisers, rejected their note as unsatisfactory grammatically.§ He said that the construction, " begin to," would require a finite verb followed by a participle, rather than a participle followed by a finite verb. Field was attracted to the idea of supplying " garment " and " head," viz. " putting a garment on his head, he wept." Such a practice was customary when weeping, especially for a man. However, Field provided no exact parallel, and we have to supply over much with

* See the evidence in Moulton-Howard-Turner, *Grammar*, vol. III, p. 49f.
† See p. 68.
‡ *A Grammar of New Testament Greek*, Prolegomena, 1906, p. 131 ff.
§ F. Field, *Notes on the Translation of the New Testament*, Cambridge, 1899, pp. 41–43.

the verb. Commentators have largely despaired, among a welter of suggestions. It is an unresolved enigma, according to one of them ; and yet another bids us " be content to share the ignorance of all the ages."

The wisest course is to consult an authority very close to St. Mark in time. St. Matthew might know, better than most, what St. Mark meant by *epibalōn*. If he expressed the concept differently in his own gospel, it was not because he disagreed with the earliest evangelist on any facts concerning St. Peter's weeping, but because he wished to make St. Mark's phrase less ambiguous and colloquial. At any rate, he did substitute the words, " he went outside." This I believe to be the correct translation of *epibalōn*, because the verb *ballein* (from which it is compounded) belongs to a small group of transitive verbs which in Hellenistic Greek are used intransitively. The usage is quite prominent in the New Testament itself. Already St. Mark had used *epiballein* in this way : a great wind arose, and waves *epeballen* into the boat. There is no object ; the waves pushed themselves. These are instances of the way in which Hellenistic writers prefer a reflexive idea to the object with this particular transitive verb—and with a small number of others too.* St. Peter pushed (*ballein*) himself onwards (*epi*). Perhaps he threw himself on the ground (C. H. Turner), but it is more likely that he threw himself outside, for that is how St. Matthew chose to interpret it.

Did Jesus say " Yes " at his trial ? (*Matt.* 26[64])

Before the crucifixion Jesus faced two major interrogations. The first, before the Jewish high priests, was a hostile business ; that before Pontius Pilate began with the outward appearance of a fair trial. In both he was invited to answer a question about his identity and, strictly speaking, the question was not about claims. Caiaphas commanded him to declare, under oath, whether he was the Messiah. St. Matthew relates that Jesus replied, " *You* have said." The evangelist conveys, I think, that *you* is emphatic, as he uses the pronoun *su*, which was not compulsory unless emphasis was intended (26[24]). It would not be the answer " Yes."

Strangely enough, Caiaphas had refrained from asking, " Are you *claiming* to be Messiah ? " His question was, " *Are* you Messiah ? " That is not quite the same, and the answer of Jesus is a gentle reminder that the high priest was putting the words into his mouth. " You are saying so. You are not even suggesting that I might be making a false claim. You are saying that I could be the Messiah, and you want me to tell you whether I am."

* For these, see Moulton-Howard-Turner, *Grammar*, vol. III, p. 51 f.

It does not matter whether *plēn*, which follows, means " but " or " and," although there have been long debates on it.* Either is logical enough, on the suppositions we are following. " You are saying so. But (or " And ") I will tell you this. . . ." " But " certainly implies a contrast between " you say " and " I tell you," suggesting that Jesus's answer is not " Yes." The usual view is that *plēn* has this adversative meaning (" but "). The point is not very significant, since either meaning fits fairly well whichever answer Jesus intended.

In the praetorium, the Roman official asked the same question, " Are you king of the Jews ? " Replying, Jesus used the present tense on this occasion, " *You* say it " (Matt. 27^{11}, Mark 15^2, Luke 23^4). The synoptic evangelists agree on the wording of this answer. Again *su* (" you ") is underlined. Simple, yet ambiguous and non-committal, the answer recalls what he replied to Judas Iscariot's enquiry before the Last Supper, " Master, is it I ? " and Jesus answered, " *You* have said."

On all three occasions, it has been alleged, Jesus intended the plain answer, " Yes." But that involves transferring the emphasis. " You *have said* it." If that is so, he was disclosing the Messianic secret to top people on the eve of Calvary, revealing himself very publicly as Son of God. However, the emphasis is not so placed. It is, " *You* are saying this, not *me*." For the meaning " yes," the personal pronoun *su* is pointless. In splendid isolation, the pronoun places full responsibility on the questioner (" you "), dissociating Jesus from the assumptions of the question, neither affirming nor denying. He often answered one question by posing another. " Do you think so ? " he seems to say. " Ask yourself." To Judas also : " I do not call you a traitor, but what is *your* opinion ? " To his judges : " The Messiah ? What do *you* think ? "

It will be countered, first of all, that St. Mark does not so understand Jesus's answer to Caiaphas (14^{62}). He reports him as answering, " I am,"—a plain Yes. What is not so generally recognized is, that there is some rather strong textual evidence against this reading. The early branch of manuscript transmission, known as " Caesarean," reports the same answer in Mark as Jesus is reported to have given in Matthew and Luke. The Caesarean reading could well be correct, for it is reasonable to suppose that the words, " you have said that," have been omitted accidentally or designedly before the words, " I am." Thus Jesus said, " You have said that I am " (as in Matthew and Luke). At a very early date in Christian history, Origen quoted the longer phrase, and that is how it appears in the Georgian and

---

* M. E. Thrall, *Greek Particles in the New Testament*, Brill, 1962, pp. 20–24, 70–78.

Armenian versions.* Dr. Vincent Taylor accepted it as the true reading in his commentary. B. H. Streeter favoured this. " Now ordinarily one would suspect this reading as due to assimilation from Matthew. But here again the obscurity of the expression, or the apparent hesitancy it might seem to imply in our Lord's acceptance of the title Christ, would favour its omission. Moreover, the view that the words originally stood in Mark explains the language of Matthew and Luke."†

If the submission cannot be sustained, it is evident that St. Mark is using a peculiar tradition concerning the Caiaphas trial, for St. Luke's account conforms with the submission we have made. " You say that I am." It may have had the intonation of a question, and in this gospel Jesus is reported as giving a reason for withholding a positive answer : " If I tell you, you will not believe " (22⁶⁷).

---

* In detail, support for the longer reading in Mark 14⁶² is as follows (for deciphering of Symbols reference should be made to S. C. E. Legg, *Novum Testamentum Graece . . . Evangelium secundum Marcum*, Oxford, 1935, pp. following Preface) : Θ fam¹³ 543 472 565 700 1071 Geo Arm Origen. The shorter reading (" I am ") is based on the mass of textual authorities. Dr. Thrall assumes (*op. cit.* p. 72) that because " there are at least ten instances where two or more of these witnesses have added to the Marcan text a word or a phrase derived from the parallel verse in Matthew," there is " a strong probability that the same thing happened " in Mark 14⁶². But among the ten instances, Dr. Thrall's choice of Mark 14³⁵ (=Matt. 26³⁹) is unfortunate because there is a further harmonization in that verse on the part of א B etc. (προελθών). There is no denying that these authorities harmonize considerably ; the best of them do it, even א CD (see Mark 14³⁰, where the authorities suspected by Dr. Thrall of harmonization actually refrain from it by retaining συ : Θ fam¹³ 543 565 1071 Geo), א (see 14³⁰·³⁵·⁷² 15²⁴·³⁶), even B (see 14³¹·³⁵ 15¹⁰·²⁰·³⁵). Further evidence of the weakness of Dr. Thrall's argument is afforded by the fifteen occasions in the Passion narrative where two or more of her suspect witnesses preserve an unharmonized text of Mark against these very witnesses which preserve the shorter text of 14⁶². Thus the ten instances brought forward by Dr. Thrall are more than counterbalanced by these fifteen : (1) 14¹⁰ : Θ 565 are among supporters of the non-harmonizing reading " Iscarioth " against D Old Lat Vulg Syr. (2) 14¹⁹ : Θ 565 700 Geo Arm Origen support the addition of καὶ ἄλλος· μήτι ἐγώ, against א BC etc. which harmonize with Matthew. (3) 14²⁰ : Θ 565 add ἕν before τρύβλιον. (4) 14²⁹ : Θ omits αὐτῷ. (5) 14³¹ : Θ 565 have the word-order με δέη, while the majority harmonize with Matthew. (6) 14³¹ : Θ adds δέ. (7) 14⁴³ : Θ 565 700ᵐᵍ 1071 Geo Origen add " Iscariot ", against א BCW etc. (8) 14⁶⁸ : Θ 067 fam¹³ 543 565 700 1071 Geo Arm add καὶ ἀλέκτωρ ἐφώνησεν, but the majority harmonize with Matthew. (9) 14⁷² : Θ 543 565 700 1071 fam¹³ Arm add δίς, while א C*W etc. harmonize with Matthew and Luke. (10) 15¹² : Θ 700 1071 Arm add θέλετε, against א BCW etc. (11) 15²⁰ : Θ fam¹³ 543 700 1071 add ἴδια but BC etc. harmonize. (12) 15²⁹ : Θ 471 565 Geo omit ἐν against א BC etc. (13) 15³⁴ : Θ 565 1071 Geo Arm read λαμά, while א CL etc. harmonize with Matthew. (14) 15³⁵ : Θ 565 read non-harmonizing παρεστώτων but BA harmonize. (15) 15⁴⁰ : Θ Geo Arm read Μαριάμ.

† B. H. Streeter, *The Four Gospels*, Macmillan, revised 1930, p. 322.

It may be objected that " You have said " is an Aramaic expression and that it may mean " Yes." But even if it is credible that Jesus used Aramaic in Pilate's court, the presence of the emphatic pronoun in Greek is a presumption in favour of an emphatic pronoun having been used in the equivalent Aramaic. Dalman's alleged parallel from the Babylonian Talmud—without the pronoun—is therefore less potent evidence for the real meaning. Moreover, other rabbinical scholars, Chwolson and Abrahams, take the opposing view. The phrase occurs in a story in the Talmud, from which the reader is as well placed as anyone to judge just what " you have said " might have meant in Aramaic.

One day two learned rabbis disputed on the necessity for the ceremonial washing of hands and feet under certain conditions. Ought one to wash before entering the space between porch and altar in the temple ? Simeon argued against it. His disputant was Eleazar ben Hyrcanus, noted for his overbearing methods. " I myself," confessed Simeon, "once went between porch and altar without washing hands and feet." Eleazar replied disdainfully, " Who is more important, you or the high priest ? " Simeon was silent, and Eleazar pressed the point. " You are too ashamed, are you not, to admit that even the high priest's dog is more important than yourself ? " Simeon was roused by the taunt. " Rabbi, *you have said it*," was his reply. " I wonder," said Eleazar, " how you managed to evade the temple watchman. By the liturgy ! Even the high priest would have had his head split open ! "

Simeon would be pretty abject if he intended a plain Yes. The parallel is therefore too dubious to carry weight.

Privately Jesus believed himself to be Son of God and made the claim before his disciples. Nevertheless it is reasonable to suppose that publicly he preserved the " Messianic secret " until the day of resurrection finally made the position clear.

It may be said, against these grammatical submissions, that the classical emphasis or contrast involved in the use of the nominative case of personal pronouns is no longer upheld in Hellenistic Greek. There are indeed one or two instances in the New Testament itself where the pronoun is inserted apparently gratuitously. " Take heed to yourselves," and " Take ye heed " (Mark 13[9.23]), are among them. Herod says, " John have I beheaded." without special emphasis on the word " I " ; no one else was likely to have beheaded the Baptist. Yet after all there is some emphasis, however subtle. " *I* beheaded John ! *Mine* is the guilt." Moreover, the apparent exceptions are very rare, and it is possible in every instance to appreciate some emphasis at least.

Soldiers' scorn and robbers' reproach

Pilate's men, having scourged, robed, and crowned Jesus, cried mockingly, " Hail, King of the Jews ! " (John 19³). Literally, it was, " Hail, *the* King of the Jews ! " It is vocative with the definite article. When the construction occurs in the Greek of the New Testament, there is usually good reason for it. It was not the writers' imperfect skill in the language, but his neat method of expressing the scorn of the soldiers.

Basically the definite article was a mildly demonstrative adjective, not necessarily implying scorn, although there is a good case for it in this context. A finger is pointed. " *This* king of the Jews ! "

Manuscripts supply a variant reading in St. Matthew's version of the incident, because although Codex Sinaiticus and the Byzantine tradition have the definite article (as in John), it is absent from the Alexandrian, Western, and Caesarean textual traditions. One may be a harmonization with St. John's gospel ; or the other an attempted improvement of the grammar. In Mark, however, the Byzantine text appears to represent a harmonization with the other gospels, and it is therefore unlikely that St. Mark or St. Matthew express any scorn on the part of the Roman soldiers.

Further discrepancies appear in the crucifixion narratives. St. Matthew apparently records that both robbers reproached Jesus on the cross, while St. Luke tells us that one of them showed sympathy to the extent of defending Jesus. But the ancient Latin fathers, Jerome, Augustine, and Ambrose, were alert to a grammatical point which modern writers have missed. By the principle of *pluralis categoriae,** it is evident that St. Matthew did not intend his reference to " robbers " (plural) to be taken literally (27⁴⁴). English idiom demands the translation : " the robber who was crucified with him reproached him." St. Matthew has every excuse for using his peculiar Greek idiom, for his mind was dwelling on robbers as a class. " The idea of *robbers* reviling Christ ! " We come to the resurrection and we find him referring to some women (28⁹) of whom he writes that " *they* came and held him by the feet," although it is clear from other sources that it was St. Mary Magdalene alone.† The evangelist uses " crowds " in the same way as we do, meaning but one crowd ; he goes further than we and refers to " many " crowds for one big one (4²⁵ 8¹·¹⁸ 13² 15³⁰ 19²), but doubtless he has in mind the very derogatory sense of *hoi polloi* in Greek and means " the masses." That the rabble resorted to Jesus was something worth recording by an ex-publican who had once himself

---

* See p. 47.

† My own reference to " other sources " is a *pluralis categoriae*, for only St. John is intended ; he alone describes the *noli me tangere* scene with Mary.

been relegated to that particular class—supposing that the first gospel depends in any way upon Matthew the publican.

" He is dead ? When did he die ? " (Mark 15⁴⁴)

Good Friday evening, when day came to an end, was the Preparation of the Sabbath. An honourable councillor named Joseph approached Pilate for permission to remove Jesus. Raising no objection, the procurator expressed surprise that the prisoner *was already dead* and then summoned the centurion who was on duty at Golgotha. To him Pilate put one question, " *Did he die* some hours ago ? "

Now it is important to observe that the procurator in these two remarks used the same verb in different tenses, according to the evangelist's reporting. It is too readily assumed that the breakdown of perfect and aorist was so complete at this period that it cannot be relied upon for New Testament exegesis. The method of reporting Pilate's words is an indication that this is not so, and it is supported by clear examples of the old distinction between perfect and aorist in the contemporary Common Greek. Papyri written by uneducated men, however, present a different picture on the whole, especially when the Ptolemaic period passes into the Imperial.* In the first three centuries A.D., indiscriminate use of either tense in order to express past time is a feature of the mass of uncultured papyri. The New Testament is not in line with this. St. Mark is too careful, and so is St. Paul.† Both writers retain the original " resultative " force of the perfect tense which implies that the results of an action which is part are still vividly present at the time of speaking. At a definite moment in the recent past, Jesus had died ; St. Mark reports Pilate as wishing to know exactly when that moment occurred, and so he employs the aorist. At that instant, while Pilate is speaking, Jesus's lifeless body hangs upon the cross. It is fitting then that in referring to this Pilate should change the tense from aorist, the *punctiliar*, tense. His expression of surprise is voiced in the perfect tense. " He is dead ! "

St. Mark is quite far removed from the average standard of the popular Koine language of his day, for his report of the scene is not only naturally expressed but is also neat and correct.

15. THE RESURRECTION AND AFTER

Parenthesis in the resurrection story (Mark 16¹⁻⁸)

I have urged‡ that parenthesis is characteristic of St. Mark's style, and that for this evangelist parenthesis is not merely a matter of

---

* Moulton-Howard-Turner, *Grammar*, vol. III, p. 68.
† See pp. 112ff.   ‡ See pp. 64ff.

insertion but of insertion in the wrong place, so that often a false impression of his meaning is given. The application of this knowledge is useful in the story of the resurrection.

In one part of this story the accepted practice among translators is to follow St. Mark's word-order literally and to read : " They said among themselves, Who shall roll us away the stone from the door of the sepulchre ? And when they looked, they saw that the stone was rolled away : *for it was very great* " (verses 3 and 4). The parenthesis, I suggest, is in italics. One may imagine that by some lapse of memory St. Peter omitted this detail about the size of the stone and therefore did not insert it at the appropriate place, after " sepulchre," but recalled it when he had finished the next sentence and inserted it there, in the manner characteristic of less articulate people even in English. It makes no sense where it stands, if it is taken closely with the immediately preceding remark. I recollect a friend describing orally how he narrowly missed being appointed to a coveted post. Had he written the story he would doubtless have transposed the last two sentences. " The train arrived late at the station and was dreadfully slow. I missed the interview and did not get the job. You see, it was foggy." Probably St. Peter spoke like this, with delayed parenthesis, and St. Mark has preserved his words exactly, whereas the following reconstruction would have been more logical : " And they said among themselves, Who shall roll us away the stone from the door of the sepulchre ? (For it was very great). And when they looked, they saw that the stone was rolled away."

It is both startling and gratifying to have a vivid glimpse of the way in which the great apostle might have spoken. Only a recording of his voice could bring him closer to us.

It leads us also to a more acute insight into the real motive behind certain remarks in the gospel of St. Mark.

Before the resurrection, in sorrow on the mount of Olives, Jesus had promised the disciples that one day he would die, rise from death, and leave his place of burial to arrive home in Galilee before they could do so. He is not reported as saying that they would see him in Galilee, although they may have read this message into his words. The detail helps to trace another instance of delayed parenthesis in the style of St. Mark's resurrection narrative. Within the sepulchre, a young man spoke to the three women who had brought spices. " Go your way," said he, " tell his disciples and Peter that he is going before you into Galilee : there you'll see him, *as he said to you* " (verse 7). Again, the italicized words are a delayed parenthesis, and they should occur after " Galilee." This is because in 14[28] St. Mark had not recorded that Jesus promised they would see him. Logically the parenthesis belongs elsewhere : " Go your way, tell his disciples and

Peter that he is going before you into Galilee (*as he said to you*) : there you'll see him."

St. Matthew also had misgivings about St. Mark's order as it stands and he took the liberty of smoothing things out by reporting the angel himself as saying, " Lo ! I have told you."

Does this build too much on the assumption that we necessarily have an accurate account of Jesus's words ? The foundation of the argument is not that at all, but rather the fact that St. Mark had his own words before him in 14[28] and on the strength of them the angel's reported words in 16[7] are incompatible with what Jesus is reported to have said, except on the hypothesis of delayed parenthesis.

Eyes are opened (*Luke* 24[31])

The superfluous use of "his" and "her" came into post-classical Greek and is very pronounced in the biblical language, where doubtless Semitic influence was decisive.*

On one occasion St. Luke pressed the tendency even further and placed " their " (*autōn*) in the most emphatic position possible—at the beginning of the sentence. " *Their* eyes were opened " (24[31]). Here is double emphasis : first, to use *autōn* at all, and then to place it so emphatically. However, the emphasis is not pointless when we view the sentence in relation to what goes immediately before. " He took bread, blessed and broke it, and gave it to them (*autois*). Their (*autōn*) eyes were opened, and they knew him." The evangelist has placed the two like-sounding pronouns together : *autois, autōn*, and the clue to correct interpretation is mentally to unite the pronouns as closely as possible and to understand the concept underlying the story of the Emmaus road to be the enlightening capacity of the breading of bread. As many as (*autois*) receive the broken bread, these are the ones (*autōn*) who gain enlightenment. Appropriately, *autōn* is placed first for emphasis.

This was certainly an interpretation which was current in the early Church. For there is a very ancient textual variant, which agrees with it, in what is known as the Old Latin tradition—a valuable and early testimony to the Bible text. After the statement that Jesus took bread, broke it, and gave it to them, comes the addition : " After they had taken the bread from him, their eyes were opened."

Such may not be the true text of Luke, and it looks like an interpretation by Origen, indeed, the correct interpretation. Perhaps it found its way into the text of the gospel, by means of a marginal note, and so became part of the Old Latin tradition.

* Moulton-Howard-Turner, *Grammar*, vol. III, p. 38.

The interpretation is symbolic. The sacred mysteries of the body and blood open the eyes of believers to see the risen Lord in the midst and to recognize him as Jesus.

The forgiveness of sins in the Christian ministry
(Matt. 16[19], John 20[23])

What is the essence of the perfect tense in Greek ? Perhaps the easiest, if not the most accurate, definition would be that it expresses a state of affairs which came into being at some point in the past but which is still true at the time of speaking. The moment when it came into being would be expressed by the aorist. The continuance at the moment of speaking would be expressed by the present. The perfect tense, therefore, has to express two truths at once : the previous inception of the condition and the present continuance of it.

There are parts of the New Testament where this axiom of grammar must have important theological significance. For instance, were the apostles granted the responsibility of selection in the forgiveness of sins (John 20[23]) and in the " binding and loosing " (Matt. 16[19]) ?

In Matt. 16[19] St. Peter was promised the keys of the kingdom of heaven and was told that whatsoever he should bind on earth would be bound (perfect participle) in heaven and whatsoever he should loose on earth would be loosed (perfect participle) in heaven. Here the real significance of the perfect tense is all-important. The interpretation of W. C. Allen* ought to be challenged : " Whatsoever thou bindest shall remain bound, shall never be loosed." This is to lay the main emphasis on the future, which is implied only in the auxiliary verb *estai* (" it shall be "), but the participle *dedemenon* is perfect and looks back as well as forward. On the strength of our statement concerning the essence of the perfect tense, a better interpretation would be : " Whatsoever thou bindest shall already have been permanently bound." It takes away the responsibility of human choice, and therefore uninformed choice, and represents St. Peter as acting in these solemn binding and loosing matters always under the infallible guidance of the Holy Spirit. The deaths of Ananias and Sapphira are probably early instances of this promise.

The issue is clearer still in the other, the Johannine, passage, where the tense is perfect and not even future-perfect. " Receive the Holy Ghost : whose soever sins you forgive, they have been forgiven

---

* W. C. Allen, *The Gospel according to St. Matthew* (I.C.C.), T. & T. Clark, 3rd. ed. 1912, p. 177.

(perfect) ;* whose soever sins you retain, they have been retained."
The question is whether, in spite of the absence of a future element,
the perfect tense here ought to be understood in the sense of a futuristic
present ; the futuristic present is widely used and the perfect tense
was originally present in meaning, in that it expressed the *state* of
the subject.† " They are forgiven (with the nuance, " they will be
forgiven ") is no less possible than " they have been forgiven." But
examples of the old present-perfect tense are in fact very rare in the
New Testament period and tend to be confined to a few stereotyped
forms which are well known.‡ The perfects *apheōntai* (if this is correct)
and *kekratēntai* in John 20²³ cannot be intended as present-perfects,
especially with this author and particularly at a period when the old
intransitive perfect was so surely giving way before the active,
transitive and resultative perfect.§

However, in neither context is it safe to assume that the process
has gone a stage further and that the perfects are already aoristic-
perfects. The New Testament indeed has a large number of these ;
but the contexts so often‖ make it clear that the perfect is being distinguished from the aorist. St. John is singularly anxious to preserve
the reality of the resultative perfect, for he has seventy-seven instances,
compared with twenty-nine in the other three gospels together. " We
may ascribe this to the peculiar style of the Fourth Gospel, its love of
emphasis and solemnity, its stress on the abiding significance of everything."¶ It is clear then that in the Johannine and Matthean contexts
the perfect tenses used by our Lord (or represented to be so used)

---

* This is actually debatable, since it depends upon the reading *apheōntai* of codices
Alexandrinus and Bezae, the original hand of Vaticanus and the corrector of
Codex Sinaiticus, which is widely accepted by editors. However, many will prefer
the reading of the Textus Receptus (*aphientai*), the present tense of the same verb ;
it has the advantage of support from a very important textual tradition, represented by the Koridethi manuscript and the Freer Gospels. It is easy to appreciate that *apheōntai* is a correction, as the perfect was felt to be more in harmony
with the other perfect in the sentence.

† " Originally it had no resultative force but simply expressed the subject's state;
this had been arrived at by some previous activity, but the state arrived at was
represented by the perfect as so permanent that the perfect can be said from long
before the New Testament period to have present meaning." Moulton-Howard-
Turner, *Grammar*, vol. III, p. 82.

‡ E.g. ἀπόλωλα in Matthew and Luke ; ἀνέῳγα in John and Paul ; πέποιθα and
ἕστηκα in the gospels ; and of course οἶδα.

§ To accept *aphientai* as the correct reading would make little difference to the
argument, as the writer (or Jesus) evidently intended the verb to be parallel in every
way with the perfect *kekratēntai*, and so it is a perfective-present ("they are already
forgiven ").

‖ E.g. Pilate's careful distinction of the tenses ; see p. 77. Also St. Paul's, when
he was discussing Christ's resurrection ; see pp. 112ff.

¶ Moulton-Howard-Turner, *Grammar*, vol. III, p. 83.

ought not to be read as if they were aoristic-perfects. We must not, in effect, paraphrase like this : " Whatsoever you shall bind on earth will be from that moment bound in heaven, and whatsoever you shall loose on earth shall then be loosed in heaven " (Matt. 16[19]) ; " whose soever sins you forgive, they will at that moment be forgiven, and whose soever sins you retain they will then be retained " (John 20[23]). This is to jettison a wealth of meaning. Matt. 16[19] and John 20[23] do not give a presbyter authority to decide which sins deserve forgiveness.

I would only add that in the Johannine context our Lord makes special reference to the Holy Spirit. That is surely the clue to real understanding of both passages. Later on, Peter and John especially were destined to create important precedents and loosed many from the bondage of sin. They saved from death and they consigned to death. They baptized Samaritans and Gentiles. They dealt severely with Simon the magician. In none of this were they conscious of personal decision, but of an over-ruling and inspired guidance. On one remarkable occasion the Holy Spirit said to a reluctant Peter, " Get you down and go with these men, for I have sent them." In the baptism of Cornelius which followed Peter's vision a flood of Gentiles entered the Church by a decree already made in heaven. It was not in any way humanly planned or devised.

CHAPTER THREE

SAUL OF TARSUS

1. WHERE WAS SAUL BROUGHT UP?

In a recent translation of a Dutch monograph one may read the interesting argument that St. Paul had not merely been educated in Jerusalem, but even brought up there—and not in Tarsus, as is more generally supposed.*

Tarsus was a Hellenistic city, and it is often assumed that it was here that the apostle derived whatever Hellenistic elements are to be found in his writings. If St. Paul was exclusively brought up and educated in Jerusalem many influences which might otherwise seem to be Greek in his thought must be explained entirely within the possibilities of Judaism.

The argument turns mainly upon two passages in the Acts of the Apostles.

(1) In the first (22³), all seems to depend on the right connotation of the words, " this city." Is it Jerusalem or Tarsus ? But first, van Unnik has a suggestion concerning the correct method of punctuation. He rejects the method of the A.V., which has become standard, followed by Westcott and Hort and even by the R.S.V. in recent times : " I am a Jew, born at Tarsus in Cilicia, but brought up in this city at the feet of Gamaliel, educated according to the strict manner of the law of our fathers." Such a punctuation suggests that although the apostle was a native of Tarsus, he had been brought up and educated in Jerusalem under Gamaliel's care. Van Unnik thinks it unlikely that Gamaliel would have " brought up " Saul, understanding that word correctly, and prefers a punctuation which links the education closely with Gamaliel, like that of the N.E.B. " ' I am a true-born Jew,' he said, ' a native of Tarsus in Cilicia. I was brought up in this city, and as a pupil of Gamaliel I was thoroughly trained in every point of our ancestral law.' " From this translation is still not clear (as in the Greek) whether " this city " ought to refer to Tarsus or Jerusalem.

Unless " this city " refers to Tarsus, St. Paul contradicts what he is reported as saying to Claudius Lysias, when he emphasized his origin in the Greek city of Tarsus and on the basis of so respectable an

* W. C. van Unnik, *Tarsus or Jerusalem : The City of Paul's Youth*, English translation by G. Ogg, Epworth Press, 1962.

83

association, political and cultural, he had begged leave to address the crowd (Acts 21³⁹). Moreover, if the punctuation suggested by van Unnik is accepted it seems to me that the words " brought up " go very closely with the word "Tarsus," for we may render the sentence thus : " I am a Jew, born at Tarsus in Cilicia and brought up in this city ; I was trained, under Gamaliel, in exact knowledge of our ancestral law " (Knox version). Here we are following both the punctuation and sense of the Latin text, according to the Sixtine and Clementine Vulgate : " ego sum vir Iudaeus, natus in Tarso Ciliciae, nutritus autem in ista civitate, secus pedes Gamaliel eruditus iuxta veritatem paternae legis." Notice the pronoun *ista*, meaning " that " and making the reference to Tarsus rather definite. Against a punctuation like this it must be admitted that the pattern of participial clauses is such that they usually precede the words with which they are associated : this means that the participle " brought up " ought to be associated closely with " at the feet of Gamaliel," after which there would be a comma. However, we must not argue from a hypothetical pattern, since there is no consistent pattern throughout St. Luke's writing ; a very large number of passages might be quoted to illustrate that St. Luke does not invariably place the participle first in its phrase (e.g. Acts 1³. ¹⁵ 2³³ᵇⁱˢ 3². ²⁶ 6¹ 7⁹ 8³ 10⁹. ²³ 11¹² 13³⁹ 14¹¹. ¹³. ¹⁷ 15⁵. ²¹ 16²⁵. ³⁷ 18¹⁸ 19³⁴. ⁴⁰ 21¹⁵. ²⁴. ²⁶). Therefore the phrasing, " at the feet of Gamaliel educated," is stylistically possible for St. Luke.

As far as 22³ is concerned, the evidence does not require that " this city " must refer to Jerusalem. Tarsus has just been mentioned, and the clause containing " this city " goes all the closer with it, if van Unnik's punctuation is adopted, and we read : " I am a Jew born at Tarsus in Cilicia *and* brought up in this city. At the feet of Gamaliel I was educated according to the strict manner of the Law of our fathers." So the argument that Tarsus played no part in the early education and training of the apostle lacks conviction.

(2) The second passage is Acts 26⁴. " All Jews know my manner of life from the very beginning, as a child, both among my own nation *and* in Jerusalem." Does " my own nation " refer to the Jews in general or to the people of Cilicia where he was born ? The latter is more natural, in view of the contrasting phrase, " and in Jerusalem." For this reason, van Unnik seeks to establish a different translation (" among my own nation, *including* Jerusalem "), avoiding the contrast that the word " and " would imply.

Two points of language appear. What is the meaning of *ethnos* (the Jewish people ? or the Tarsus people ?) and does *te* mean " and " in this context ?

In the plural, *ethnos* always refers to the Gentiles, as one would expect, but the singular is almost exactly divided between Jews and

Gentiles in its New Testament usage, and once (Acts 8[9]) it is used of Samaria.* However, " my nation " on the lips of St. Paul meant the Jewish nation on two occasions (Acts 24[17] 28[19]). But for *te*, it might well be conceded that the Jewish nation is intended in the passage at present under discussion.

Moreover, the question arises whether *te* ought to be omitted. As a copulative particle it was declining in normal use, only to be revived later as a stylistic artificiality, especially during the life-time of the scribes of our oldest New Testament manuscripts. " It is not surprising that in textual transmission scribes and editors were unable to resist introducing τε sometimes at the expense of δέ."† But one cannot in this way account for every occurrence of *te* in Acts ; a hundred and seventy is too large a number. In this verse, *te* is well attested.‡ On internal grounds it would be more likely that omission took place in order to procure better sense,§ than that *te* was inserted by stylistic scribes ; it is more difficult, and therefore more probable. We are impelled to a reconsideration of the meaning of *ethnos*. Accepting *te*, and assuming that it means " and," we will more naturally take *ethnos* of a Gentile nation (the Cilicians) than of the Jews.

It seems then that *te* is a genuine stylistic feature of the author. To support the exclusively Jerusalem upbringing of Saul it will have to be argued that *te* is not so much " and " as " including " or " actually." But there is a long tradition, from Plato to Polybius, supporting the use of simple *te* (without *kai*) as a copula meaning no more than " and," and linking together both words and clauses.‖ The best suggestion would be that St. Luke from time to time varies his style by means of this simple copulative particle. He is not alone in this peculiarity, for would-be " literary " men, such as the author of Hebrews and Jude, employ the device, and so does St. Paul.

On this occasion St. Paul apparently meant by " my nation " something different from his meaning on a previous and a future occasion. He is referring not to his present position but to the situation of childhood days before he went for his education to Jerusalem. Before that, he would naturally have thought of his " nation " as being the people in the home town of which he was so proud, Tarsus, " no mean city."

* Of Gentiles : Matt. 21[43] 24[7] (= Mark 13[8], Luke 21[10]), Acts 2[5] 7[7] 10[35] 17[26], Rev. 5[9] 7[9] 13[7] 14[6]. Of Jews : Luke 7[5] 23[2], John 11[48ff.] 18[35], Acts 10[22] 24[3.10.17] 28[19], Rom. 10[19], I Pet. 2[9]. † Moulton-Howard-Turner, *Grammar*, vol. III, p. 338.
‡ It is omitted only by Codex Ephraemi (5th. century) and by four uncials of the ninth century, among MSS. of any importance.
§ " Among my nation in Jerusalem " is easier than " among my nation *and* in Jerusalem " if the scribes thought " nation " meant the Jews.
‖ H. G. Liddell and R. Scott, *A Greek-English Lexicon*, 9th. ed. by H. S. Jones and R. McKenzie, Oxford, 1940, vol. II, p. 1763 (A. I. 4).

2. Autobiography in St. Paul's Epistles

Seemingly personal references by St. Paul should not be accepted at their face value nor used biographically. He may well be employing a trick of rhetoric, common in Greek literature from Demosthenes onwards, to make a point vivid by means of the first and second personal pronouns, " I—thou," without intending any direct reference either to his readers or himself.

This is important in the epistle to the Romans. In the discussion concerning the believer's struggle with evil powers in his own nature both before and after conversion, St. Paul presents an extreme case to make the point more clear. He speaks of lust as a personal experience (7^7), and apparently makes his own confession, " Sin wrought in me all manner of concupiscence " (7^8). The former Pharisee was not living a secret sin-life, and none of his Greek speaking readers would take this as a confession. " With the flesh I serve the law of sin," is not autobiographical, but conventional, rhetoric. He shared the experience of all Christians, but he envisages an extreme case rather than his own. " Thou " too is not a personal reference to Jewish Christians in Rome.

Nor need many of the apparent complaints in the Corinthian letters be taken as personal attacks upon the apostle. Rhetorical devices would come naturally to one who was dictating (I Cor. 16^{21}). For instance, " Why am I evil spoken of ? " means, " Why is such a Christian evil spoken of ? " (10^{30}). If he says that *he* pleases all men in all things, this is a precept for Christians in general (10^{33}), rather than a private technique of evangelism.

Another autobiographical feature demands the clarification of grammar. St. Paul owned a special call from God to go to the Gentiles, as St. Peter's was to evangelize the Jews, He spoke of " the gospel of the uncircumcision " (Gal. 2^7). This is just another of the apostle's genitives. Objects are often direct, but not necessarily. The phrase is intelligible immediately if the objective genitive is indirect (" to " or " for "). The gospel of the uncircumcision then is " the good news *for* the uncircumcision," as one may have long suspected without appreciating the subtlety of the Pauline genitive.

3. Saul's Conversion

" I tried to make them blaspheme " (*Acts* 26^{11})

Early Christians in Jerusalem were victims of Saul's zealous rage, but to many readers of our best known and best loved English version it comes as a shock to discover that these believers were made to blaspheme, and that the incipient rabbi succeeded in his dreadful attempt. " I punished them oft in every synagogue and compelled them to blaspheme " (A.V.). The R.V. and subsequent versions have rectified the fault by allowing the full force of the Greek conative imperfect. With due modesty, Saul actually said, " I *tried* to make them blaspheme," and one must not infer that his vicious onslaught achieved anything beyond the further spread of the new faith.

Only Saul understood the voice (Acts 9⁴)

Among the nice grammatical distinctions of the classical period, now blurred in the Hellenistic of the New Testament, is the difference between the accusative and genitive cases to denote an object after the verb " to hear " (*akouein*).

Much use might be made of the distinction for Bible interpretation, if only one could be quite certain that it were still a valid one. The furthest we may go is to say that when the verb " to hear " is followed by a participle (e.g. " we hear that some are walking ") there is then some real difference between the accusative and genitive. It would appear that the accusative transforms the participle into a subordinate clause of indirect speech (e.g. " Jacob heard *that* there was corn in Egypt "), while the genitive influences the participle to indicate the sound that was directly heard : e.g. Jesus " heard them reasoning together," not " *that* they reasoned together " (Mark 12²⁸) ; and " we heard him say," not " *that* he said " (14⁵⁸) ; the blind man therefore actually heard the noise of the multitude passing by, not *that* it was passing by (Luke 18³⁶) ; at Pentecost, too, every man heard the apostles actually speaking in his own language, and it was not a rumour that went round.

It follows that, at Saul's conversion, he heard a voice speaking directly to him, for this is indicated by the use of the genitive in the second account of the conversion (Acts 22⁷). It is somewhat perplexing to find that in the first and third accounts St. Luke chose to use the accusative to convey exactly the same meaning, thus confounding the old classical niceties. On one occasion St. Mark too does this, but he has never received the same reputation as St. Luke as a writer of good Greek, and in his instance it happens to be the compound verb " overhear " (*parakouein*) : " Jesus overheard the word that was spoken " (Mark 5³⁶). According to the rules this should be : " Jesus overheard *that* the saying was being spoken." This is almost, but perhaps not quite, nonsense.

The discrepancy in the accounts of Saul's conversion has led to some attempts to overcome it grammatically and so vindicate St. Luke's consistency. To this end, the further classical distinction is invoked, namely that the accusative case really denotes not the *specification* of the object, but the *extent* of it. In the accusative, one does not so much hear *a* sound as hear the gist of it. The inference is that there is a slight change in the meaning of the verb, from " hear " to " understand." Such a distinction, if it could be sustained for the Greek of the New Testament, would not only neatly resolve the grammatical difficulty in the conversion accounts, but would introduce a meaningful sidelight into the story and enhance St. Luke's reputation for linguistic dexterity.

J. H. Moulton considered that the " old and well-known distinction " was valid for the New Testament,[*] and received the support of A. T. Robertson in America[†] and the Roman Catholic scholar, Maximilian Zerwick, S.J.[‡]—besides the margin of the R.V. Such an estimate of St. Luke's powers is the more plausible because he may have deliberately corrected St. Matthew's unclassical accusative to the genitive in the phrase, " Whosoever heareth these sayings of mine " (Matt. 7[24]). Physical hearing is involved, not understanding, and so the genitive is more strictly correct.

In the same way, St. Luke in describing Saul's conversion (Acts 9[7]) states that the servants heard the voice, and correctly uses the genitive as he presumably intends merely to specify that a voice was heard, and no more. Equally correctly, on this theory, when St. Luke is reporting St. Paul telling his own story to the mob in the temple precincts (Acts 22[9]), he makes use of the accusative case, because here it is said that the servants did *not* hear (i.e. " understand ") the voice. There is no contradiction between 9[7] and 22[9] since the case alters the meaning of the verb. The servants therefore heard *a* voice (genitive of specification) according to 9[7], but they did not understand its meaning (accusative of extent) according to 22[9]. They looked through a glass darkly ; he saw face to face, and heard with understanding. The vision was directed at Saul alone.

There is much to be said against so neat a theory. A case could be made out that normally St. Luke is following a simple but different rule that the accusative denotes the *thing* heard, and the genitive the *person* heard.[§] There were exceptions enough to this in classical

[*] *Prolegomena*, p. 66. The opposing view was taken by W. H. Simcox, *The Language of the New Testament*, Hodder, 1889, p. 90. The distinction is not admitted either by F. Field, *Notes on the Translation of the New Testament*, Cambridge, 1899, p. 117 ; nor by C. F. D. Moule, *An Idiom Book of New Testament Greek*, Cambridge, 1952, p. 36.

[†] A. T. Robertson, *A Grammar of the Greek New Testament in the Light of Historical Research*, Hodder, 1914, pp. 448 f., 472, 506.

[‡] M. Zerwick, *Graecitas Biblica*, 3rd. ed., Rome, 1955, §50.

[§] *Expos. Times*, vol. LXXI, no. 8 (May, 1960), pp. 243 ff. Liddell and Scott imply that it is the " proper " classical usage.

authors, and too many in St. Luke. There are Acts 9⁷ 22⁷, for instance, where the genitive is used of the *thing* heard.

Abandoning such an idea, it is worth examining in greater detail the view that the accusative involves an *understanding* of the object while the genitive merely records the physical *hearing* of it. It may be tested in other contexts. Acts 3²³ (genitive) : " every soul which will not *hear* that prophet " ; i.e. which refuses even to let a prophet speak, and there is no question of *understanding*. Matt. 10¹⁴ (accusative) : it is not enough that the householders merely *hear* the apostles, but they must take heed and *understand*. On the other hand, there are numerous exceptions : several accusatives occur when there must be no idea of *understanding*, merely physical perception. E.g., it was not enough for the high priest that his ears had caught the sound of blasphemy : see Matt. 26⁶⁵, Mark 14⁶⁴ (except where some MSS have substituted the genitive). Nothing more than the physical sound of St. Mary's voice, as she entered her cousin's house, inspired the unborn babe to leap in her cousin's womb (Luke 1⁴¹) ; nothing that Mary had said caused the flutter of excitement, simply the sound of her voice. Although there appear to be few exceptions to the rule in the fourth gospel, generally it is less certain in the rest of the New Testament, particularly in Acts and Revelation. It may simply be that the accusative is by now encroaching on the preserve of the genitive, without having completely ousted it. Nevertheless, I doubt whether the instances just given are exceptions after all. The accusatives, which appear at first to involve no more than physical perception, each bear a more subtle interpretation. The high priest was after all addressing scholars, and to detect blasphemy in one so evidently holy and harmless needed careful consideration, not to say casuistry ; it is less than certain that Jesus, heard by the pious but untutored Jew, would appear blasphemous. So much so that the accusation of Caiaphas on this evidence is distinctly puzzling. A claim to Messiahship is not blasphemous. In view of this, one is tempted to keep the true force of the accusative and interpret the high priest's words as follows : " You have *detected* (not merely *heard*) the blasphemy of his reply. What do you think ? It is blasphemy, is it not ? " Jesus's self-accusation was not immediately clear, and the high priest needed to give direction to the jury and to appeal to trained minds rather than to trust to the immediate reaction of their ears.

The other apparent exception is St. Mary's voice at the visitation. Was it merely the excitement of hearing her young cousin arrive, which produced the movement in Elisabeth's womb ? Much more was involved, and when the Virgin entered Elisabeth's home that day, Elisabeth may have known more than is apparent in the incredibly restrained narrative. She knew why she herself was pregnant and so must have known what brought another woman, mother of a greater Child, to her side. " Blessed woman ! " she exclaimed. " Blessed child that lives in you ! " Like Saul of Tarsus, she had *heard* her voices and like him had *understood*. The Virgin's salutation was interpreted as well as heard. " The mother of my Lord has come to me ! " Elisabeth understood.

4. SAUL AND HIS READERS

" *You know very well* " (*Acts* 25[10], *II Tim.* 1[18])

Exasperated by the cunning of the procurator Festus, St. Paul urged, " I am guilty of nothing against the Jews, as you know *very well* " (Acts 25[10]). In calmer mood to St. Timothy he wrote, " You are *very well* aware of all that Onesiphorus did for me at Ephesus " (II Tim. 1[18]).

The bishops of the Most High and Mighty Prince James knew far less than we about Hellenistic Greek, but in this instance they did better than the N.E.B. translators. Hellenistic writers tended to depart from classical standards by using the comparative degree of the adjective in place of the superlative.* One of the functions of the superlative is elative. That can be expressed in English by using the word " very " ; e.g. the normal superlative is " biggest," while the elative superlative is " very big." It applies to adverbs as well as adjectives. By taking *beltion* as a comparative adverb in the classical fashion, the N.E.B. translators expand the word by translating it, " You know *better than I could tell you.*"

The Revisers of 1881 knew enough of Hellenistic Greek not to follow the lead of commentators like Ellicott, Holtzmann and Huther, who urged that *beltion* be rendered as in classical Greek : " you know better than I can tell you." Such a rendering had the weighty support of Winer's *Grammatik*, the syntactical oracle of the period, but Winer did suggest the slight variation, " better than I." However, the R.V. and most subsequent English versions, in view of the vagaries of comparison in Hellenistic Greek, commendably retain the translation of the A.V., which in turn depended upon Tyndale and Coverdale over against Wiclif and the Rheims Bible.

Attention should also be drawn to Acts 24[26] where the previous procurator, Felix, hoping for a bribe, *repeatedly* sent for St. Paul to parley with him : the word has the form of a comparative (*puknoteron*), but it must have the elative meaning, " very often."

More important still is Gal. 4[13] where the most far-reaching results of this point of syntax are seen in historical criticism. It helps to

* See pp. 58f.

decide the vexed question between North and South Galatian theories of the destination of the epistle to the Galatians. The expression *to proteron* was more likely to have been intended by the apostle as elative superlative, and less likely as the true comparative. It should have been *to prōton* in classical Greek. The meaning then is " originally," " at the very first." It is precarious to suppose that St. Paul refers to the first of only *two* visits (i.e. comparative). Nor need the word be non-elative, i.e. " the first of at least three times." Unfortunately, the observation robs this particular verse of any positive weight in the Galatian controversy, but scholarship must often progress merely by eliminating impossibilities.

" His favourite converts " (Phil. $1^{3.5}$)

Grammar sheds a ray of light, of a slight but human interest, on the apostle's relations with the Christian believers in Philippi.

The problem of the genitive case, whether it is to be interpreted as subjective or objective, comes up frequently in St. Paul's letters. In Phil. 1^3 he writes to his favourite converts : " Upon *your every remembrance* I thank my God " (the literal translation). But does he mean, " whenever *I* think of *you*," or " when *you* remember *me* " ? Perhaps it is of no consequence, and even includes both thoughts, as when St. Paul spoke of the " love of Christ " constraining us : this was mutual, Christ's love for us and ours for him.

These friendly Christians at Philippi are reminded of their " fellowship *in* the gospel " (Phil. 1^5). But this phrase needs some revising in the light of grammatical knowledge. The word " in " is *eis*, and, unlike many writers in the Hellenistic period, St. Paul and St. Matthew avoid confusing the prepositions *eis* (into) and *en* (in). The significance of this for exegesis has been appreciated by the Jesuit grammarian Zerwick.* If St. Paul really was as meticulous as we think, he must have intended something more than the A.V. rendering, " your fellowship *in* the gospel." The R.V. is better : " your fellowship *in furtherance of* the gospel." But this is still not quite what *eis* implies, in spite of the support of Ellicott and Lightfoot, for *eis* involves a movement or development towards a goal.

The Philippians receive a compliment in return for their generous fellowship. This gift seemed to St. Paul to be quite disinterested and spiritually inspired. Its goal was simply that gospel preaching might continue. St. Paul thanked the Philippian Christians for their money ; to him it had been " fellowship *as a contribution towards* the preaching of the gospel."

* M. Zerwick, *op. cit.*, §§77, 78, 79.

Why he wished to see Rome (Rom. 1¹⁵)

I know of no Bible (except the Greek Testament) which fails to report St. Paul as saying that he looked forward to preaching the gospel to Christians at Rome (Rom. 1¹⁵). It is doubtful whether that was his meaning. In the first place, he might think it a waste of time to preach the gospel to the converted. Again, grammatically, the passage has for long presented difficulties. There is the phrase, " as much as in me is " (*to kat' eme*) ; the translation is legitimate, although for this St. Paul might more probably have said *to ex emou*. Assuming the correctness of this rendering, presumably the Greek word (translated " I am ready ") is to be understood as a main verb by supplying the auxiliary verb *eimi* (" I am "). Moreover, we will then have to accept the textual authorities which have the nominative as against the accusative case.

I would plead, however, that the phrase *to kat' eme* is not adverbial but nominal, which means that it may stand in place of a noun and form the object of the verb, " preach." As to the verb itself, to render it " preach the gospel " (as A.V., R.V., R.S.V., and others) is not the only conceivable way. It is granted that in the next sentence St. Paul uses the word " gospel," as if he had been reminded of it by this verb. Nevertheless, " gospel " is not fundamental to it, and the verb is used in biblical authors without that connotation. Indeed, in the Septuagint passage which is quoted in this epistle (10¹⁵) the object of the proclamation is not a " gospel " but " good things," and in this context also St. Paul is reminded to use the word " gospel " in the next sentence (10¹⁶). This would not prove, against the general evidence of biblical Greek, that " gospel " in its technical sense is essential to the verb in St. Paul's vocabulary, or that it is inadequate in some contexts to translate it by " preach " or " announce," quite simply.

If, at this stage, the meaning of the phrase, *to kat' eme*, might be settled, there would be an object for the verb, " preach." Part of the phrase is the preposition *kata*, and joined with the accusative case it has in biblical Greek the characteristic meaning, " according to." It could well mean, therefore, " the news about me " or " my version of things," and adequately fit the context. St Paul was evidently looking forward to giving the church at Rome " my version of things."

He had heard of their Christian life and beliefs ; they too would have heard of his. He wanted to exchange experiences and teachings with them, and so he writes, " I owe much both to Greeks and barbarians . . . and therefore I am anxious to tell you in Rome also my own point of view."

"*My own hand*" (*Gal.* 6[11])

The device known as the epistolary aorist is used by Greek letter
writers fairly often ; a past tense occurs in a letter where a present
tense is more idiomatic in English.   For instance, " I *sent* Tychicus "
(Eph. 6[22], Col. 4[8]) probably means, " Herewith I *send* Tychicus—with
this letter."   The Greek method is logical in a sense : by the time that
Tychicus arrives the actual sending will of course be in the past.   The
same is true of St. Paul's remarks about Epaphroditus in Phil. 2[28]
and the slave Onesimus in Phm. [12].

However, it must be remarked that St. Paul did not use the verb
" to write " in this idiom.   In I Cor. 5[9, 11] he says *egrapsa* (" I wrote "),
and far from being the epistolary idiom that meaning is clearly that
in the past he had written a previous letter, which had given rise to
questions which he now was preparing to answer.   In Rom. 5[15], the
reference is to the same letter as he was then writing but the past
tense is deliberately used to mark a change of tone or re-assessment of
his previous words in the same letter.   It is not an epistolary aorist ;
on the contrary, when St. Paul intended that the verb " to write "
should be epistolary he did in fact use the present tense (*grapho*).   So
in II Cor. 13[10], II Thess. 3[17].

The serviceability of all this for the exegete is that in the ambiguous
instance of Gal. 6[11] he can be the more confident that the aorist,
egrapsa, is not epistolary but is a true past tense.   On the usual view
that this is epistolary, meaning, " See with what large letters I *am*
writing to you with my own hand " (R.S.V.), we have to visualize that
at this point St. Paul took the pen from the scribe, finishing the letter
himself in large handwriting.   St. Paul did have a scribe, Tertius, who
is said in Rom. 16[22] to have been " the writer of this letter " and to
have united his own greetings with those of others.   Moreover, at the
close of three other epistles (I Cor. 16[21], Col. 4[18], II Thess. 3[17]) St. Paul
seems to have taken up the pen of a scribe and to have added greetings
in his own hand.   He went so far as to say, when completing II
Thessalonians, that such an appendix was his trademark in every
letter that he wrote.   Dictation indeed was a very common practice
and this is something important to bear in mind when the style of
individual authors is being considered.   Although a system of short-
hand was usually employed, we can never be quite sure to what extent
the amanuensis functioned as a reviser as well.   However, it should be
seriously questioned whether St. Paul did use any kind of secretary at
all when he wrote to the Galatians.   There is no change of style at this
point in his letter.   If he did write it himself, he wrote under sufficient
difficulty to account for the large characters.   This may be explained

be bad eyesight, but there is very little evidence for this. There is no less evidence for the explanation that he had damaged his hand. That would at least make the writing big, whereas failing eyesight more normally brings the face closer to the paper. There is an emphatic reference to " my own hand." It would be hasty to see in this a contrast with someone else's hand, when it could as easily be emphatic in a slightly different way—a pathetic reference to " my poor hand."

It may be thought that the suggestion that St. Paul had actually been crucified at Perga in Pamphylia, by Jews who resented his charges that the Jewish people had crucified their Messiah, is too fantastic. This was just before he went inland to visit the Galatians, and might sufficiently have scandalized the young St. Mark to make him return to Jerusalem and home. Something more than a fever attack or the danger of robbers in the Taurus mountains influenced the youthful John Mark, and before the suggestion is dismissed outright consideration must be given to the fact that in the same context in which St. Paul referred to his ungainly handwriting he contrasted himself with those foes who shrank from the crucifixion. That is followed by an outburst, almost of pain. " God forbid that I should boast save in Jesus Christ our Lord's cross, by which *I have been* (perfect tense) crucified. . . ." (Gal. 6[12f.]) It need not be metaphorical. Moreover, there is a reference to the *stigmata* of Jesus in his own body immediately after this. He had preached to the Gentiles on a background of physical suffering (4[13]) and they had received him as if he were Jesus Christ himself. He had reminded them in this letter that he has been crucified " with Christ." " And yet I am still alive ! " he added (2[20]). We read on, " O foolish Galatians . . . , before whose eyes Jesus Christ has been placarded among you, crucified ! " (3[1]) The verb, " I have been crucified with," is the same as that which describes the co-crucifixion of the two robbers with Jesus (*sunestaurōmai*). The famous " stake in the flesh " which has given rise to so much controversy (II Cor. 11[24f.]) is consistent with the theory of crucifixion. Lastly, it should be recollected that St. Paul was to remind the Corinthian Christians that always he carried about in his body the putting to death of the Lord Jesus (II Cor. 4[10]). One wonders whether this is all metaphorical.

5. Syntax and Saul's Journeys

Tact and tenses (Acts 15[37])

For some reason, the Jewish youth had deserted his seniors on the first missionary journey at the moment when they reached its most dangerous stage, about to set off from Perga northwards for a hundred miles through robber-infested uplands to Galatia. So when plans were

mooted for the second journey, John Mark's relative, Barnabas, tentatively expressed the wish that they should take him with them again
(Acts 15[37]). The narrative of the Acts of the Apostles represents the
ensuing quarrel between friends as very bitter, enough to undermine
their plans to travel together (15[39]).

However, if the author understood Barnabas correctly, his suggestion
to take John Mark was but a tentative one, at first. That must be the
significance of the imperfect tense (15[37]) where normally the aorist
would serve. " Barnabas wanted " must mean " Barnabas was
desirous " ; or better still, " Barnabas had half a mind to." It is a
frequent use of the imperfect.

The tenses are very important, for what Barnabas actually wanted
to do is now reported in the aorist tense and not the present. He had
half a mind " to take John Mark with them." That is, Barnabas
refrained from assuming that John would stay with them all the time ;
the present infinitive would have implied it. All was tactfully broached,
and Paul's reply was equally mild, as can be seen by the tense he used.
The imperfect, *ēxiou*, means that Paul merely " requested," and not
even pressingly ; many instances in the New Testament illustrate that
a demand which expects fulfilment needs the aorist tense. He set out
in full the reasons for his hesitant request : John Mark had " departed
from us in Pamphylia and did not go with us to the work." The
request itself follows. " Do not let us have this man with us all the
time." Although he used the same verb as Barnabas, he deliberately
altered the tense from aorist to present, because he envisaged that
John Mark might continuously or regularly travel with them, which
was the very thing he wished to avoid. Perhaps it was his intention
to give the young man a rest and take him on a subsequent journey.
No other explanation adequately accounts for the conspicuous change
to present infinitive in 15[38]. The change is slight, involving the insertion of very few letters : *sumparalabein* into *sumparalambanein*. The
subtlety may well have escaped Barnabas. At any rate, what seems
at first to have been a reasonable and hesitant difference of opinion
eventually flared up into a " paroxysm " (Greek *paroxusmos*), so violent
that old friends parted. The outburst is usually thought to agree
perfectly with St. Paul's quixotic temperament and his point of view
is condemned as unforgiving and mistaken. If we are to take grammar
seriously the whole position must be reviewed and credit given to St.
Paul for at least as great a weight of tact and restraint as St. Barnabas,
who, apparently, without waiting for the church's blessing, sailed off
home to Cyprus at once with John, while the supposedly hasty man
made choice of another helper and did not leave until he had been
commended to the grace of the Lord by the Christian brethren. This
much must be said in the interests of justice and grammatical truth.

A sort of command (Acts 16²²)

The mystery of one small item in the adventures of Paul and Silas at Philippi during the second missionary journey can be resolved by appreciation of another subtle stroke of St. Luke's pen. Why did not Paul and Silas, as Roman citizens, plead the fact to the magistrates against their unlawful beating and imprisonment ? When Paul protested on the following day, and the nervous officials apologized in person, it was too late. He did not usually covet bruises or welcome martyrdom, and later on in Jerusalem took good care to plead his citizenship and claim its privileges.

The answer may be that Paul and Silas did in fact make known their Roman citizenship, only to be over-ruled deliberately by the Philippian magistrates in deference to powerful commercial interests. Apollo's priests were requiring strong action against two mischievous strangers. The clue is given unconsciously by the author himself, who placed the magistrates' charge to the gaoler to flog the prisoner in the imperfect tense (16²²). Whenever the imperfect is used with Greek verbs of asking and commanding, it imports the idea of incomplete action in the past ; there is a feeling of attempt without achievement, of command without confidence of being obeyed. It has already been seen how Barnabas " had half a mind " to take Mark, and Paul " hesitatingly requested " that they should not. Not that the Philippian magistrates gave a definite command to the gaoler in so many words : " They must be flogged ! " The gaoler would know it was contrary to the law. What they did was to give him a sort of command, a wink, a nod, or a hint. " Do the usual with these men." St. Luke carefully avoids saying that they had explicitly and peremptorily ordered the flogging. The tense of his verb represents a mere pretence at command, satisfying the plaintiff commercial interests, and yet not constituting a technical breach of Roman law. The magistrates possibly hoped that the gaoler might have the good sense not to carry out what they had diplomatically but half-heartedly commanded. Next day, when St. Paul let them know that the order had been literally fulfilled, they came in alarm to beg that the prisoners move on.

Why had not St. Paul protested to the gaoler and refused to accept the punishment ? Almost certainly the protest would have been ignored. If, as we suppose, the magistrates had given no more than a veiled command, it would seem pointless to pass a message to them. The gaoler was expected to relieve them of responsibility.

In this connection it is interesting that the " Western " text of Acts, in 16³⁹, adds that the magistrates came " with many friends into the prison and begged them to come out, saying, ' We did wrong at your *trial*, because you are innocent men,' and they brought them out and begged them, saying, ' Go away from this city, in case the mob make a tumult against us, crying out against you.' "

The confession, " We did wrong at your trial," accords with the suggestion that has been put forward. The magistrates had deliberately broken the law in some way, and had not acted in ignorance. But this translation needs some defending against the usual rendering : " We did not know, concerning your affairs, that. . . ."* Although a very frequent meaning of *agnoein* is " not to know," it often means " to act amiss " in Polybius and other writers. Ignorance of the facts was a lame excuse for magistrates, and an abject apology for an utter injustice committed under pressure of powerful opinion is conceivable. *Ta kath' humās* is an adverbial accusative (" at your affairs," i.e. " at your trial ") ; similar expressions abound in St. Paul's writings and in contemporary Greek.† Indeed the phrase must mean the " case in court " when Festus is reported as laying St. Paul's case before king Agrippa (Acts 25¹⁴).

Opinions widely differ over the precise value of the " Western " text of Acts. It is represented very largely by the famous manuscript in the University Library, Cambridge, the gift of Theodore Beza, a Reformation scholar. " Western " is a misnomer, for it represents a definite type of text of an early date in textual transmission. Some scholars think that this is actually the original version of Acts as it left the author's pen—perhaps a rough draft before he, or someone else, revised it, and as a matter of fact many " Western " additions are true to the style of St. Luke himself, as far as we can verify it.

Agrippa's interruption (Acts 26²⁸)

King Agrippa II's avowal as he listened to St. Paul's apologia at Caesarea has been variously rendered and explained. " Almost thou persuadest me to become a Christian," will be immediately recalled from the A.V., but it is apparent that something is wrong, either with the translation or the text, the moment one turns to the R.V. The best British scholarship of 1881 produced : " With but little persuasion thou wouldest fain make me a Christian." What has happened ? First, the words *en oligō* (literally, " in a little "), which had hitherto been understood as an idiom meaning " almost," were now taken differently ; *en* was the instrumental *en*, " by means of " and not literally " on," and the phrase became for the Revisers " by means of a little." The further alteration, in the second half of the sentence,

---

* R. B. Rackham, *The Acts of the Apostles*, Westminster Commentaries, Methuen, 14th. ed., 1951, p. 286.

† Moulton-Howard-Turner, *Grammar*, vol. III, pp. 14 f.

stemmed from superior manuscripts on which the Revisers based their version, and which had not been available to king James's bishops. " To become " (*genesthai*) was substituted for " to make " (*poiēsai*) by copyists in the earliest days of the transmission of the New Testament text, because it was more intelligible. Although their wording conforms to contemporary English, the makers of the N.E.B. of 1961 have not substantially altered the R.V. : " You think it will not take much to win me over and make a Christian of me." Then may one assume that king Agrippa's famous remark no longer presents any difficulty ? Not while the rendering commits such violence to the syntax of the Greek, of which a literal construe reads as follows : " In a little you are persuading me to make a Christian." It requires harsh manipulation (emending *peitheis*, " you persuade," to *peithē*, " you are persuaded ") before this can be made to justify the R.V., and even more to justify the N.E.B., for their renderings are comments unrelated to any grammatical interpretation of the true text, and doubtless the Greek construction was untranslatable by either committee.

One escape from the grammatical difficulty* is to see the Greek phrase, " to make a Christian," as an idiom meaning something rather different, i.e. " to play the Christian," in fact, to be a Christian. There is a precedent in the fact that the Greek translators of the first book of Kings (21[7]) had used this phrase (with " king " in place of " Christian ") to express a Hebrew text which meant " to play the king "— not " to make a king." Very much later in Greek literature the phrase appears again in this sense, but there is no contemporary evidence that there was an idiom like this in the speech of St. Paul's day, and when he makes his retort to Agrippa it is obvious that he himself regards *genesthai* (" to become " or " to be made ") as the passive of *poiesai* (" to make "), which thereby becomes an active and not an intransitive verb, for otherwise St. Paul, to give any point to his retort, would have had to say, " I would to God you *played my part* (*poiesai*, not *genesthai*)."

The Septuagint evidence is unimpressive. The Greek translation of the books of Samuel and Kings is notoriously literal and not always efficient, and there can be no doubt that " to play the king " (which is found only in the Codex Vaticanus and one cursive manuscript) is a literal translation of an earlier Hebrew text of the Old Testament than the current Massoretic text. The latter is reflected in the reading, " to carry out sovereignty " (found in Codex Alexandrinus and several other Lucianic and Hexaplaric authorities) which represents a literal translation of our present Hebrew text. The point is that these are literal

---

* Accepted in Dr. F. F. Bruce's Tyndale Press commentary (1951) and in the new Peake's Commentary (1962), following Lake and Cadbury in *The Beginnings of Christianity*, vol. IV, p. 323.

translations and no authority for idiomatic Hellenistic syntax. As for the other evidence, taken from writers of the Byzantine period, it is centuries later than St. Luke and has comparatively little value as interpretation of his language, especially as in fact there is no reason why he should not have been using a legitimate construction of classical Greek. St. Paul makes a dignified defence before royalty and his language is of the highest tone. In this speech occurs the only certain instance, apart from questions, of the old-fashioned potential optative, which is sometimes called "urbane" on account of its stilted tone. St. Paul says, "I could pray" (26[29]). The presumption is therefore that Agrippa's interruption is not a colloquial idiom which is found nowhere else in contemporary Hellenistic literature, but it can be classified as thoroughly correct and worthy of a man who was educated in Rome, was an intimate of the emperor Claudius, and whose own speeches (if we can believe the reporting of the historian Josephus) were so classical in style as to be reminiscent of Thucydides.

This thoroughly classical construction is well known to grammarians. When a governing verb has an object and this object is at the same time the object of a dependent infinitive, then that object, whether noun or pronoun, is not repeated in the infinitival clause.* This is exactly the construction in Agrippa's avowal: " You are trying to persuade (this is the governing verb) me (the object) that you (the subject of the governing verb, but not repeated in the infinitival clause, in accordance with classical style) have made (the dependent infinitive) me (the object of both verbs, but not necessarily repeated in the infinitival clause in classical Greek) a Christian in a short time (or easily)." There is a precise parallel in Xenophon's *Memorabilia* (I, 2, 49) where the Greek historian represents Socrates as using the very same governing verb as Agrippa (*peithein*) : " Socrates . . . trying to persuade (governing verb) his disciples (the object) that he (subject, but not stated) will make (dependent infinitive) them (the object, but not stated in the Greek) wiser than their fathers."

To see this expressed in tabular form is probably the simplest way to appreciate how closely Agrippa's idiom follows the classical pattern.

---

* See for instance, Kühner-Gerth II, §476. 2 fin.

Analysis of sentence-structure

AUTHOR	MAIN CLAUSE				DEPENDENT CLAUSE			
	subject	governing verb	object of the governing verb *expressed in the Greek*	link with dependent clause *not needed in Greek*	subject *not expressed in Greek because same as subject of governing verb*	dependent verb (infinitive)	object *not expressed in Greek because same as object of governing verb*	predicate
1. St. Luke (Acts 26²⁵)	You	are trying to persuade	me	that	you	have made	me	a Christian in a short time
2. Xenophon (Mem. I. 2. 49)	Socrates . . .	trying to persuade	his disciples	that	he	will make	them	wiser than their fathers

CHAPTER FOUR

ST. PAUL'S TEACHING

I. Practical Pastoralia

Marriage and divorce (I Cor. 7¹⁰⁻¹⁶)

To many converts at Corinth the continuance of the married state was a real difficulty, and St. Paul dealt with the problem with guidance as from an inspired apostle.

In general, no man was to divorce his wife, nor a wife her husband, even on grounds of unfaithfulness (as opposed to Matt. 5³²). In any event, there must be no re-marriage while a spouse is living. Presumably he spoke of unions where both spouses were Christian believers, and he followed Christ's own teaching.* Nevertheless, the circumstances of a Christian partner living with a pagan spouse may make the continuance of the married state very difficult, and the pagan spouse may demand separation. Only in this situation would St. Paul permit separation ; even so, he appears to hope that the demand would not be made. His emphasis is on the possibility of reconciliation. Potentially at least the pagan spouse belongs to God simply by virtue of the Christian link ; children, too, in the mixed marriage enjoy the blessing of Christian fellowship.

To a point, therefore, reconciliation is the goal. Yet if a pagan spouse seeks a dissolution of marriage it should be granted and both parties should be at liberty to re-marry. There was little point in preserving the outward semblance of a union, and the chances of converting the pagan to Christianity he thought very slender. Good grammatical exegesis interprets him like this : " How do you know whether you will save your spouse ? " And he must be understood not to have said, " How do you know whether you will *not* save your spouse ? "†

St. Paul declared that our Lord's words about the indissolubility of marriage do not apply to instances such as these (I Cor. 7¹²). Nevertheless it is difficult to believe that Christ was legislating only for future Christians in unmixed marriages.

Dean Alford ascribed the discovery of the true rendering of verse 16

---

* Mark 10⁹, Luke 16¹⁸. See chapter 2 in the present work, pp. 60 f.
† This is the impression given by the R.S.V., N.E.B., and other renderings.

to Lyra (fourteenth century) and noted its subsequent adoption in 1614 by the Roman Catholic scholar Estius, by Meyer, De Wette and (the Roman Catholic) Bispring. Some commentators* still regard verse 15 as parenthetical between verses 14 and 16, whereas a change of subject at 15 is more natural, with 15 and 16 going closely together. It is not necessary to take 15 as a parenthesis. Moreover, Alford considered that the order of Greek words favoured his interpretation, since " husband " and " wife " each occur in an emphatic position in the sentence, so that the sense must be : " Wife, how do you know whether you will convert your *husband* ? "

What must certainly be resisted is the attempt of Lightfoot and Findlay† to justify the rendering, " whether you will *not*," by means of the Septuagint. This Greek version of the Old Testament uses a similar phrase to that of St. Paul, to express the Hebrew " it may be," " perchance " (literally, " who knows ? ").‡ However, although this is similar to what St. Paul wrote, it is not the same, and it need not be his idiom. Instead of the Hebrew " who knows ? " St. Paul wrote, " What do you know ? " It may be objected that, in that case, the translation, " How do you know . . . ? " is mistaken, because " what " is not " how." The answer is that the Greek *ti* (" what ") is actually used for " how "§—which is not so very different from its frequent meaning, " why."

The mistranslation of St. Paul's dictum, which was taken for granted for centuries before Lyra, and even later, must have occasioned misery to many a Christian spouse who, like Queen Bertha of Kent or the Merovingian Clotilda, adhered to what appeared to be the strict letter of apostolic teaching. These ladies were fortunate in winning over a pagan spouse, but of others it can be truly said, " How do you know whether you will save your husband ? "

Even when the apostle is correctly interpreted, the whole position which he adopted is too unsatisfactory to be applied to present conditions. Almost anyone in our society might claim to be a Christian burdened with a pagan spouse, and to have become a Christian since marriage. Almost any spouse might claim to be unequally yoked with a Christian. The church could not scripturally forbid divorce if these claims were advanced. How does one define a Christian ? A member of a recognized Christian group ? a churchgoer ? an upright godfearer ? The time is long past when St. Paul's words could carry weight except

---

* E.g. E. Evans, in the Clarendon Bible.

† J. B. Lightfoot, *Notes on I Corinthians i-vii*, Macmillan, 1895;   G. G. Findlay, *Expositors' Greek Testament*, Hodder, 1895.

‡ F. Brown, S. R. Driver, C. A. Briggs, *A Hebrew and English Lexicon*, Oxford, 1906, s.v. מִי, f. (d). Especially Esther 4[14] (" who knows if you have come to the kingdom for such a time as this ? " The meaning is : " perhaps you have . . .")

§ Septuagint of Hosea 11[8]. " How (*ti*) shall I give thee up ? " (twice).

in their very general sense of " Be reconciled if you can. If not, do not restrict your liberty." Even so, it is more than any state permits at present.

" Seize your opportunity to be free ! " (I Cor. 7²¹)

Well established grammatical principles govern the use of imperatives in Greek. " The aorist imperative is more or less restricted to precepts concerning conduct in specific cases. . . . On the other hand, present imperatives give a command to do something constantly, to continue to do it."*

The principle should solve once for all the old problem of St. Paul's advice to the Corinthian Christians about slavery. " Art thou called being a slave ? care not for it : but if thou mayest be free, use it rather " (I Cor. 7²¹). Unfortunately, the familiar words of the A.V. may be understood in either of two ways. The object of the word " use " is either " freedom " or " slavery." St. Paul is saying either, " Even if you have the opportunity to be free, use your slavery (to the glory of God) " ; or else, " If you do have the opportunity to be free, use it." The first interpretation suits the tone of what the apostle has been urging upon his readers in the immediate context, i.e. " Let every man abide in the same calling wherein he was called." It was also the interpretation of the Syriac Peshitto version, which has, " Choose for thyself that thou mayest be a slave."

Although St. Chrysostom had heard of the second interpretation, nevertheless he chose the first on the ground of what he called " the method of Paul." One may be surprised that the N.E.B. relegates the traditional interpretation to a footnote and favours the second one in the text, although the latter is of course more consonant with modern sentiment. " If a chance of liberty should come, take it." Some consider that the rendering ignores the particles in the Greek conditional clause, which may be translated : " Even if a chance of liberty should come." On the other hand, it does take full account of the grammar of tenses in the imperative mood, for the present imperative would have been needed if St. Paul had advised them to continue using their opportunities as slaves to the glory of God. He selected the aorist imperative, " Seize your opportunity ! "

The question of the precise meaning of the conditional particle— whether it is " if " or " even if "—is not actually relevant to the discussion, since ei kai is capable of either meaning, and one must there-fore be guided by the other feature of grammar, even against the context.

* Moulton-Howard-Turner, *Grammar*, vol. III, p. 74.

2. CHRISTIAN UNITY

One loaf represents our unity (I Cor. 10[17])

" For we, being many, are one bread, one body."

This way of interpreting St. Paul, the usual way, seems to me as unintelligible as it is unnecessary grammatically. The verb " to be " is supplied legitimately ; "are " corresponds to nothing in the Greek, but St. Paul omits the verb " to be " when it is a mere copula, and sometimes when it is stronger than that. It is stronger, and yet omitted, in I Thess. 5[3] (" *there is* peace and safety ") and in about thirty other passages.*

It makes the statement about Christian unity in I Cor. 10[17] more intelligible if the ellipse is understood as involving something more than a mere copula. Then one reads it like this : " Because *there is* one bread, we the many are one body." The apostle's reasoning has been that Corinthian believers should have no fellowship with idolatry, on the grounds that they already have fellowship with Christ in the bread and in the cup of the Lord. One cannot at the same time have fellowship with him and with devils. Here is a dichotomy : there are two families, the Lord's and the devils', each family having fellowship with its deity, a close bond uniting each within itself. The one loaf of bread symbolizes it. Because there is but one loaf, the many believers who come together to the Lord's table are one body. This is not to say that they are one loaf. More correct is the marginal reading of the R.V. : " seeing that there is one bread, we, who are many, are one body." The Revisers' hesitation to place it in the text may have been inspired by grammatical objections, an uneasiness about attributing to St. Paul the practice of omitting the non-copula verb " to be," unaware that he omits it about thirty times in his letters.

Members of the Body (Col. 3[5])

However stilted it sounds for a writer to address the members of his own body in the vocative case, as though they were living persons, the alternative may be no less difficult.

The usual translation of Col. 3[5] refers to our members " which are upon the earth," but it can scarcely be correct when the sentence proceeds to list those members as " fornication, uncleanness, inordinate affection," and so on. Such being failings of the body, but hardly members of it, the translation is far from satisfactory, and one is

* Moulton-Howard-Turner, *Grammar*, vol. III, p. 303.

tempted to suggest the expedient of departing from standard versions and construing " members " as a vocative, as if St. Paul were addressing his own body. The presence of the definite article is by no means unusual with a vocative.

The suggestion amounts to this. An adjectival phrase (" which are upon the earth ") now changes itself into a noun phrase (" the things which . . .") and becomes the object of the imperative verb, " mortify." The phrase reads, " Members of my body, mortify the things that are on earth : fornication, uncleanness, inordinate affection. . . ." It may perhaps be more significant, in this context, to understand " members " as members of the Body of Christ. St. Paul may refer to Christians in general and to his readers in particular. " You, as members of the Body, must mortify the things that are upon earth. . . ."*

3. The Apostasy of Judaism

Sinners in spite of everything (Rom. 2²⁷)

A Greek preposition, without losing anything of its normal meaning, will gain an additional nuance from its context. It would be a pity to miss this in translation, as much as in exegesis.

I have in mind *dia* (with the genitive case) which is fundamentally " through," whether of space or time. The context may modify it to mean " in spite of " in both languages. The English sentence, " He came to his glory *through* suffering," shows how the preposition may gain the derived meaning, " in spite of " or " in face of." It is no less true of Greek, and an important example is St. Paul's indictment of the Jew in Rom. 2²⁷.

In the words of the A.V., St. Paul writes, " And shall not uncircumcision . . . judge thee, who *by* the letter and circumcision dost transgress the Law ? " *By* the Scriptures and a Mosaic ordinance, divinely given, one could not transgress the Law ; so we must not give *dia* a meaning such as " by," which at once suggests " by means of." Rather, the Greek preposition, whose primary meaning is " through," has the derived meaning here of " in spite of." This makes perfect sense. " In spite of your letter (i.e. the Scriptures) and in spite of circumcision, you transgress the Law."

Although they missed the point here, the bishops saw it in another place where there is a parallel phrase, " through (*dia*) uncircumcision." The A.V. of Rom. 4¹¹ renders it, " though they be not circumcised " —which of course implies that *dia* means " in spite of."

* Charles Masson made the suggestion that " members " be regarded as vocative, and he understood it as members of the Body, the Church. *Commentaire du Nouveau Testament*, Neuchatel and Paris, 1950, in loc.

Would that translators had seen the point at Rom. 2²⁷. The basic argument of these early chapters is that not only the Gentile, but even the Jew, has sinned, in spite of so many advantages and privileges beyond the Gentile.

The superiority of the Jew (Rom. 3⁹)

When he compared the advantage of Jews over Gentiles in God's sight, St. Paul, as a Jew, put forward the proposition : " What then ? are we better than they ? " (Rom. 3⁹ A.V.)

The translation is based on the Vulgate and is a good one. Field and the Revisers, with Vaughan's and Olshausen's support, bring needless complexity into the discussion by proposing that the verb is passive, and so arriving at the precisely opposite meaning, " Are we excelled ? " Vaughan did admit that a passive of this verb was " most unusual, perhaps unique," and he would have expected the active voice. Unfortunately Vaughan did not suggest that St. Paul might have been using the middle voice rather than the passive—with, of course, its active nuance (" to excel ").

Grimm-Thayer's lexicon, little used now by students, expresses impatience with the pedants. " It does not make against this force of the middle in the present passage that the use is nowhere else met with, nor is there any objection to an interpretation which has commended itself to a great many and which the context plainly demands." Among the " great many " Grimm-Thayer might have classed Bishop Westcott and Dean Alford, as well as Bengel from a previous century, and what Sanday and Headlam call " the majority of commentators, ancient and modern " ; and Grimm-Thayer were destined to have great names like Vaughan, Field, and Sanday-Headlam ranged against them. It is strange that Vaughan confessed that the passive was " perhaps unique," for Field found an instance in Plutarch. In the Egyptian papyri no example of either middle or passive has been found. Vaughan and Olshausen, however, while insisting that the verb is passive, somehow reached a translation which presupposes an active or middle. " Are we preferred ? " They felt that the context clearly demanded that sense, and this is something which Field overlooked.* While it is true that the lexicons provide no example of the middle voice being used in an active sense, the New Testament abounds in instances where a middle voice is used when there is an active form of the verb available ; indeed, the middle is often used in the very sentence where its active form occurs with the same meaning. New Testament writers are not happy in their understanding of

---

* However, he was justified in dismissing a third suggestion, that of R.V.ᵐᵍ·, as grammatically untenable.

the middle voice, at any rate by classical standards, but they are not prevented from using it ; they almost kill it with kindness. Moreover, the evidence from very early commentators and glosses is weighty in itself, as indirect testimony to the meaning of the middle. In this connection there is a variant reading of venerable antiquity, which may be an early gloss, a comment in the margin of a manuscript, explaining the meaning of the text for the reader's benefit, this comment being accidentally copied into the text subsequently. The original (uncorrected) text of Codex Bezae (fifth century) and Codex Boernerianus (ninth century) probably represents one of these glosses : " Are we better than they ? " So the gloss interprets the verb in an active sense, and it was made at a period when the meaning of this verb in the middle voice was better known than is possible to-day with the scanty evidence at our disposal.

Jewish faith will save the world (Rom. 3[30])

Elsewhere* I ventured a warning against assuming too many fine distinctions in this kind of Greek, suggesting that the translator should look twice at the " theology of prepositions " because Hellenistic writers tend to use them indiscriminately. It is essential always to keep the context in mind.

That was a general assessment of a tendency and not a categorical denial that there is any theological significance in, say, St. Paul's transfer from the use of one preposition to that of another in the same context. It is a very different thing. Indeed, the translator " must guard against the assumption that the N.T. writers have nothing significant in mind when they vary a phrase from one verse to the next, even if the difference does not seem significant to us."† A good instance is the extreme liberty which some take in translating the word " in " (Greek en) to suit the particular context regardless of linguistic principles.

One may wonder then what St. Paul had in mind when penning Rom. 3[30]. In one verse appear two parallel phrases, but with a different preposition in each. " God will justify the circumcised ek faith, and the uncircumcised dia faith " (literally, " from faith, . . . through faith "). One asks whether God has two different ways of regarding the faith of Jews and Gentiles. Many will agree with Canon C. F. D. Moule that it is straining credulity to adopt a distinction between ek and dia in the verse,‡ in the way that Sandy-Headlam

---

* Moulton-Howard-Turner, *Grammar*, vol. III, Introduction.
† *Bible Translator*, vol. X, no. 3, July 1959, p. 120.
‡ C. F. D. Moule, *An Idiom Book of New Testament Greek*, Cambridge, 1953, p. 195.

sought to do.* They suggested that *ek* denotes the source, and *dia* the attendant circumstances, but without making it very clear how the distinction works out in practice as to Jew and Gentile respectively ; and it is not clear how from this distinction they arrive at the following paraphrase : " God, Who requires but one condition—Faith, on which He is ready to treat as ' righteous ' alike the circumcised and the uncircumcised—the circumcised with whom Faith is the moving cause, and the uncircumcised with whom the same Faith is both moving cause and sole condition of their acceptance " (p. 95). What is meant, presumably, is that, for the Jew, circumcision was the *ostensible* ground of justification (in the sense of an *opere ex operato* formality), while the real ground (*ek*, denoting the source) was the personal faith of the Jew, although he did not appreciate this ; and for the Gentile, on the other hand, there is one only ground of justification, the ostensible ground (*dia*, denoting attendant circumstances), which is personal faith.

The makers of R.S.V. may perhaps have been pursuing the same line of reasoning when they too introduced a distinction : " he will justify the circumcised on the ground of their faith and the uncircumcised because of their faith." More likely they were reduced to the mechanical expedient of rendering two apparent synonyms in Greek (*ek* and *dia*) by two near synonyms in English (" on the ground of " and " because of ").

On the assumption that St. Paul chose his words carefully, one is tempted to be bold and to interpret this and the following verses in an entirely new way. The supposition is endorsed by two grammatical principles.

First, St. Paul has placed no definite article with " faith " at its former mention, i.e., when he wrote, " God will justify the circumcised *ek* faith." Nevertheless, at its second mention he has resorted to the article, i.e., when he wrote, " And the uncircumcised *dia* faith." It is no more than the normal use of the Greek article in anaphora,† for the article on the second occasion refers back, like a demonstrative adjective, to the immediately previous mention of the word " faith." In view of the semi-demonstrative character of the definite article, we ought to translate the phrase, " God will justify the Jews as a direct result of their faith and then will justify the Gentlles by means of *that same* faith." It satisfies both the distinction of the prepositions and the force of the anaphora. Moreover, it brings out the important point that the faith of which St. Paul was speaking is not the faith of the Gentiles, not even the faith of both Jews and Gentiles, but

---

* W. Sanday and A. C. Headlam, *The Epistle to the Romans*, I.C.C., T. & T. Clark, 5th. ed., 1902, p. 96.

† For further discussion of anaphora, see p. 10.

unexpectedly enough the faith of Jews alone. The Gentiles are saved by means of the faith *of the Jews* ! One of the pivotal themes of the epistle to the Romans is that God's plan of salvation involved the justification of the Jews first and then, through the Jews, the justification of the Gentiles ; the two world-divisions are interdependent, because whereas the Jew is provoked to return to God by the conversion of the Gentile, in turn the Gentile reaps the blessings which flow from Israel's faith in God. Therefore in 11[15] St. Paul was able to reason that God's temporary rejection of Israel has brought about the reconciliation of the whole world to him, and the blessings to the world will be correspondingly greater when Israel's own faith brings her back to God. Such blessings he could describe as nothing less than " life from the dead " for the Gentile. I believe that St. Paul already had this thought in mind in 3[30] and was even there emphasizing the interdependence of the Jew and the Gentile under their " one God." The Jews are justified by their faith, and the Gentiles by the faith of the Jews.

The next words (verse 31) do not shatter this thought if they are rendered in a way different from the conventional. The conservative way is: "Do we therefore make light of the Law because of Faith? God forbid ! We establish the Law." It is a poor translation, missing so much that must have been in the background as St. Paul reasoned against his imaginary opponent. Above all, it misses his significant play on words. The truth is, that the grammatical consideration of anaphora once more throws a ray of light. Now it is by a reverse argument, because the article is absent.

The word *nomos*, meaning either " law " or " principle," occurs twice, without the article, and this would suggest that as there is now no anaphora the *nomos* in each instance does not refer to the same thing. In other words, the second *nomos* cannot mean " the same law." St. Paul in fact took advantage of a fairly common literary device to use a word twice in a sentence, but with a different meaning. It is difficult to bring this out in English ; we have no word which will bear quite the same two senses of " law " and " principle." Our prosaic translation must be : " Are we then (by our argument that Jews are saved by faith, not the Torah) setting the Torah at nought ? Oh, no ! At least we have established a *principle*." The principle is that Israel's faith will be the means of the world's salvation. He avoided all suspicion of disrespect for the ancient Law of Moses, but asserted that if his reasoning did after all involve the end of that Law (sad thought for a proud Jew !), yet he exalted a far more important principle : Israel's faith will save the world.

Can so much be distilled from the two grammatical principles that anaphora is very important and that *ek* expresses a direct source while *dia* indicates the means ?   Even if St. Paul dictated his letters, the erstwhile rabbinical student would choose his words very carefully.

4. FAITH AND WORKS

" *The faith of Jesus Christ* "

St. Paul affirmed that the righteousness of God was manifested through " the faith of Jesus Christ " to all who believe (Rom. 3[21-25]). It is not easy to determine the significance of that phrase, but everything depends on the force of the Greek genitive, whether it is objective or subjective in relation to the noun on which it depends.   If the English reader is unacquainted with this double function of the genitive case, he will be surprised to learn that the phrase may well mean " faith *in* Jesus Christ "—not Christ's own faith, but the faith which finds its object in him.   For this reason grammarians know it as the objective genitive.   The subjective genitive would give " the faith (or, perhaps, faithfulness) belonging to Jesus Christ."

A most important and difficult problem of interpretation is the correct assessment of the Greek genitive.   In this particular instance the A.V. evades the issue because it is based on the Vulgate's non-committal simple genitive which literally renders the Greek, " the faith *of* Jesus Christ."   This sounds in English like a subjective genitive, his own personal faith.   On the other hand, the N.E.B. came down on the side of the objective genitive, by its rendering, " faith *in* Christ." The issue is vital.   If salvation is wholly dependent on the faithfulness (faith) *of* Christ, regardless of faith *in* Christ, too much weight attaches to God's exclusive part in the drama of redemption.   Redemption cannot be complete until there is some response from man's side, and that response is faith *in* Christ.*

It may be that the Old Testament meaning of *pistis* really is " faithfulness " rather than " faith " ; nevertheless, if we are to take sides at all in this issue, it seems to me more probable that as far as St. Paul's language is concerned the genitive which is governed by *pistis* is objective, and St. Mark also seems to understand it in this way in the similar phrase, " have the faith *of* God " (11[22]) which surely must mean, " have faith *in* God."   Moreover, a similar phrase must be so interpreted in II Thess. 2[13] (" faith *of* the Truth "), as it can scarcely involve a subjective genitive ; God has chosen us for salvation by way of our faith in his Truth.   Such must be the meaning, since immediately before this the writer refers to the damned " who believe not the Truth."

* See the discussion between T. F. Torrance and C. F. D. Moule, in *Expos. Times*, vol. LXVIII, pp. 111, 157.

Against this, the phrase, " the faith of God," in Rom. 3³ gives better sense in its context if it is understood as " God's faithfulness," for it is contrasted with man's lack of it.

The problem of the genitives remains insuperable as long as we elect to decide for the one interpretation against the other. A genitive might equally well in the author's mind be subjective and objective, and we need not sacrifice fullness of interpretation to an over-precise analysis of syntax. The following composite paraphrase indicates the way one might interpret what St. Paul had to say about the role of faith and faithfulness in the drama of man's redemption : " God's act of redemption is seen to be motivated not only by the willingness and faithfulness of Christ by offering himself on behalf of all those who believe in him, but is seen also in the response of men who put their faith in Christ (Rom. 3²¹⁻²⁵). A man is not set right with God by keeping the Law but by his faith in Jesus Christ and by Christ's own faithfulness (Gal. 2¹⁶). I owe my life both to his faithfulness in giving his life for me and to my own complete trust in the Son of God (Gal. 2²⁰). To everyone who believes in Jesus Christ there is a promise made, and made because he was faithful (Gal. 3²²)."

It may look like a grammatical compromise, to resolve a deadlock, but with a mind like St. Paul's, quicker than his own pen or a scribe's, it will not be unreasonable to distil every ounce of richness from the simple genitives of abstract qualities which abound in his epistles. If he had been asked to elucidate, he would have excluded entirely neither the objective nor the subjective sense.

Paul v. James

The supposed discrepancy between the views of two New Testament authors on the way of salvation has often provoked comment. Martin Luther did not like the epistle of St. James, which he felt had little to say to the Christian as compared with the epistles to the Galatians and the Romans. The Pauline epistles leave no doubt that justification is by faith alone ; St. James appears to take the opposite view that one is saved by good works and not solely by faith.

However, it is difficult to appreciate that anyone could read Gal. 5⁶ with a correct understanding of the verb *energoumenē* (middle voice) and subscribe to the view that disagreement, let alone friction, existed between the two apostolic writers. For both of them, justification is by means of a faith which produces good works. St. James undoubtedly insisted that he could test a man's faith by his works. St. Paul preferred not to speak of " works," but he did make use of the word " love " repeatedly, in this connection, and that amounts to what St. James means by " works," for love is an active benevolence towards others

Indeed, St. Paul placed love above faith when he insisted that it would outlive faith and its absence made the strongest faith valueless (I Cor. 13). In the epistle to the Galatians he tempers an urgent appeal not to trust in works with an almost verbal repetition of the practical message of St. James. In the Christian religion nothing matters save one thing : " faith, which works by showing love." It is " faith, which expresses itself in love " (J. B. Phillips).

This " bridge " (as Bishop Lightfoot called it*) " over the gulf which seems to separate the language of St. Paul and St. James " is rein-forced when the full force of a grammatical point is appreciated. The participle *energoumenē*, although passive in shape, must not be taken in a passive sense. St. Paul never used this verb elsewhere in the passive and if he used it so in this place his meaning would have to be, " faith, which is provoked in other people by our loving them." Although Tertullian read it in that way, and the N.E.B. (like the R.V.) puts this interpretation in the margin, it cannot be the meaning. I prefer to take the form of the verb as that of the middle voice, which in this particular tense has the same form in Greek as the passive. In the New Testament there is a number of verbs which, in spite of having a middle form, are active in meaning in an intransitive sense : e.g. " to be in doubt," " to be inferior." All of them have, in the New Testament, an active as well as a middle form ; there was much con-fusion at this period between the active and middle voices, and the middle, being a luxury, was dispensed with in time. Indeed, the New Testament authors were rapidly losing their grip on nice grammatical distinctions in voice.

The grammatical argument is clinched when we look deeper into St. Paul's theology and find the same word *enērgeito* used in a corres-ponding way concerning what happens before conversion. Then " sin-ful passions *operated* in us, provoking deadly fruit " (Rom. 7[5]). That thought should be linked with Gal. 5[6] : " faith now *operates*, showing love."

It is the very gospel insisted upon by St. James.

5. RESURRECTION

Sometimes a writer asserts that the difference between the aorist and perfect tenses has broken down in the New Testament period of Greek. This is far too extreme, since the biblical authors are often punctilious in maintaining it, and they would seem to be deliberately giving solace to their readers by this means. So St. Paul appears to shout aloud the truths of the Gospel.

An impressive instance lies in the discussion of the resurrection in

* J. B. Lightfoot, *Epistle to the Galatians*, Macmillan, 10th. ed., 1890, p. 205.

I Cor. 15. " Christ *died* for our sins " is too final and funereal a translation. The N.E.B. has missed an opportunity to proclaim the apostle's
message with all the vigour which the Greek aorist affords. It is,
" Christ *did* die (once in the past) for our sins." " He *did* suffer burial."
These are aorists, momentary, non-committal. Then comes that
significant perfect. " Now he *is* risen from the dead, ever since the
third day." Sensitive overtones deserve sensitive translation, a higher
fidelity treatment than they receive in our English versions. Dull
renderings dehumanize the apostle, blurring the sharp edge of his
nicely poised dialectic.

St. Paul is seldom careless with his tenses, and it would be particularly difficult to deny this when he is treating of the death and
resurrection of Christ which to him were events of great moment,
leading to conditions for the believer which are equally important.
The resurrection as a historical event is described in the aorist in I
Cor. 15[15]. " He brought Christ back to life." The hope that believers
will be brought back to life (futurative present tense) depends entirely
on the historicity of Christ's resurrection, i.e. on whether it *did* take
place (aorist tense, again). But St. Paul's next sentence introduced a
new tense and with it a new and deeper theme. Whether the effects
of that one historical act *continue* to be effective (perfect tense, now)
is proved only if the dead shall be raised. So St. Paul expressed it all
like this : " God once carried out the act of raising Christ from the
dead ; if you insist that the dead will not be raised, then I say that
God did not do this act of raising Christ. But I go further and say
that Christ is still alive ; he must be alive, because the dead are going
to be raised. If Christ is not alive still, your faith is vain and you are
still in your sins. Moreover, those who fell asleep in Christ (aorist,
because this is not a continuing state) have perished, if that is so
(" perished " is aorist ; i.e. for a moment they perished). All through
our present life we have constantly been trusting in Christ. That by
itself is valueless. If Christ is not alive now (perfect), no amount of
constant trust will help us. But he *was* raised from the dead and *is*
alive. He is the first fruits of those who have been sleeping." (I Cor.
15[15-20])

Moreover, in our passage it is not only the careful selection of tenses
which is important. The position of the adverb *monon* (" only ") in
verse 19 is accurately selected. St. Paul did not mean, " If in this life
only. . . ." In Greek word-order an adverb tends to follow very closely
upon the verb or adjective or other adverb which it is intended to
qualify. In this sentence the adverb *monon* occurs, not after the words
" in this life," but after the verb, indeed after the whole sentence.
There is no contrast intended between having faith while we are in
this world and having it in some other. The contrast is rather between

having faith *only* and having faith supported by the reality of Christ's present risen life. Such are the careful grammatical *minutiae* which ought to be faithfully reproduced in a translation. Incidentally the same use of a subtle chiaroscuro of language is seen, not only here in the sphere of syntax, but also in the vocabulary which St. Paul employed when discussing the resurrection, for he distinguished between the " dead " and the " sleepers." Where Christ was concerned he spoke openly and boldly of " death," but where we are concerned he spoke of " sleep "—as if he were sparing our feelings. When the mention of the resurrection has supervened, to give reassurance, as it were, he spoke plainly of the " dead." But when the context refers only to hope (e.g. the first-fruits), he spoke more gently of " those who sleep."

The point was noted as long ago as the ninth century by Photius, bishop of Constantinople.

6. THE END OF THE WORLD (I Cor. 10[11])

In the A.V. St. Paul is reported as saying that the Old Testament is a kind of parable " written for our admonition." The important thing is the reason why special attention should be paid to this parable. Upon us " the ends of the world are come."

Much discussion has centred upon the phrase, " the ends of the world." Can it mean the final Catastrophe ? It is thought not, because in the Greek original " worlds " is a plural word (*aiōnes*). The suggestion has arisen that an " end " might be a " frontier," and this, allied to the fact that *aiōnes* may sometimes mean " ages " or " dispensations," gives the meaning, " the frontiers of the ages," " the no-man's land between one age and the next." Then St. Paul may well be reminding his readers that they in their lifetime stand at the boundary between old and new dispensations, at the place where Old Testament meets New Testament, where Law ends and the Age of the Gospel begins. If the suggestion is a little eccentric, at least it does justice to the two plurals, " ends " and *aiōnes*.

However, this is an occasion for recalling that in both the Greek and Semitic languages circumstances exist in which a plural noun is used where in English there is a singular. " Heavens " is one important instance and " worlds " (*aiōnes*) is another. Except in poetic speech we do not have this idiom and in normal English St. Paul should be represented as saying, " They are written for our admonition, upon whom the End of the *World* is come." St. Paul shared a vivid expectation of the Parousia with all his early converts.

Languages have their own peculiar idiosyncrasies in the use of singular and plural, and even to-day among representatives of the Indo-

Germanic group the idiomatic plural in one language will be translated by a singular in another. It is a point which the makers of English versions have largely overlooked. In this instance, the translators of 1611 (" world ") saw the point which those of 1961 missed (" ages ") ; recent grammatical study has shown that in a number of such instances of the Greek plural there is no true plural idea present in the Greek.*

The word which is often translated " ages " affords a notable example. It is indeed a true plural when it refers to the seven Ages of time, but in other circumstances the Greek word is plural only because the writers were influenced by a Hebrew word which stands idiomatically in the plural and thereby receives an intensification of meaning in a characteristically Hebrew fashion.† In biblical Hebrew, the word in its plural form meant " everlastingness," " eternity." But post-biblical Hebrew developed a new meaning, viz., " world " ;‡ and there is no doubt that in some books of the Bible it had already acquired this meaning. It is true that the word was usually singular, but the Greek translators of the Old Testament had become accustomed to the the Greek plural, aiōnes, which they had used in translating the biblical Hebrew plural, and apparently they set a precedent by retaining it to translate the Hebrew for " world." So it was that a new plural word, having a meaning as if it were singular, became current in biblical Greek. There is a passage in the thirteenth chapter of Tobit where a Greek translator actually wavered between singular and plural and also between the two meanings of the word :—" eternity " (verse 1) and " world " (verses 6 and 10 : according to manuscripts Sinaiticus and Vaticanus). The contents of Tobit's prayer make it clear that the context of the word in verses 6 and 10 is that of praising God among other nations ; he is God of the *world*, in fact, and not of *eternity*.

It all provides ample enough precedent for the New Testament passages and in particular for this reference to the Parousia by St. Paul. It need not be supposed that the apostle was reminding his readers that they were nicely poised at the frontiers of the two separate dispensations in the history of the world. His view of history was not quite like that, at least not at this point in his ministry. It was dominated by the expectation of the imminent return of Christ and the end of the universe as we know it, of human life as we live it. There could be no better description of such a cataclysm than to call it the End of the World.

---

* For precedent in classical Greek, see especially J. Wackernagel, *Vorlesungen über Syntax*, Basel, 1926, vol. I, pp. 97 ff.

   † See F. Brown, G. R. Driver, C. A. Briggs, *op. cit.*, under עוֹלָם 2. 1.

   ‡ M. Jastrow, *Talmud Dictionary*, London and New York, 1903, vol. II, p. 1052.

7. The Solidarity of the Human Race

The title will at once call to mind the epistle to the Romans. The argument of St. Paul is complex at times and interpreters of this epistle have followed quite different lines of explanation, but his concept of salvation is so fundamentally opposed to the individualism that has long been traditional in the West, that unless the reader penetrates the philosophical barrier dividing him from St. Paul he will long continue in the dark. Pauline soteriology is based on a view of humankind which is wholly corporate. Everything depends on the concept of membership.

It is shocking to the western mind that divine grace and salvation should be pressed to the extreme where the apostle seems to say, " By virtue of our membership in the human race we inevitably sin." Is it legitimate to push him so far ?

Behind the theological question is a grammatical problem. According to many critics, including Sanday and Headlam,* the Greek words *eph' hō* in Rom. 5[12] mean no more than " because," as indeed they do in II Cor. 5[4]. There are grammarians who entertain serious doubts about this,† and prefer to take the Greek words in their literal meaning, " in whom." The point affects the theological question whether St. Paul teaches that death came to all men " because " all sinned (fair enough to the western mind), or whether St. Paul is putting forward an uncompromising conception of the solidarity of the human race— so extreme that it involves mankind mechanistically in the sin of its first parent, or, to demythologize, involves mankind in sinning just because it is mankind. All is bound up with one's opinion concerning *eph' hō*, or should we not rather say that opinion concerning *eph' hō* is coloured by one's reading of St. Paul's theology in general ? Those grammarians who insist on taking the words literally (" in whom ") will translate the whole context : " As by one man sin came into the world, and death by sin, so death passed upon all men through him *in whom* all men sinned." I am bound to say that this seems more consistent with the apostle's main argument when one reads the epistle to the Romans as a whole. The descendants of Adam, once irrevocably united to him in sin and death, now belong to the New Adam. That is the way their salvation in all its completeness is accomplished. It is not by virtue of their " works," but because they are " in Christ."

Romans (International Critical Commentary), 5th. ed., T. & T. Clark, 1902, p. 349.
† Reference should be made to an article by S. Lyonnet in *Biblica*, vol. XXXVI, 1955, pp. 436–456, who takes a different view from Sanday and Headlam, and usefully reviews the exegesis of the Greek fathers.

Not in this epistle only, but everywhere it is a theological presupposition on which St. Paul leans heavily. " As *in* Adam all die, so *in* Christ shall all be made alive " (I Cor. 15^{22}). The Greek fathers found the doctrine of the re-creating Christ so real that there was no difficulty in the phrase in Rom. 5^{12} and they did not particularly dwell upon it in commentaries. Nevertheless it is true that St. Cyril of Alexandria substituted *kath' hō* for *eph' hō* and appeared to lay the emphasis on the particular acts of sin of each man rather than on the racial solidarity which would be involved in the phrase " in whom," He urged that we are imitators of Adam " inasmuch as " we have all sinned like him (*P.G.* LXXIV, 784 C). St. Theodoret was even more explicit : " Not by the fault of his ancestor, but by his own fault each man receives the sentence of death " (*P.G.* LXXXII, 100 B). So much is pointed out by Sister Cornelia Rozemond in her interesting christological study,* but she does admit that by the time of St. John of Damascus the other interpretation gains currency among the Greek fathers. These interpreted *eph' hō* as if it were *di' hou*, meaning " through whom." Such is St. John's interpretation (*P.G.* XCV, 477 A) and that of Oecumenius (*P.G.* CXVIII, 416 D), and it is all one with their implicit belief in the solidarity of the human race through Adam in sin and in death, with the compensating corollary of the solidarity of the race in salvation and blessing through Christ who unites man and God in his own person. In this way, they believed, the incarnation displays God's " philanthropy "—his lovingkindness to mankind. In the same way, according to Irenaeus, Basil, Gregory of Nyssa, and Cyril of Alexandria, the grace of baptism (that is, the putting on of the new Adam) restores us to that state of integrity which the first Adam originally enjoyed.

All this is characteristic of, but not peculiar to, the fathers of the Greek Church. The same deeply spiritual interpretation of Pauline soteriology passed into English evangelicalism and the genius of Isaac Watts has made poetry of the figure of the two Adams.

> " Where he displays his healing power
> Death and the curse are known no more ;
> *In* him the tribes of Adam boast
> More blessings than their father lost."

Such an interpretation is consistent with St. Paul's general conception of sin and atonement. There remains the question of the grammatical justification for this interpretation in Rom. 5^{12}. What does *eph' hō* really mean ? The difficulty lies in the very wide use of the

* *La Christologie de Saint Jean Damascène* (Studia Patristica et Byzantina, 1959), p. 9.

preposition (*epi*, appearing in elided form here as *eph'*). Sometimes it has the local meaning (" in "), as appears in Eph. 1¹⁰ (" in heaven "), but I would offer a suggestion based on the fact that even in classical Greek, and much more so in the New Testament period, the distinctions between the cases with this preposition are difficult to maintain. The variability is evident in St. Paul's very interesting use of this preposition with the genitive when he writes to St. Timothy and states that Jesus Christ witnessed a good confession *epi* Pontius Pilate.* He means " under the power of " or " within the jurisdiction of " Pontius Pilate, and one readily sees the conformance of this to what St. Paul has to say concerning the fate of man in Rom. 5¹². Man is " under the power of " and " within the jurisdiction of " his prime forefather. Man is said to inherit death because he belongs to Adam's jurisdiction, where the rule is death. If it is objected that such a meaning of *epi* with the dative, as opposed to the genitive, would be unique, one can at least refer to *epi* with the dative in St. John Chrysostom, when he says, " I leave this to (in the power of) your judgment."† Moreover, there is further support in the aorist tense of the verb in " all men sinned "—not the tense of continuous or habitual action, but that which tends to emphasize the action itself. Now, if the meaning should be that death has come to all *because* all sinned, the imperfect tense would be expected. The aorist then refers to a single past action, i.e. the sin of the whole of mankind, realized in anticipation when Adam sinned. The reference is not to the multiplicity of sins which men commit continually and which are peculiar to each man, but to that once-and-for-all sin of which men are guilty simply by virtue of being sons of Adam.

This way of taking *eph' hō* is that of Origen, of the Vulgate (*in quo*), of St. Augustine, and of Beza. It is uncertain how St. Chrysostom understood the phrase, but there is no doubt that he wrote, " When Adam fell, even those who did not eat of the tree all became mortal because of him." But St. Theophylact leaves no doubt that *eph' hō* is not a conjunction meaning " because," but the *hō* is a relative pronoun referring the reader back to Adam, the " one man " by whom sin entered the world.

8. The Mystical En

Much has been written about the theology of prepositions, which will be regarded as suspect in these days. Nevertheless, the student of biblical Greek grammar must acknowledge a peculiar usage of the

---

* I Tim. 6¹³.
† *Homilies on Images*, 357, 46. See M. Soffray, *Recherches sur la Syntaxe de St. Jean Chrysostome*, Paris, 1939, p. 74.

preposition *en* which is theologically important. It is neither the instrumental *en* (" by " or " with "), which increased its vogue in the post-classical language, nor is it simply the local meaning of " in." It is mystical, if that would be understood not as metaphorical or spiritual, but as secret and invisible. To be " in Christ " is not to be taken in a local sense, which is crude and meaningless, but neither is it a metaphor. It is what certain theologians have termed " Christification," a sharing of the *physis* or nature of Christ—an adumbration of what in later theology was known as the *theosis* or deification of human nature, having as its ultimate goal the consummation which is described by St. Irenaeus as *anakephalaiōsis*, the " recapitulation " of all men in Christ, adopting the verb used in Eph. 1[10].

This is the full flower of which the seed alone may have been in the mind of St. Paul and of the author of the phrase, " partakers of the divine nature " (II Pet. 1[4]). However, it is probably not fortuitous that certain features of St. Paul's style point in this direction. Designedly, he chose substantives rather than verbs or adjectives to describe Christ's relationship with those who are *en Christo*, and delicately turned away from activity to existence, his idiom subconsciously following his theology. What was once activity and growth and movement has now become identification. Verb and adjective cease to be appropriate, supplanted by the substantive idiom. Christ no longer *gives* life. He *is* Life (Col. 3[4]). He *does* not sanctify or redeem. He *is* sanctification and redemption. Neither is he sanctifying, living, or redeeming ; these attributive qualities are rejected in favour of equivalent substantives. He does not make us wise, but *is* to us wisdom. The unusual and unidiomatic parade of substantives is consistent with St. Paul's doctrine of the union and indwelling of the believer. Identification renders activity and attribution redundant, for they would represent a relationship between separate entities. Christ and the believer, like Christ and the Father, are one—a substantive whole. Predication alone is feasible and a new idiom is demanded where " Christification " has taken place—the predication of an abstract noun to a personal name.

It is not only Pauline Christianity that used the idiom. St. John refrained from saying that God is *loving*, preferring the mysterious declaration that " God *is* love."

The mystical union with Christ, described as *en Christo*, is also explained in complementary terms as Christ or the Spirit existing *in* the believer. It is a reciprocal indwelling. " You are not in the flesh but *in* the Spirit, if the Spirit of God dwells *in* you " (Rom. 8[9]). The idea of mutual indwelling is real enough to those who actually live inside this new sphere of spiritual existence. It was real enough to St. Paul and many of his readers. Indeed, it is difficult to find any other way of explaining the *en* which occurs in the first Epistle of St. John. Men walk *in* either of two spheres : in darkness, lies and hate, on the one hand, or in light, truth and love on the other. God's Word is *in* us, his love is perfected *in* us, and we in our turn abide *in* God, as well as he *in* us. Pauline theologians, as notable as Père L. Cerfaux,* have argued that St. Paul intended nothing mystical by the *en*-formula, and that the preposition expresses no more than simply a faith-connection with Christ, for all that we share *in* is no more or less than the life of Christ through faith. There is no mutual indwelling, and anything spatial about the term, " in Christ," is dismissed as a vague and pantheistic mysticism in which Christ is reduced from a person into the status of a spirit or " mana." Père Cerfaux for instance argued that the phrase, " to put on Christ," is only a metaphor, not to be understood realistically ; it is the equivalent of the phrase, " to be like Christ." Theology apart, I would feel uneasy about such an interpretation of the grammar. It does scant justice to the rich pre-cision of Pauline syntax, and, from a theological standpoint, one fears that this is not the first time in Christian history that mysticism has been too easily equated with pantheism.

The debate whether St. Paul's experiences are those of the mystic is a fruitless excursion into terminology. Denials that they amount to mysticism have to be qualified in the next breath in a way that makes the previous denial simply academic. According to Dr. Martin Dibelius, for instance, " We can feel the passionate ardour of the won-derful new life when he testifies, ' If anyone is in Christ, he is a new creation '."† The fact that St. Paul can say of every true believer (for instance, Andronicus and Junias) that he is " in Christ," does nothing to diminish the mysticism, for it is not the esoteric kind. It is Christian, and the distinction between so-called mystics and ordinary Christians is unreal. In that sense St. Paul is never " on the path of mysticism," but the experience of being " in Christ " must not be under-rated simply because he does not use the " pagan " word *apotheosis*. He repeats essentially what the " pagan " word means and accepts it for Christ. Neither does he use the word *Logos* of Christ, and yet St. John has no scruples. The name matters not, but man is being transformed into God's image. When St. Paul claims no longer to " live " independently, but that Christ lives in him (Gal. 2²⁰), this is strangely like what the accredited mystic asserts when he becomes God and God is identified with him.

Attempts to explain this *en* as having merely an instrumental meaning (" by " or " with ") should be resisted, for the predominant

---

* See the chapter with this title in his *La Théologie de l'Église suivant S. Paul*, Paris, 1947.

    † *Paul*, English tr., Longmans, 1953, p. 107.

meaning is still " in," " within," " in the sphere of," at this period.   In
a paper on the preposition *en*,* I set out its basic spatial meaning and
proffered a warning against too flexible an interpretation of the
passages. Sometimes, where at first sight it seems not possible that
en can mean " in," a closer look and deeper insight into the primitive
Christian viewpoint brings awareness that this is more than the excep-
tional instrumental *en*.   An example would be John 13[35]. The best
known translation, " if ye have love one to another," assumes that *en*
means " to," not " in."   But there is no reason at all why the Greek,
which is *en allēlois*, should not be construed, " if you have love *among*
one another," for the sphere " in " which the love is exercised is
Christ's redeemed community.   The tendency to give to *en* so little
of its primary force, without reckoning with the mystical sense of
" within," is unfortunate.   By way of baptism, a Christian comes into
the new atmosphere which is the Body of Christ and ceases to be " in "
darkness or " in " the flesh.   That being so, St. Paul described himself
in Eph. 4[1] as " the prisoner *in* the Lord," and not " the prisoner *of*
the Lord " (A.V.).   He lived in Christ, in hope, in consecration, in
peace.   They are spheres or atmospheres, air, which the Christian
breathes.   No one, having examined I Thess. 4[7], would charge St.
Paul with anything short of precision in his use of prepositions where
the finer points of theology are at stake.   In the same sentence he
distinguished *epi* from *en*, but, bluntly insensitive, as often, King
James' bishops failed to make the same sort of distinction in English.
It is easy to make it : " God has not called us *to* uncleanness, but his
call is addressed to us *in our state of* sanctification."   The call to believe,
too, comes to us in this same sphere of Christian sanctification and
redemption.   Adolf Deissmann, grammarian and theologian, made it
clear a long time age in his *Die N.T. Formel " in Christo Jesu "* (1892) ;
he showed that the verb, " to believe," when followed by the preposition *en*, means neither to believe in a person nor to believe a person ;
where that is demanded by the context the verb is always followed
either by different prepositions (i.e. *eis* or *epi*) or by a simple dative.
When the verb is followed by *en*, a new situation is in mind, and I
suggest that it is the mystical conception of Christification once again.
We do not therefore " believe in the gospel " (Mark 1[15]), nor does
" everyone who believes in him " have eternal life (John 3[15]).   What
we ought to read sounds revolutionary : " In this gospel dispensation,
you must repent and believe " ; and " every believer whose life is hid
in Christ possesses eternal life."
    These highly mystical phrases, " in Christ," and " in the Lord,"
occur as many as forty-two times in two epistles of St. Paul.   But, in

* *Bible Translator*, X, no. 3, 1959, pp. 113–120 ; against Mr. W. R. Hutton. See
also Moulton-Howard-Turner, *Grammar*, vol. III, pp. 260–265.

addition, it was felt that Christian experience demanded several others of the same kind, such as : " in the Truth," " in the Spirit," " in the Name."

Interchangeable with the "in"-formula in this mystical sense is a characteristically Pauline genitive construction. He spoke of " all the churches *of* Christ "· (Rom. 16¹⁶) in the same manner as elsewhere he refers to " the churches *in* Christ Jesus " (I Thess. 2¹⁴, Gal. 1²²). It is doubtful whether any difference was intended by such an obvious parallel but the construction in St. Paul's epistles deserves a careful interpretation.* The syntax volume of Moulton's *Grammar* gives further examples of the " mystical " genitive : II Thess. 3⁵ " steadfast loyalty *in the Body* of Christ " (not " the patience *of* Christ "), Rom. 3²²⁻²⁶ " faith *exercised within the Body* of Christ." The controversial phrase, " the faith of Jesus Christ," is an instance where careful interpretation of the genitive proves to be rewarding ; we have already found that it was difficult to comprehend it within the limits of either the subjective or objective genitive exclusively, and suggested that it shared in the qualities of both.† This may be the occasion to raise the question whether it may not also be an instance of St. Paul's " mystical " genitive. That is to say, it is not merely subjective, objective, nor even both. It may be one of those characteristically Pauline genitives.

9. PRŌTOTOKOS

" *Archetype of all creation* " (*Col.* 1¹⁵)

It is not my present purpose to quarrel with whatever the mechanical computers may declare about the authorship of the epistle to the Colossians, but I refer to " St. Paul " for convenience sake.

The epistle was canonical from the earliest period of which there is any record and its contents are equally important at the moment when atheism often goes thinly disguised. St. Paul's theme is knowledge of God. He contrasts the Power of darkness with the Kingdom of God's beloved Son ; deliverance from the first is achieved by " his blood." God's Son is " the image of the invisible God, the first born of every creature." " He is before all things."

The enemy, in St. Paul's opinion, was a humanist philosophy which had become fashionable at Colosse, all the more disquieting because it posed as the genuine Christian gospel. It was based on physical science and was materialistic, like the philosophy of our own age of

---

* " Indeed, so rich is Paul's compression of language with genitives that the attempt to define too narrowly the various types of genitives is vain ; they all denote a relationship which is amplified by the context." Moulton-Howard-Turner, *Grammar*, vol. III, p. 212.   † See above, pp. 86, 91.

Enlightenment, and like it too, it had its superstitious side : fixed holidays scrupulously observed, moral expediency, astrological curiosity, and the black arts.

Against it all St. Paul promoted Christ as sole deliverer from dark powers, for he is " the firstborn of every creature " (1^{15}), a phrase which is capable of two meanings in Greek. One of them is endorsed in the text of the N.E.B. : " His is the primacy over all created things." The alternative meaning is in the margin : " He was born before all created things." All turns on whether the reader understands the genitive ("all created things ") as objective (therefore " *over* all created things "), or as a genitive of comparison, understanding the adjective " firstborn " as an adjective of the comparative degree, perfectly permissible in this kind of Greek (therefore " he is born *before* all created things "). Doubtless the two titles are equally appropriate for Christ : he is both " first in rank *over* all created things " and also " born *before* all created things." The former represents a primacy of status, while the latter is a temporal priority. The *prōtotokos* phrase has divided commentators into two camps. although a few make the attempt to unite both : e.g. " born first, before all the creation " (Moffatt).

Prōtotokos occurs in the Greek Old Testament, II Kingdoms (II Samuel) 19^{43}, where the context requires the interpretation, " I was born before you," but this is not really a parallel. Since *prōtotokos* is not followed by a genitive, it supplies no assistance in deciding which kind of genitive St. Paul was using with *prōtotokos*.

Bishop Lightfoot felt that St. Paul's construction could not be a genitive of comparison, for it would be straining syntax to connect the genitive with only the first part of the compound word *prōtotokos* ; it ought to depend on the whole of the word, whatever it means. And what of the meaning ? Is it primacy in status and sovereignty, or primacy only in time ?

A new tendency among critics* favours the idea of status and sovereignty, and it well accords with an early conception of Christ as reflected in the literature of the New Testament. Christ is the Alpha (Rev. 1^{11} 21^{6}), the Beginning, and the context makes it clear that this is more than temporally understood, as when the seer wrote, " Jesus . . . is . . . the *Prōtotokos* of the dead and the prince of the kings of the earth. . . . To him be glory and dominion " (Rev. 1^{5}). St. Paul wrote of him, " He is the head of the Body, the Church : who is the Beginning, the *Prōtotokos* from the dead ; that in all things he might have the pre-eminence " (Col. 1^{18}). So from every theological point of view,

---

* Specimens of recent views include : A. W. Argyle, *Expos. Times*, LXVI, 2, p. 62 (in favour of temporal primacy) ; H. G. Meecham, *ibid.*, LXVI, 4, p. 124 ; C. Masson, *L'Epître de Saint Paul aux Colossiens*, Paris, 1950, p. 99.

the word is clearly concerned with sovereignty, and the phrase should mean "Sovereign over all created things." As St. Theodore of Mopsuestia commented, "This concerns not time alone, but is also a matter of pre-eminence." It is what Dr. T. K. Abbott alleged was impossible (International Critical Commentary, p. 211), and he preferred the view that only priority in time and distinction from creation itself was intended, quoting Theodoret and Chrysostom in favour. "The meaning is not of power and glory," wrote St. Chrysostom, "but only of time." This is commendable. Although the contexts of the word involve the theological conception of sovereignty, one must beware of importing it into the word itself. On the other hand, the construe which Dr. Abbott suggested is not the only alternative, for the genitive may be neither objective nor comparative, both of which, as our discussion reveals, leave much to be desired when taken closely with *prōtotokos*. Might it not rather be the partitive genitive? "Among all created things." I would retain the manifest meaning of *prōtotokos*, "firstborn"—but in the sense that the Messiah was said to be firstborn—and interpret the word as closely identifying Christ with the family of which he is head, i.e. the whole of creation which looks eagerly for redemption. It has a parallel in the epistle to the Romans where St. Paul again described him as a new Adam, closely identified with believers as an Archetype of a fresh stage or leap forward in the collective evolution of all the creatures of God, in the onward march towards the goal of achieving what Christ is himself—the "icon of the invisible God." In I Corinthians the thought re-appears : he is the First-fruit of them that sleep in death.

Suppose then that *prōtotokos* does not express superiority so much as indentification, and it is little wonder if later, when the Church was facing the Arian heresy, her teachers felt that the title had its dangers. This was because the significance of Christ as the universal Archetype was not sufficiently realized. It had been St. Paul's answer to the speculative intellectuals of Colosse. It concerned salvation as well as christology. It was the characteristic way in which St. Paul linked salvation with christology—through him who was identified with humanity as its new Leader and all nature's First-fruit on the one hand, and as the "icon of the invisible God" on the other.

When St. Paul immediately proceeds to say (1^{16}) that all things heavenly and earthly were created "in" Christ, the preposition must be taken literally and not instrumentally.* Christ embraces them all, having become their *prōtotokos*, so that they are his icon in the same sense that he is God's. For he is "in" God, and they are "in" him. There is much in common with the Johannine theology of true pantheism.

* See the discussion, pp. 118–122.

" They have been, and are being, created " (Col. 1¹⁶)

The soteriological significance of *prōtotokos*, discerned in the previous section, is surely the reason for the spectacular change of tense in the next verse (16). At the beginning is the aorist *ektisthē*, and at the end the perfect *ektistai* ; it is a puzzling change, of which no account is taken in any translation in any meaningful way ; for merely to distinguish " were created " from " have been created " is not helpful.

St. Paul was pursuing the intimation of verse 15, that Christ is God's icon and our archetype. The two tenses are thus explained by the fact that the *prōtotokos* conception necessarily involves two other conceptions, viz. (1) a past act which is punctiliar (grammatically) because one aspect of creation is past for ever, and (2) a second action which is not merely punctiliar but also perfective. Of this second action, the results are with us still, since we and all creation are not yet in actuality the icon of Christ, as he is of God. Although the process has been soundly set in motion, it will proceed while all nature continually renews itself in him until it reaches his entire perfection. Aptly using the perfect tense, St. Paul could close the verse with the words, " All these things were once created by his instrumentality (*dia*, " through " ; not *en*, " in," as at the beginning of the verse) and they continue to be created now towards (*eis*) him." He meant towards his perfect image ; closer to the intended pattern. St. Paul did not often confuse the prepositions *eis* and *en*, and indeed in Col. 1¹⁶ he set both together in a context which requires that their meaning is not at all synonymous : " in (*en*) him were once created all things that are in heaven and upon earth, the visible and the invisible, thrones, lordships, powers, authorities ; all these *have been* created (and now exist) by his continual support (*dia*) and he is their goal (*eis*)."

The view admittedly represents a deviation from the grammars,* but the verbs are very close together and the thought seems too profound to suppose that St. Paul had no reason for the change.

The development of his icon-theology in other epistles deserves close attention. It has an ethical aspect, in that the Christian who is becoming increasingly conformed to the icon of Christ puts on " a new man " which is visible in the increment of good deeds and true holiness ; lying becomes less a habit, anger lasts for a day at the most and stealing becomes a thing that is past (Eph. 4²⁴ ᶠᶠ·). But the practical aspect is based on a deep mysticism which concerns transformation of the human personality. St. Paul promised the Corinthians that if Jew

* Including Moulton-Howard-Turner, *Grammar*, vol. III, p. 70, where it is said that a subtle distinction between *ektisthē* and *ektistai* is doubtful in Col. 1¹⁶, " but the exegete could hardly be blamed for suspecting it."

and Gentile turned to Yahweh with face unveiled, the resulting vision would be glorious ; yet it would be glory of the looking-glass rather than reality, and man has to be transformed from this glory to another which is final, involving the whole race in one united Body of Christ, the Church, the perfect icon of God (II Cor. 3¹⁸). At present Christ alone is that icon, but his glory is at least seen by those who believe, whereas the minds of unbelievers seem to be deliberately blinded by " the god of this world," so that they cannot see anything at all of the light of him who is the icon (II Cor. 4¹⁴). In a terminology which sounds fatalistic, because he was strictly brought up within Judaism, St. Paul said that God had " fore-ordained " that believers should resemble the icon of his Son and eventually receive his glory ; so once more Christ is the *prōtotokos* among brothers (Rom. 8²⁹).

The resurrection was never far from his thoughts whenever St. Paul wrote about the final glory, as is shown by his mention of the heavenly icon in the resurrection-chapter (I Cor. 15). The icon is a garment which has to be worn (15⁴⁹). In Colossians he was to speak of Christ wearing the *earthly* icon as a garment. My next chapter develops this theme.

10. The Glory of Yahweh :
" Glory Through the Looking-glass "

Among the more theological of St. Paul's letters is the second to the Corinthians, written during or just after a period of severe strain. The outward circumstances of the apostle may account for some of the deep insights of the epistle. One of them has provoked more than ordinary questioning. " Now the Lord is that Spirit : and where the Spirit of the Lord is, there is liberty. But we all with open face beholding as in a glass the glory of the Lord, are changed into the same image (Greek *eikōn*, whence " icon ") from glory to glory, even as by the Spirit of the Lord " (3¹⁷ f. A.V.).

On quite other grounds (3¹⁷, it is suggested that St. Paul equated or confused the risen Lord Jesus with the Spirit. Little wonder if this passage provides powerful corroboration. " The Lord is that Spirit," and the end of the passage might well be translated, not as the A.V., but, " even as by the Lord, the Spirit." This is the R.V., following Alford and Wordsworth. Ought it to be conceded then that St. Paul's conception of God was binitarian rather than trinitarian ? Was the risen Lord, who *sent* the Holy Spirit to lead his disciples into truth, none other for him than that same Holy Spirit ? As far as their influence in Christian experience is concerned, St. Paul does appear to envisage a complete identification. The coming of the Spirit is the promised return of Christ himself. It must be granted that in this passage St. Paul avoided discussing essential distinctions within the godhead and would have considered it inappropriate at this time to raise with the Corinthians the deep questions which were vital to the Church later on. He referred to the lifting of a veil, an experience in which Christians turn at one and the same time to the Lord Jesus and to the Spirit and find that, for their needs, the two Persons are one and the same. I doubt whether St. Paul needs so much apology. It has been too readily assumed that for him the Lord Jesus is the Spirit. To quote one commentator—Anderson Scott in the original Peake's *Commentary on the Bible*—" Here, as elsewhere with few exceptions, ' the Lord ' is Christ." Perhaps this is another " exception." There is a point of grammar which a theologian or two has missed, namely, the anaphoric use of the Greek definite article. Normally in St. Paul's way of speaking, *ho Kurios* with the article is Christ while *Kurios* without it is Yahweh, the God of Israel revealed through most of the Old Testament. While that must be conceded, there is nevertheless the complication that in the passage under discussion (II Cor. 3^{17-18}) the use of the definite article is likely to be anaphoric,* taking up an immediately previous reference. Thereby the article becomes virtually demonstrative. The immediately previous reference to *Kurios* will be found in the preceding verse, and it refers of course to Yahweh. It has no article, and the discussion centres on Exodus 34^{34} and on the veil that was taken away when Moses went towards him. " Yahweh is the Spirit," St. Paul proceeds with a boldness which seems unique until we find that he makes a parallel identification of Yahweh and Jesus Christ when he writes to the Philippians (2^{11}). Yahweh is sometimes the pre-existent Lord Jesus, and sometimes the Holy Spirit, in the interpretation of these Old Testament theophanies. It is not surprising that Yahweh should be referred to as *Kurios* throughout our passage, or that St. Paul should be envisaging here a pre-Christian experience. He explains that the Jews would have seen the glory of Yahweh and the veil would have been lifted from their faces if they, like Moses, had turned to Yahweh, seeking him with their whole heart. " When a man turns to Yahweh, the veil is removed " (verse 16). At this point only, St. Paul introduces and compares the Christian experience when he says, " But we," and intuits the new conception of twin glories, Jewish and Christian. " We are changed from glory to glory "—from the Jewish vision of Yahweh's glory to the Christian vision of the glory of the new dispensation. The relation between Judaism and Christianity is very much in St. Paul's mind. " We are all changed," Jew and Gentile alike, and must all turn to Yahweh, with face unveiled. Still that vision is not the final glory, but glory through a looking-glass. Its final form will be when Jew and Gentile in one Church

---

* For discussion of anaphora, see Moulton-Howard-Turner, *Grammar*, Vol. III, pp. 172–174.

become the united image of God himself, because the true Church as well as being the Body of Christ is the icon of God.

This may be the place to put forward, very tentatively, a suggestion for looking at a part of this passage in an entirely new way. It is the suggestion that the sentence translated, " where the Spirit of the Lord is, there is liberty," has been misunderstood for a very long time, even from the earliest centuries of textual transmission. The Greek word for " where " is *hou*, but the aspirate must of necessity be very doubtful because the first manuscripts probably had no breathings or accents. Omitting the rough breathing (i.e. the aspirate) we have the common Greek negative (*ou*). By now perhaps the reader wonders whether there is any good reason for reading *ou*, after centuries in which Christian scholars of both East and West read the word as *hou*. The answer is partly exegetical, partly grammatical. Exegetically, the sentiment that where the Spirit is there is liberty seems out of place in St. Paul's difficult argument. Grammatically, the subordinate clause introduced by " where " would be a local clause. Among local clauses, those introduced by "whence" never in all their fifteen instances in the New Testament occur before the main clause and those introduced by " where " almost always occur after the main clause. There are twenty-one instances, including two in St. Paul's epistles. In view of this we ought to feel some doubt about the alleged local clause in II Cor. 3[17] because it precedes the main clause, and I think we may justifiably look for an alternative interpretation. Now, if *hou* is read as *ou* very good sense results. The genitive *Kuriou* must be separated from the noun *Pneuma* and connected closely with *eleutheria*, which besides meaning " liberty " can also denote " independence." Thus we no longer have the phrase, " the Spirit of the Lord." The whole sentence now reads, " But the Spirit is not independence of Yahweh," and it is to be understood as a rhetorical reiteration of the truth of the previous sentence, " Yahweh is the Spirit."

11. EARTHLY AND HEAVENLY GARMENTS (II Cor. 5)

Endless comment has arisen from the first ten verses of II Cor. 5. From the time of H. A. W. Meyer at least, it has been alleged that there is a contradiction between St. Paul's sentiment in verses 2–4, where he seems to fear a disembodied state between Christ's *parousia* (second coming) and the resurrection, and his sentiment in verses 8–10, where he says it is better to leave the body and to be present with Christ, presumably in that same disembodied state. It is an apparent contradiction, but not very remarkable in a system of reasoning as subtle and versatile as St. Paul's.

The argument of the whole passage is that Christians are not to lose heart because death is at work in their midst, for this was clearly a problem in the Christian community at Corinth. St. Paul reminded them that there is a constant drain on the outward part of our nature while the inner nature is as rapidly gaining strength. Visible things perish, but the invisible part of man does not ; and the distinction corresponds to that between two kinds of dwelling : a tent, which is fragile and impermanent, and a permanent divine edifice which belongs to a heavenly, supernatural order of things. St. Paul conceived that the Christian could never be really happy in his tent. It is made with mere human hands, like the tents which Paul sewed at Corinth. The Christian devoutly longs for an *additional* dress ; that is to say, while he does not want to lose his earthly body he is eager that it should be subsumed in the glorious resurrection body which he will receive from the sky when Christ comes. This body is the *oikētērion* in St. Paul's terminology, and he assumes that the reception of it will end the disembodiment which perhaps to some Christians at Corinth was a matter for dread. They feared to be found " naked." Being burdened, they groaned, because (*eph' hō*) they had no desire to divest themselves of the earthly " tent " ; rather, by escaping death at the *parousia* of Christ, their desire was to put on additional clothing. They wanted the mortal to be swallowed up in the real life. " But," said St. Paul, " God has designed us for this very thing and he gives us the guarantee of the Spirit." The meaning is apparent. " You do not have to be distressed about a temporary disembodiment. What does it matter, if it is only for a while ? " This brought St. Paul back to his original theme, before his digression concerning disembodiment. " Therefore we always take courage and realize that while we are present in the body we are absent from the Lord. We must walk by faith rather than sight, and we take courage, and rejoice rather to be absent from the body and to be present with the Lord." Nevertheless, the bodily life is important ; we must please Christ while we are in it, and we shall answer to him for the way we have lived " in the body " (verse 10).

The passage is alive with interest for the grammarian, as well as for the exegete. There is the question : why did St. Paul, in one and the same breath refer to the building *in* heaven (verse 1) and *from* heaven (verse 2) ? Why is it " heavens " (plural) in the first instance and " heaven " (singular) in the second ? Moreover, why is the building itself referred to as *oikodomē* in verse 1 and as *oikētērion* in verse 2 ?

The easiest thing would be to dismiss the differences as a stylistic aberration, arising out of a writer's love of variety. Nevertheless it seems perverse to confuse his readers in the interests of a literary virtuosity which he claimed to have renounced in his dealings with the Corinthians ; and this is in a passage which has every appearance of being carefully and precisely penned in the interests of pastoral care

and teaching. The critic must be reluctant to make short work of dis-
criminations in syntax and vocabulary, especially when significant
issues are involved.

So let us take the first point : " in the heavens " (verse 1) and
" from heaven " (verse 2). As in the case of " world " or " age,"* the
Greek plural ought to be rendered by the singular in English idiom,
and never by " heavens "—with the obvious exception of those technical instances where the plural in Greek refers to all or some of the
Seven Heavens of Jewish cosmology. This is the plural of majesty
and means " heaven," in the sense of God's abode. The Greek Bible's
use of the plural is due to the plural form of the Hebrew word which,
in the thought of the writer, lies behind it. In the New Testament
the Greek word is usually singular when " sky " is meant, rather than
heaven. But not always. Witness the plural in the sense of " sky "
in Matt. 3[16 f.] (= Mark 1[10 f.]), 24[31], Acts 7[56]. When " heaven " is
intended to convey the dwelling-place of God, the Greek word is plural
with the notable exception of the singular in the fourth gospel and
Revelation—one of many indications of the unity of authorship. St.
Mark carefully distinguishes singular and plural within the limits of a
single verse : " The stars shall fall from the *sky* (singular), and the
powers in *heaven* (plural) shall be shaken " (13[25]). The evangelist was
no scholar, but one always has the impression that he was systematic
with what Greek he did know.

From this digression on the use of the plural we return to St. Paul's
thought in II Cor. 5. When he used the singular of *ouranos* he must
have meant " sky," for he was always careful with the subtleties of
syntax. " For we know," he wrote, " that if our earthly house of
this tent were dissolved, we have a building (*oikodomē*) of God, an
house not made with hands, eternal in *heaven*. For in this tent we
groan, earnestly desiring to put on (as an extra garment) our house
(*oikētērion*) which we will receive from the *sky*." To counter the
strange seeming of this interpretation, we should recollect St. Paul's
view of the second advent of Christ and its chronology relative to the
resurrection of Christians, as expounded in I Thess. 4. Christians who
die before the Lord's coming will be brought to resurrection by Christ
himself and take precedence over those who are still alive. " The
Lord himself will descend from the *sky* (this is the singular again) . . .
and the dead in Christ shall rise first ; then we that are alive, who are
left, will be caught up with them in the *clouds* " (verses 13–18). Not
surprisingly, then, in II Cor. St. Paul could refer to the future " garment " of Christians as being received from the " sky." That garment
is the *oikētērion*, whereas the *oikodomē* is said to be " in heaven "
(verse 1). Now the *oikētērion*, according to Greek usage, would be

* See pp. 114 f.

simply a habitation, a place where one lives,* and aptly describes the resurrection body received in the twinkling of an eye, an outer garment which is placed over the mortality which the Christian had previously worn. On the other hand, an *oikodomē* would be the result of a long period of growth and preparation ; in some contexts it means the act of building. It is used of the elaborate " buildings " of Herod's temple (Matt. 24[1]), and St. Paul used it of the Church and Christians as " God's handiwork " (I Cor. 3[9], Eph. 2[21]). It is heavenly, but not in the sense that it comes down from the sky, like the *oikētērion* ; it belongs to eternal realms and represents the whole process of transformation into the icon of Christ which the Christian undergoes daily, and to which the technical name of Christification is given. The sudden assumption of the *oikētērion* is but one stage in the process of *oikodomē*.

All this answers some of our grammatical queries about the passage, but it leaves the notoriously difficult *eph' hō*, which generated so much discussion concerning the effects of Adam's sin (Rom. 5[12]).† It seems to me that in this passage, but not in Romans, the oldest exegetical tradition which it is possible to trace accepts the meaning " because." The paraphrase submitted above reveals that it makes the best sense. Thus the Christian is anxious *because* he does not want to remain " unclothed " in some intermediate state between death and resurrection, but hopes for the resurrection body. Of course, *eph' hō* often meant " on condition that " in earlier Greek and in some texts of the Common Greek, but it makes no sense in this context unless we gratuitously add to St. Paul's words, e.g. " We are anxious [but we are only justified in being anxious] provided that we do not want to be unclothed." Surely so large an addition is indefensible. What St. Paul actually said was, " We are anxious," not " We are justified in being anxious." It was possibly some local anxiety in Corinth, like that in Thessalonica, which necessitated his digression to deal with their anxiety about becoming disembodied. St. Paul has no anxiety on this score : even in the disembodied state he will at least be " with Christ," and it is all part of that long process, which God has designed, of being changed from glory to glory, of being conformed more and more into the likeness of Christ, a process by no means restricted to this life.

12. OBJECTIVE EVIL

" The darkness which hides " (*I Cor.* 4[5])

A langauge in which, for example, " the known thing " is used for " knowledge " and " the kind thing " for " kindness," may seem rather curiously strained ; but in fairly cultured speech of classical and

* It is used of the proper " dwelling " of angels in Jude[6].   † See pp.116 ff.

Hellenistic Greek it was not unusual to express abstractions by means of an adjective in the neuter gender preceded by the definite article.

In biblical Greek, this substantival expression was nearly always followed by a noun in the genitive. There is the expression, " the known thing of God " (Rom. 1[19]), which is almost certainly one of these abstractions. Even so, it is still capable of a double interpretation : either " God's knowledge " or " the knowledge about God." Origen and St. Chrysostom accepted the latter, knowledge about God or that which may be known of God ; and it serves the context better than the first. But Dr. Rudolf Bultmann* has given us a different lead, by directing attention on the person in the genitive case and transforming the expression into " God in his knowableness " (" Gott in seiner Erkennbarkeit ").† Bultmann applied the method further in Rom. 1[20] where he transformed " the invisible things of him " into " he the invisible." The genitive is therefore objective : God is the object of the knowing and the seeing. However, close examination of the similar phrase in I Cor. 4[5], " the hidden things of darkness," reveals that here the genitive ought to be subjective ; darkness cannot be hidden, but it can hide. What exactly did St. Paul conceive that God would one day bring to light ? Was it the things which darkness hides, or was it not rather the concealing darkness itself ? His reasoning, closely followed, is this. In a world where decisions are reached by biased judgment, and where motives are mixed, it may be impossible to judge fairly because of an ignorance and prejudice which amounts to blindness. It is not simply that man falls short of omniscience or some facts are hidden from him when he makes a decision, but the situation is far worse. There is a positive darkness which poisons and misdirects the mind, to be removed only by the brightness of the Lord's *parousia*, not by the mere acquisition of further knowledge. So St. Paul was suggesting that Christ will dispel " the darkness itself which hides," and that was a more radical remedy than the mere dispelling of " the things which darkness hides." At Corinth he was on trial for his stewardship, and if it were only a matter of revealing facts of which his accusers were ignorant, that could soon be put right. It did not need the *parousia* to bring new facts to light ; yet only the *parousia*, nothing less, could dispel the deep prejudice which is " the darkness which hides " the truth deliberately. This is surely correct, for in the same sentence St. Paul refers to it as " the scheming of hearts."

* So also Moulton-Howard-Turner, *Grammar*, vol. III, p. 14. A reviewer, objecting to the interpretation as unusual and highly improbable, gave no further enlightenment and ignored Bultmann altogether. *Journal of Theological Studies*, N.S., vol. XV, April 1964, p. 120.
† G. Kittel, *Theologisches Wörterbuch zum Neuen Testament*, Stuttgart, vol. I, 1933, p. 719.

St. Paul and evil spirits

The apostle had heard, probably from Epaphras, that false teaching among the Colosse church members was becoming dangerous. It professed to be a system of philosophy, but he saw it as deceitful, uninspired and intellectually gauche. In Christ alone, he wrote to them, lies the perfection of godhead, and for that reason he is superior to all the angels worshipped with Jewish rites by these false teachers. Christ's work is so complete it makes circumcision unnecessary. In Christ the believer is raised by baptism from death to life. He began this argument in verse 8 of chapter 2, and reached a climax in verse 15, saying that Christ has " spoiled " (A.V.) the powers and authorities —that is, the angels worshipped by the heretics—and has made a public example of them, triumphing over them while on the cross. The details of this tremendous climax are worth studying.

The word " spoiled " (A.V.) is difficult. Its correctness depends on taking a verb in the middle voice as if it were active. It means to " undress " in the active, but here it is middle, and that normally means to " undress oneself." The Revisers of 1881, with their sensitivity to exact scholarship, had followed the lead of Dr. Alford with bishops Ellicott and Lighfoot, putting forward a translation which truly represents the middle voice : " having put off from himself the principalities and the powers."

There is the further possibility, envisaged by the margin of the R.V., and originating in the Latin fathers, Hilary, Ambrose, Augustine, that the principalities and powers are understood not as objects of the verb to " divest himself," but are transferred as objects of the verb in the next sentence. However, the Latin fathers then proceeded to a more dubious expedient ; they supplied the words " his body " after the verb " divest himself," reading as follows : " He divested himself of his body and made a public example of the principalities and the powers." That is too much to supply, and one suspects that these fathers used a text like the Latin and Greek text of the ninth-century Codex Boernerianus which actually has the insertion, " his flesh."

Linguistically, there is most to be said for the rendering of the R.V. itself, which is in fact how the Greek fathers* understood St. Paul's words, and they were probably more conversant with his Greek than we. Firstly, although the middle voice of this verb is sometimes found in literature in an active sense† (i.e. not to " divest oneself," but to undress someone), nevertheless it is more natural to

---

* Chrysostom, Severianus, Theodore of Mopsuestia, Theodoret.
† Examples in G. Kittel, *op. cit.*, vol. II, p. 19, and W. Bauer, *Griechisch-Deutsches Wörterbuch*, 5th. ed., 1952, col. 151.

take the verb in its true middle sense. Secondly, immediately after this, in the same epistle, St. Paul used this verb in the middle voice with no doubt about its true middle meaning (to " undress oneself ") ; so in 3⁹ he wrote, " You have divested yourself of the old man." Linguistic acumen and theological insight led the Greek fathers safely through a tangle of interpretation, to the conclusion that St. Paul said that Christ divested himself of the principalities and the powers.

Presumably these are the evil angels which were part of the repertoire of the false Colossian teachers. St. Paul nevertheless did not dismiss them as fairy tales, as airy nothingness. They exist. Evil spirits dwell withing human nature simply because it is fallen and distorted human nature. But Christ put the nature on himself and wore it as a robe, conquering in it the evil powers, for he was tempted in all points, but victoriously, and the moment of final deliverance and victory was at the moment of death upon the cross, divesting himself (middle) of that robe of weak humanity, at his glorification, lifted from the earth, drawing all men to him. Then he divested himself of temporary mortality, and in that moment of nakedness upset the sway which evil beings had previously held over mankind.

It was regrettable when western Christendom, under St. Anselm's and Martin Luther's influence, ceased to think of Christ on the cross as Christus Victor and began to see him instead as Christ the Victim. St. Paul had encouraged the Colossians to think of the cross as a victory over evil powers, without a hint of juridical satisfaction, the placation of an angry Father or a demand that his offended honour be repaired. That was a light in which St. Paul rarely, if at all, viewed the crucifixion, for he referred only indirectly to the sorrows of the Redeemer, not noticing the pain and saying nothing of the nails and crown of thorns. At the cross, he saw salvation, the power of God, the victory over evil spirits.

The great message to the Colossians was echoed by St. Chrysostom, who declared in a powerful sermon, " I call him king, because I see him crucified."*

---

* *P.G.* XLIX, 413.

CHAPTER FIVE

SAINT JOHN

1. St. John Personally

Who is the Other Disciple ? (*John* 1⁴⁰)

Amid the intricasies of the Johannine problem attention has been focussed on one or two cryptic remarks which must be due to the author's modesty. In 1³⁵ St. John the Baptist was standing with " two of his disciples " when he saw Jesus approaching. These two disciples left John to follow Jesus (1³⁷), and in a moment we are told the name of one of them, Andrew, Peter's brother (1⁴⁰). But the other's name is not disclosed. One suspects that he was the evangelist himself, and as he was evidently one of the earliest disciples it might well be St. John the fisherman. Rudolf Bultmann* described the suggestion as " arbitrary," adding that " the wish is father to the thought," and forbearing to discuss what has for long been said on the other side, namely that one of the most important members of the Twelve is never otherwise mentioned in a gospel which is abnormally precise and appears to be based on the recollections of an eye-witness ; the passage under discussion, for example, mentions the time of day. An alternative explanation of such features in the fourth gospel has never been given.

Within this context there is a problem of grammar which enlightens the larger problem of authorship. It concerns Andrew who, in verse 40, is named as one of a pair of disciples, and of whom the evangelist says, " He *first* finds his own brother Simon . . . and he brought him to Jesus." The doubt all centres round the word " first." The manuscripts give a choice of three possibilites : (1) *Prōton*, treated as an adverb and meaning " firstly " ; this is the way the N.E.B. takes it (" the first thing he did was to find his brother Simon "). (2) But *prōton* is also an adjective in the accusative case, and on that supposition one must translate : " the first person he found and brought to Jesus was his brother Simon," thus raising the question whom he brought " second " or subsequently. If this is the correct grammar, one has to move on to verse 43 and, instead of understanding Jesus as

---

* R. Bultmann, *Das Evangelium des Johannes* (H. A. W. Meyer's *Kritisch-exegetischer Kommentar*), Göttingen, 1941, p. 70.

the subject of the sentence, " he finds Philip," one takes Andrew as the subject and realises that Philip is the *second* person whom Andrew brought, Simon being the first. There may be an objection to the syntax of this, because Jesus is the subject of the previous clause and it is unnatural to revert back to Andrew as subject in verse 43. (3) But some important manuscripts and textual authorities provide a variant to *prōton*,* which throws new light on the narrative of St. John and which may be of equally early origin.†

This variant is *prōtos*, a masculine adjective in the nominative case, thus agreeing with the subject of the sentence. " Andrew was the first person to find his own brother and bring him to Jesus." The variant makes it much easier to understand why St. John, as distinct from the synoptists, appears to ignore the call of the brothers James and John, for the evangelist is saying that Andrew was the *first* person to introduce his brother, the implication being that there is another who did the same. The Other Disciple, mentioned in verse 35, was the *second* person to introduce his brother to Jesus. The introduction is not actually described. That would have involved the evangelist himself, whose reticence provides nothing more than hints of his own identity.

It is a novel suggestion, but support is provided by a curious feature in the style of the passage : the use of the adjective *idios* in connection with " brother." Classical Greek makes this emphatic ; even more than " his own brother," *idios* would mean " his own peculiar brother." The course of the years weakened the meaning, so that first it became a reflexive adjective (" his own ") and ultimately no more than a simple possessive pronoun (" his "). The tendency is true only of some parts of the New Testament, and it has tempted critics to assume too much. St. John never used *idios* in this completely vacuated sense, but always with some content of peculiarity. " He came to his *own* people " (1^{11}) ; " a prophet has no honour in his *own* country " (4^{44}) ; " he called God his *own* Father " (5^{18}) ; " if another comes in his *own* name " (5^{43}) ; " he that speaks about himself seeks his *own* glory " (7^{18}) ; " when he tells a lie, he speaks of his *own* " (8^{44}) ; " his *own* sheep " ($10^{3.\ 4.\ 12}$) ; " his *own* people in the world " (13^1), " the world would love its own " (15^{19}) ; " each man shall be scattered to his *own* " (16^{32}) ; " the disciple received her into his *own* home." It is strong evidence that for St. John the emphatic sense of *idios* must

---

* The generally accepted reading is *prōton*. It is in Westcott and Hort's text and rests on the authority of a correction in Codex Sinaiticus, of Codex Bezae, the Koredethi Codex, supported by the Old Latin and Vulgate, and (more recently) by the Bodmer papyrus (p[66]) of very early date, and by a quotation in Origen which is very early textually.

† The original handwriting of Codex Sinaiticus has *prōtos* and so does the important Washington Codex (the Freer gospels).

not be ignored, for it " was always as vital as our English word *own*."*
On the general evidence of Johannine usage one concludes that
Andrew found his own brother. " Andrew set a precedent by bringing
(literally, " was the first to bring ") a brother to Jesus. He brought
his own." The inference is that a son of Zebedee was to follow the
precedent and bring his brother too.

This supports the reading *prōtos*. Some early copyist altered *prōtos*
to *prōton*, and it is easy to see how : the next four words all end with
n, and the immediately next word ends with-*ton*.

Most probably then the Other Disciple is the son of Zebedee, the
fisherman John, the traditional author of this gospel. It is but a
small step from this to turn to the Other Disciple mentioned in 18¹⁵,
and infer that he whose influence brought Peter into the high priest's
court was the son of Zebedee, no other than that mysterious Disciple
whom Jesus loved, who was near to Jesus at the Supper and by the
cross. If the three anonymous figures represent one man, he is the son
of Zebedee. It is fair to suppose that he was also the author of the
gospel in view of the remark in what some look upon as the appendix
to the gospel. " The disciple whom Jesus loved . . . bears witness to
these things and has written these things." Even assuming that the
appendix is by another hand, the editor at least testifies that John the
fisherman wrote at least the main body of the gospel.

The Beloved Disciple

The question of fourth gospel authorship is pursued more closely by
turning attention on the Beloved Disciple.

The previous section provided grammatical reasons for identifying
this anonymous person, referred to at the Supper, with John the
fisherman son of Zebedee. However, many critics, conceding that the
Beloved Disciple may have written the gospel, do not identify him with
the apostolic fisherman.

The Beloved Disciple could be the unknown person who saw the
crucifixion and " bare record, and his record is true ; and he knows
that he speaks the truth " (19³⁵). The science of grammar may be
applied once more. It has been proposed that the first " he " in the
verse (" he knows ") is not the same person as the second, and support

---

* J. H. Moulton, *Grammar*, vol. I, p. 90. " Not even in the Byzantine papyri
have we a single case where ἴδιος is not exactly represented by the English *own* "
(p. 88). He rightly concluded : " One feels therefore quite justified in adopting
the argument of Westcott, Milligan-Moulton, etc., that the emphatic position of
τὸν ἴδιον in John 1⁴¹ was meant as a hint that the unnamed companion of Andrew,
presumably John, fetched *his* brother " (p. 90). Too many commentators still
uncritically follow the incomplete presentation of Blass-Debrunner, *Grammatik
des neutestamentlichen Griechisch*, Göttingen, § 286, 1.

can be got from the Greek, which has *ekeinos* (" that man ") for the first " he." One could suppose that two persons are involved, the author of the gospel and Another. The author is referred to as *ekeinos* (" that man ") ; the Other is said to be an eye-witness of the crucifixion and he may well have been John the apostle himself, the Beloved Disciple. From him may be derived the facts on which the gospel is based ; it is suggested that the apostle did not himself write it, in view of the author's statement here. " The eye-witness is the guarantee of all this, and his witness is reliable : there is another who can vouch for the truth of it."

I do not find this very convincing, even if it is permissible to bring in Aramaic usage as a precedent. An Aramaic origin of the gospel is debatable, and the use of the word *ekeinos* has no significance for authorship. Its force in the Greek that St. John was using was considerably weakened,* so that more often than not it must be understood in what the grammarian calls an anaphoric sense, referring back to a subject already mentioned, and taking it up once again with no strong emphasis (merely " he "). Decidedly it does not introduce a new subject. It is best therefore to understand *ekeinos* as referring neither to a mysterious " author," nor to God, nor to Jesus (which has been suggested). It more naturally refers to the eye-witness previously mentioned who is the author as well. " An eye-witness," he says, " has written this record. A true record it is ; the eye-witness can vouch for its truth."

2. The Logos Philosophy

The Logos is life (John 1³ᵗ·)

There is no doubt that, in the Word (*Logos*) of God, St. John finds the instrument of creation, if not the author of all life. All things were made by the Logos, or through him. Doubt arises in connection with the next words in the Prologue. One way of interpreting them is : " Without him was not anything made that has been made. In him was life." All depends on the punctuation, and the earliest manuscripts seldom give any guidance on this point.† There is a more likely alternative, following a punctuation adopted by the earliest fathers,‡ which would read like this : " Nothing was made without

---

* Instances in Moulton-Howard-Turner, *Grammar*, vol. III, p. 46.

† The above punctuation is found mainly in very late manuscripts, and is that of the Received Text lying behind the A.V. and R.V.

‡ There must have been a very early adjustment of the punctuation, because the oldest versions range themselves on either side. On the whole, however, this punctuation has the earliest support. It has been suggested that the other punctuation was due to the early Church's expedient against heretics who were trying to prove their point.

him. As to that which has been made, he was its life."* This translation is based upon a grammatical usage known as the *nominativus
pendens*, by no means rare in biblical Greek (there is an instance in
John I[12]) whereby a word in the nominative case occurs at the beginning of a sentence but is syntactically isolated from the rest of it.
" Creation—in it he was life."† The N.E.B. (" all that came to be
was alive with his life ") appears to be following this punctuation, and
perhaps this syntax, but it loses the stark grandeur of St. John's own
words.

On the other hand, E. V. Rieu‡ adopts a different construction of
the syntax. "What came to be in him was Life." Unfortunately
this may involve identification of the created world with life itself,
unless what Rieu means is simply, " Life was one of the things which
came into being in him." It is better to assume that the Word of God
is the life-giving principle and therefore life itself.

" Born of bloods " (John I[13])

The English version, " which were born, not of blood," embodies a
mistranslation, since it is unlikely that we have here an instance of the
late Greek use of the plural for the singular, although that is certainly,
as we have seen, a characteristic of St. Matthew and some other New
Testament authors. There is difinite point in the plural of " blood "
in this context, and there is ample precedent both in earlier Greek and
in the contemporary biblical Greek for the plural meaning of " bloods."§
St. John must have in mind the dual life-stream of male and female
which they both contribute to that of their children, and Behm quotes
St. Augustine :‖ " ex sanguinibus homines nascuntur maris et feminae
(men are born from the bloods of male and female)." Perhaps St.
John was alluding to the *spiritual* birth of believers, as opposed to that
which is physically derived from male and female " bloods." On the
other hand, he may mean that believers share mystically in the virgin
birth of Christ himself ; they have one " blood," and not two, for
they are born of a spiritual virgin birth. At a very early stage in
textual transmission, certain copyists or editors were not unaware of
the feasibility of such a mysticism and they permitted what may
originally have been a marginal comment to this effect to creep into

* The margin of R.V. and R.S.V. has a less intelligible alternative, based on the
same punctuation, which seems to identlfy the created world with life. " That
which hath been made was life in him."
† For some reason, C. K. Barrett describes the interpretation as " almost impos-
sibly clumsy ". *The Gospel according to St. John*, S.P.C.K., 1962, p. 131.
‡ *The Four Gospels*, Penguin Books, 1952.
§ Johannes Behm, in G. Kittel, *op. cit.*, vol. I, p. 172.
‖ In Joh. Ev. Tract. II, 14.

the text itself. This is the well-known variant which transfers the whole phrase to Christ and reads : " on his name, *who was born* not of bloods. . . ."

The variant is as old as St. Irenaeus, in the second century, and it belongs to the ancient Latin and Syriac textual tradition lying far behind our oldest Greek manuscripts in venerable antiquity. Possibly it is the correct reading, unless the phrase was actually invented in order to preserve the dogma of Christ's virginal conception.

" I am the beginning " (John 8²⁵)

To the fourth gospel we are specially indebted for the information that a number of Jews began to believe in Jesus as a result of long and sometimes sharp discussions.

St. Clement of Alexandria referred to the gospel as " spiritual " without intending any reflection on the synoptists, but a deepening of spiritual understanding justifies the reader's struggle with perplexing grammar and vocabulary. An instance is afforded by the controversy in the treasury where Jesus had spoken of himself as the light of the world, provoking the bitter recrimination, " Thy record is not true." When Jesus countered this with " the Father that sent me beareth witness of me," the Pharisees flung back, " Where is thy father ? " A garbled version of the virginal conception may have been known to them. Jesus replied, " I am from above : you are of this world." The Jews proceeded to ask, " Who art thou ? " (8²⁵) At once we reach not only the deep things of theology but subtleties of grammar to convey them, for the reply of Jesus is veiled in ambiguity—hence the numerous translations of the next few words. According to the A.V., Jesus said, " I am even the same that I said unto you from the beginning." The R.V. is similar, but in its margin the Revisers placed a quite different alternative, not a statement in answer to the Jews' question, but a counter-question, " How is it that I even speak to you at all ? " The objection to the interpretation in the A.V. and R.V. is that " I said " requires a past tense of the verb, instead of the present tense of the Greek.

It is obvious that there is some great difficulty in the Greek if two meanings can be got from it by the same body of translators. The Revisers followed Westcott in their second translation (the margin), and the bishop was reviving St. Chrysostom, who was archbishop of Constantinople at the close of the fourth century. " What he meant," wrote Chrysostom, " is something like this : You are not worthy even to listen to the words which fall from my lips, let alone to learn who I am." The phrase, " That I should even speak to you ! " was a Greek popular idiom very like the modern colloquialism, " I give up ! "

spoken in exasperation over someone's obtuseness. The Greek father confirms a grammatical canon which should be employed more frequently in New Testament interpretation, viz. that *hoti* has the meaning " why ? " This has proved helpful already.* Moreover, the word " beginning " (accusative case) may have quite another meaning in this context, for often in literature and speech it meant " at all " or " altogether."† St. Chrysostom was as much aware of this as we.

However, there was apparently another very early interpretation of the words, as old as the Greek father himself. It came to light by the recent publication of a copy of St. John's gospel written on papyrus and known by its owner's name, the Bodmer papyrus, an Egyptian text dating from A.D. 200 to 250. Probably it does not represent the true reading, but at least it reflects an interpretation current in Egypt in the third century. It appears to read, " I told you at the beginning what I am saying to you now." But the " Bodmer " scribe could not have meant this, for actually his words, " I told you," are in the form of a marginal correction, probably intended to be substituted for the words, " I am saying to you now," on the ground that in his opinion the present tense was unsuitable and " What I *told* you at the beginning " was required. If this is so, his interpretation is the same as that given by our English A.V. and R.V. ; but it is also an attempt to remove an obvious objection to such an interpretation—the present tense of the verb " speak."

There were then these two interpretations, both grammatically admissible, in the golden age of patristic hermeneutics. (1) St. Chrysostom's was current in Constantinople and doubtless emanated from the Antiochene tradition of Syria, for he came from Antioch. (2) The interpretation of the " Bodmer " scribe represented the Alexandrine school of high christology, coming as he does from Egypt. This is better, for Chrysostom makes the reply of Jesus sound abrupt and needlessly ungenerous, although he was provoked by his detractors' mental blindness, perversity, and determination to spin a verbal web around him. Humanly judged, his reactions are entirely understandable and it is worth observing that the Antiochene theologians notoriously dwelt on the real humanity of Christ while their rivals at Alexandria pushed the divine nature in his person to its limits. This is where textual study and patristic research combine to give a useful example of the opposing christologies of the Church's early days. For this reason I propose a different translation for the Bodmer reading from that which has been accepted.‡ If the scribe represents the Alexandrine school he probably intended *archēn* (" beginning ") to be

---

* See pp. 68, 70.
† See the evidence in Moulton-Howard-Turner, *Grammar*, vol. III, pp. 49 f.
‡ C. K. Barrett, in *Expos. Times*, LXVIII, no. 6, p. 177.

used in its more theological sense ; not as the equivalent of *holōs* (" at all "), in the way St. Chrysostom understood. The scribe's interpretation was, " I am the Beginning (the *Archē*), as I have told you." Incidentally, *archēn* is accusative by attraction into the relative clause. In support of this there is the Old Latin reading, " Initium, quod et loquor uobis (the Beginning, that indeed which I am telling you)," which Bodmer's scribe would doubtless have emended to " locutus sum (I have told you)," had he been working on the Latin text. If we could suppose that this St. John were also the author of the Apocalypse, the interpretation would be consistent with what he writes of Christ : " I am alpha and omega, the Begining and the End " (Rev. 21⁶).

The Alexandrian Christians, even so early as the days of St. Clement, held that the flesh of Jesus was not really like ours, for it was exempt from carnal desires and feelings, even the most innocent, and to their way of thinking he would not have been so angry with the Jewish opponents, that he would say what St. Chrysostom supposed him to have said. Alexandrians laid stress on Jesus as the eternal Word, the light which existed at the beginning, brooding over all history, and this was the ethos in which St. Clement pondered the problem at about A.D. 210—just at the time when the Bodmer scribe was at work.

Interpreters favour the tradition which best accords with their own christological predilections, whether they tend to the Alexandrine or the Antiochene, and it is difficult to adjudicate. Against the Antiochene interpretation (Chrysostom and R.V. margin) it has been urged* that Jesus contradicts himself if in one and the same breath he exclaims, " Why do I even speak to you ! " and continues to speak. But this is a mere exclamation.

Here then are two interpretations, neither of which involves us in the necessity of supposing that the Lord's words are a mistranslation of Aramaic. Both are intelligible from the Greek. Both are early in date. Either may have arisen as a reaction to the other.

3. GOD SO LOVED

God giving his Son confirms his love (John 3¹⁶)

A construction which is very rare in biblical Greek occurs twice in the New Testament. The consecutive clause, using the conjunction *hōste* but having its verb in the indicative mood, was well enough established in classical Greek and occurs occasionally in the Hellenistic papyri. The accepted difference between *hōste* with indicative and *hōste* with infinitive is that the infinitive subordinates the result to the cause, while the indicative makes the result co-ordinate with the main verb and relatively more important.

* C. K. Barrett, *The Gospel according to St. John*, S.P.C.K., 1955, p. 284.

There is no reason why the distinction, which is fundamentally modal and applies equally to classical and Hellenistic Greek, should be considered meaningless in the vernacular of our period, or in the style of St. John and St. Paul.

Anglican readers will recall the Comfortable Words of the communion service : " *So* God loved the world *that* he gave his only-begotten Son." God's love is so great that (here follows the consecutive clause) he gave his Son. In Greek, *hōste* serves for the two words, " so . . . that." Bearing in mind that New Testament writers prefer the infinitive after *hōste* where classical authors have the indicative (e.g. Acts 15³⁹), how does one explain St. John's motive for retaining the indicative at 3¹⁶, unless our Lord himself is directly responsible for the noteworthy syntax ? The latest editions of Blass-Debrunner's *Grammatik*, both German and American,* perpetuate inadvertently Blass's assessment of *hoti* (for *hōste*) in John 3¹⁶ as " doubly attested " (i.e. by Chrysostom and Nonnus), when in fact the authority is extremely weak. It was to no avail that Dr. J. H. Moulton protested against evidence of that kind. Blass's treatment he described as " characteristic of a method of textual criticism which often robs us of any confidence in our documents and any certain basis for our grammar."† Indeed, one would expect Chrysostom and Nonnus to have substituted the consecutive *hoti* for the true reading, because *hoti* does occur with that function in Greek which is somewhat later than the New Testament.‡ That St. John actually wrote *hōste* with the indicative there can be little doubt. The construction makes the result co-ordinate with the cause expressed in the main verb and relatively more important ; the infinitive would have subordinated the effect to the cause. St. John then intended the meaning to be : " Whence comes this act of incarnation ? It originates in the love of God." More emphasis is on the incarnation itself than on the love which caused it. The meaning therefore is not, " How does the love of God reveal itself ? " but, " What caused the incarnation ? "

The distinction is too nice for some commentators,§ but the gospel of St. John is penetrating, and the evidence clear. Moulton and Milligan‖ cited a text as near contemporary with St. John as one could expect : A.D. 37–41. " We sold 32 choes to some strangers, including a quantity of quite thin wine, at the rate of 5 drachmae, thankfully, *so that our sales have become much more favourable*, and we hope that

---

* F. Blass and A. Debrunner, *A Greek Grammar of the New Testament*, translated from the 9th. German edition, by R. W. Funk, Chicago, 1961, § 391. 2.

† *Prolegomena*, 2nd. ed., p. 209.

‡ Ibid., p. 249.

§ E.g., C. K. Barrett, op. cit., p. 180.

‖ *Vocabulary of the Greek New Testament*, Hodder, 1930, p. 704 : P. Oxy. XIV. 1672⁶.

they will become more favourable than this."* Mainly the writer has in mind the satisfactory condition of his sales and future prospects ; the first part is introduced incidentally as the cause of prosperity and the details are not primarily in mind.

Similarly in Gal. 2¹³, the only other New Testament instance of the construction,† St. Paul writes, " The other Jews dissembled likewise with Peter, *so that* even Barnabas was carried away." Of most concern to him was a colleague's failure to resist the Judaizers' deception. Quite subordinate to this is the cause, which is stated by the main verb : " the other Jews dissembled likewise with Peter." St. Paul is thinking almost exclusively of St. Barnabas.

The discussion involves a distinction between the true consecutive *hōste* and that *hōste* which stands without a governing clause simply as a connective conjunction, like the Latin *quare* and *itaque*, and the English " and so," having little causal connection with what has gone before. The simple connective *hōste* with the indicative is not, of course, rare in the New Testament, but it falls outside the range of this discussion.

Longing : coming : believing : satisfied (John 7³⁷ᶠ·)

In John 7³⁸ Jesus says, " He that believeth on me, as the Scripture hath said, out of his belly shall flow rivers of living water " (A.V.). We are informed that he was speaking of the Holy Spirit. However, another way of punctuating the verse would involve the previous verse (" If any man thirst, let him come unto me and drink "), by making a full-stop before " and drink " (which is equivalent to, " and let him drink "), and proceed : " He that believeth in me, let him drink—as the Scripture hath said." Here we make another stop and the next words form a separate sentence : " Out of his belly shall flow rivers of living water." But why make the re-adjustment ? It is a matter of Greek style, for it has been observed that in nearly every instance where there is no ambiguity, a *kathōs* clause (" as . . .") follows its governing verb,‡ and the strong presumption is that such is the position here.

Grammar opens the way to exegesis. Placing together the two re-punctuated sentences, the reader discovers the actual experience of each seeker who turns to Christ. First comes the vague longing, the dissatisfaction with the present world : " If any man thirst." Then the work of the evangelist intervenes, pointing seekers to a Saviour :

---

* Editors' translation. The italics (mine) represent the consecutive clause.

† The variant reading which has the infinitive can be ignored.

‡ G. D. Kilpatrick, in the *Journal of Theological Studies*, N.S., XI, 2, 1960, pp. 340 ff. ; Moulton-Howard-Turner, *Grammar*, vol. III, p. 320.

" Let him come unto me." After the preaching of the gospel, comes belief in Christ : " He that believeth on me." Finally, there should be the spiritual satisfaction of the believer who finds in Christ much more than a Saviour, an unending source of all blessings : " Let him drink."

So all the stages of salvation are enumerated, stages which St. Paul had already carefully described in the first eight chapters of the epistle to the Romans.

4. ST. JOHN'S IMPERATIVAL *HINA*

" *Let God's works be manifest* " (*John* 9³)

The constant expression of purpose in the fourth gospel has occasioned frequent comment. The phrase, " in order that," is a regular feature of the author's style. It may be no more than a Jew's inherited tendency to view all things as providentially ordered and over-ruled, but there is also the possibility of a strictly linguistic explanation.

The conjunction *hina* (" in order that ") had a considerably wider meaning during our period in the evolution of Greek, although the expression of purpose is still its primary function, and there are numerous occasions where St. John appears to have used the conjunction in one of these wider senses : e.g. as the imperatival *hina*, simply expressing a command in the third person, and resolving itself practically into something like a wish, so that there is no underlying fatalism in what Jesus said about the man who was born blind, when he was asked whether the blindness was due to the man's own sin or his parents'. " Neither," Jesus had replied, " but *let* the works of God *be made manifest* in him."

The hypothesis of the imperatival *hina*, therefore, releases the text from the fatalism which had obsessed it, and dissolves the picture which had become familiar through all our English versions, a man destined from birth to suffer for the sole purpose of glorifying God when he was healed.

The new interpretation is well based linguistically. Grammarians are largely agreed that there is an imperatival *hina* in the papyri, in the Septuagint, and in Epictetus ; there is no reason why the literature of the New Testament should be an exception. A good Septuagint example is Num. 11¹⁵, where the English version gives a fair translation of the Hebrew, " Let me not see my wretchedness" (a first-person imperative). The Septuagint uses the *hina* construction in rendering this into Greek. In the same book (21²⁷) Hebrew has a third-person imperative, " Let the city of Sihon be built," and for this too the Septuagint resorts to *hina*. The many Septuagint examples of this kind provide a clue as to how the imperatival *hina* came into vogue in wider circles. The Hebrews were conscious of God's over-ruling providence in the smallest matters and often saw a connection between events which had no coherent relationship of cause and effect. They found it quite natural to employ the syntax of the purpose-clause for non-causal ideas. An example can be found anywhere in the Old Testament. In Deut. 5[14] there is a purpose-clause which nevertheless is nearer, in our way of thinking, to a wish or command than to an expression of real cause and effect. The verse is a statement of the fourth commandment : no work must be done by the householder, his family, his staff, or his guests, and this is said to be *in order that* " thy manservant and thy maidservant may rest as well as thou." All God's commandments are seen as wise provisions for his People with a purpose behind each one. The Greek reader might not have the same mental tendency, and even when the clause had been literally translated into a Greek purpose-clause (with *hina*), he would still fail to think of it as more than a command or wish. There were thousands of Bible-reading Greek-speaking proselytes in Egypt, when the Old Testament began to be translated, and as they became accustomed to their Bible in Greek the *hina*-clause ceased to be merely final and gained the new imperatival connotation, for it was more natural for them to say, " *Let* thy manservant and thy maidservant rest as well as thyself." So it was by use of the Greek Bible that linguistic influences like this spread into wider circles of Greek to the extent that here and there, even in the secular language, the imperatival *hina* is found : for instance, three times in the third century B.C. papyri. Evidently it increased in influence as time went on and became significant in the development of Greek in its more popular form, for in modern Greek we see the end of the process with *na* (shortened form of *hina*) being used with the second and third persons of the subjunctive to express a command ; that is, the imperatival *hina* of biblical Greek was kept alive for centuries and became the imperatival *na* of modern Greek. Here is one indication among many that the tributary stream of Jewish Greek made a permanent contribution to the flow of the language in general from Ptolemaic through Imperial and Byzantine Greek down to the present.

Part of the process is seen in some church writings a little later than the New Testament, where *hina* is without doubt imperatival. In the third-century *Acts of Peter and Paul* 209[14], *hina* introduces the command, " Know, O king."* In the *Acts of Philip* 39[1-3], it follows immediately upon an imperative and introduces the command, " Let

---

* Irrefutable proof that it is an imperatival *hina* lies in the fact that in the corresponding passage in the contemporary or earlier *Martyrdom of Peter and Paul*, the phrase is *gnôthi*, a real imperative (164[9]).

them speak like men " ; so also at 86²¹⁻²³. In the third-century *Acts of Thomas* 253⁶⁻⁸ the imperatival *hina* immediately precedes a normal imperatival clause, " let him send." By this time then the construction was well established and there should be no hesitation in applying the knowledge to certain New Testament passages in which *hina* appears to produce poor sense as a purposive conjunction.

First, the words of Jairus pleading on behalf of his daughter. *Hina* occurs twice and I suspect that both times it is imperatival. The first *hina* introduces, " Come and lay your hands on her." The second *hina* could be a conjunction of purpose, but it is better to take it like the first : " Let her be cured ! " The R.S.V. takes it as imperatival, but the N.E.B. needlessly inserts the words, " I beg you to " (Mark 5²³).

Then there are the words of St. Paul to the Corinthian Christians (II Cor. 8⁷), soliciting their affectionate understanding : " *See that* (*hina*) ye abound in this grace also " (A.V.). The addition of " see that " (A.V. and R.S.V.) implies that something more than simple imperatival force is intended, and the N.E.B. too betrays uneasiness about the purely imperatival force of *hina* : " Surely you should show yourselves equally lavish. . . ."

St. Paul exhorts with this *hina* again in Eph. 5³³ : " A wife must love her husband." Again the R.S.V. transforms the plain imperative by gratuitously adding, " Let the wife see that . . ." (N.E.B. similarly). Such clumsy circumlocution is avoidable, for the evidence of Hellenistic syntax strongly supports the imperatival *hina*.

" Let 'the scripture be fulfilled ! " (*John* 13¹⁸ 15²⁵)

We have now seen that much of the apparent fatalism is taken from the fourth gospel by an understanding of the syntax of *hina*. Applied to Judas Iscariot the modern reader finds it especially welcome, for in the thirteenth chapter Jesus is described as washing his disciples' feet and saying, " I have given you an example. . . . If ye know these things, happy are ye if ye do them. I speak not of you all : I know whom I have chosen," and then follow words introduced by *hina*. If this *hina* is a conjunction of purpose, then the exclusion of Judas from the number of Christ's chosen ones is purposive, by God's design, and the matter reads like this : " In order that the scripture may be fulfilled, he that eateth bread with me hath lifted up his heel against me " (13¹⁸). Yet understand the *hina* in an imperatival way, and the words of Jesus reflect a very different sentiment. It is not that Judas is excluded for a purpose, but that Judas has excluded himself. " However, let the scripture be fulfilled " (*hina*).

If this consideration places the tragedy of Judas in a new light, the same may be said of a later passage concerning the unbelieving Jews who persecuted Jesus and were destined to persecute his disciples. " If I had not come and spoken unto them, they had not had sin. . . . If I had not done among them the works which none other man did, they had not had sin. . . ." At this point *hina* occurs. Its traditional interpretation would involve another piece of fatalism. It means that the testing of the Jews and their resultant sin was planned *so that* the Torah passage (" they hated me without a cause ") might be fulfilled. But neither the testing nor the sin was inevitable. Jesus was simply provoked to a sad sigh of resignation, introduced by imperatival *hina*, " *Let* the Torah be fulfilled."

Later, when Jesus had occasion to remind the Temple officers that they had neglected to arrest him when he taught there daily, the A.V. reports him correctly : " But the scripture must be fulfilled." King James's bishops recognized the imperatival force of *hina*, and the R.S.V. and N.E.B. follow the lead, so that for once all three English versions accept *hina* as imperatival !

5. THE FATHER OF LIES

Controversy with the Jews is a prominent feature of the fourth gospel. Their fundamental faith in Father Abraham was an issue between them and Jesus, provoking his counter-command, " Ye are of your father the devil " (8[44]). His subsequent elucidation presents commentators with a difficult problem, for referring to the devil he says, " When he speaketh a lie, he speaketh of his own : for he is a liar, and the father of it."

The Revisers supported the A.V. in this interpretation, but there had already been a wide variety of translation before 1881. Bengel, Alford, and H. A. W. Meyer suggested : " For he is a liar and the father of him "* (i.e. of the liar). We must record a further suggestion, however improbable it may be on the lips of our Lord or the pen of St. John. " For he is a liar, and so is his father." It refers to the devil and involves the acceptance of a mythological " devil's father." There is a grammatical point in favour of this. According to strict rules, the beginning of the verse, " Ye are of your father the devil," might be rendered, " Ye are of the father of the devil," for " father " has the definite article and should not therefore be considered predicatively (" you are of the devil, who is your father ").

Rather different was the suggestion of W. F. Moulton and Westcott, adopted in the margin of the R.V. " Whenever *a man* speaketh a lie, he speaketh of his own, for his father also is a liar " (end of verse 44). The consideration which may have influenced these dissentients among the Revisers is that " liar " lacks the definite article ; it would suggest

* Reading " him " for " it, " which is possible in Greek.

that the word is predicative to " father " in the same sentence (i.e. " his father also is a liar "). The conclusion is not inevitable, however, since " liar " might be considered predicative to the implied subject of the previous sentence. A further consideration in favour of the R.V.'s margin is that " father " (end of verse 44) has the definite article, and so strictly ought not to be a predicate, which seems to rule out " he is a liar and the father of it (*or* of him)." This was all very well in Bishop Westcott's day, when classical study was the route to the New Testament and its syntax was assessed by rules governing an altogether different kind of Greek. Two leavenings have subsequently occurred in biblical Greek studies : discovery of contemporary papyri in Egypt near the opening of the century was assessed by W. F. Moulton's son (J. H. Moulton) in England and by Adolf Deissmann in Germany, and then the reverse tendency to give to the Semitic element in the vocabulary and syntax of biblical Greek a much larger part.* The tendencies are opposed in important respects, but neither of them represents a return to the nineteenth century and no one would now draw the same conclusion as Westcott from the presence of the definite article in biblical Greek. It has been shown that under certain circumstances the predicate regularly has the definite article in New Testament writings. The hypothesis put forward in 1933 is sometimes known as Colwell's canon because an American, E. C. Colwell, demonstrated how, in sentences where the verb occurs (say John 8[44]), definite predicate nouns usually do have the article if they *precede* the verb (that is why " liar " does not have it), and they regularly do not have the article if they follow the verb.† The information is useful in the verse we are engaged with. St. John has placed the verb " is " (*estin*) between the two predicates, " liar " and " father," the first having the article and the second not. Were W. F. Moulton and Westcott living now they might be among the first to acknowledge the guidance which E. C. Colwell's argument provides for the interpretation of this difficult verse.

One more step is required for complete understanding. " He is a liar and he is its (*or* his) father." Confident as we are of the grammar, the sense is far from clear. What is the force of *autou* ? Neither " his " nor " its " is coherent. Nothing has been directly mentioned answering to " its " ; and " his " could refer only to " a liar's father " (which is nonsense) or " the devil's father " (which is puzzling, the devil being the subject). I suggest that we have the kind of pronominal sense-construction which was normal in secular Greek and

* The first transition is reflected in the first two volumes of Moulton's *Grammar*, while the second revolution tends to be the inspiration behind volume III.

† A convenient discussion and criticism will be found in Moulton-Howard-Turner, *Grammar*, vol. III, pp. 182–184.

which passed naturally into the New Testament; "Galilee" is followed by "them" (Matt. 4^{23}), Samaria and Macedonia likewise (Acts 8^5 16^{10}) ; sometimes "their" refers to an antecedent less positive, as when St. Matthew wrote, "He left that district, to teach and preach in *their* cities," i.e. in someone else's cities (11^1). Sometimes the scribes who copied the New Testament manuscripts were unduly perplexed by the sense-construction and made it more elegant. The region round about Galilee should not be described as "they" (Luke 4^{15}), and so the Cambridge manuscript, Codex Bezae, does not have the word "their" with "synagogues" but refers simply to "*the* synagogues"; so do some of the Old Latin manuscripts, including the excellent Codex Vercellensis (as old as any Greek uncial), and the equally old Codex Veronensis, with some Sahidic Coptic versions. Codex Bezae reflects another scribal adjustment in Acts 20^2, avoiding the use of "them" after "that district."

The sense-construction was used by nearly every New Testament writer, including St. Paul (II Cor. 2^{13}, Gal. 2^2, I Thess. 1^9, etc.), and doubtless there is an instance of it in our present passage. The word "its" therefore refers to an abstract conception like lying or falsehood, suggested by the concrete word "liar" immediately before.

Application of one grammatical principle after another leads with confidence to the interpretation : "He is a liar and the father of lies."

6. The Perfect Christian

" If a Christian sins . . . he cannot be a sinner " (I John 2^1 3^9)

Understanding of Greek tenses is a key to many difficulties in New Testament exegesis, but because the study is involved the results are not yet as fruitful as they might be.

The aorist stem essentially expresses the point of time of an action, or the action itself without reference to time at all. Nevertheless, the simple principle has to be qualified : verbs which by their meaning express a state or condition are employed in the aorist tense to indicate the action which is the point of entrance into that state. The essential nature of the aorist is preserved by the prominence of the *point* of entrance, but the translation of an aorist like this will be different from that of an aorist of a verb which semantically expresses action rather than state. Thus the aorist of the verb "to be a king" (a state or condition) must be "to become a king" (point of entrance) ; of "to trust" it must be "to put one's trust in." So when the aorist is used in II Cor. 8^9 it does not mean that Christ *was* poor, but that he "became poor"; in Luke 15^{32} the aorist does not mean that the prodigal son was dead and "is alive" but that he was dead and "began to live." Christ died and " sprang to life " (Rom. 14⁹, Rev. 2⁸ 13¹⁴ 20⁴), and " burst into tears " when he heard about Lazarus (John 11³⁵). Our salvation is nearer than when we " began to be believers " (Rom. 13¹¹).

Among such important instances, one is worthy of special mention— the way St. John deals with the theme of sinning in I John 2¹ and 3⁹. Without a knowledge of the Greek aorist one might suspect that the apostle is contradicting himself in the two passages, first saying that a Christian who sins has an Advocate with the Father, the propitiation for our sins, and then stating emphatically that the Christian does not sin. " He cannot sin because he is born of God." Now the contradiction is only apparent. In the first passage the verb is *hamartē*, which is aorist, and, in accordance with the grammatical principle concerning the aorist tense of verbs which express a state (e.g. " to be a sinner "), *hamartē* will mean " he began to be a sinner," that is, " committed an act of sin " ; it is only an initial step along a certain road.

In the second passage, St. John used the present tense (*hamartanein*) ; it is a verb of which the present stem means " to be a sinner," that is, it expresses a state rather than an action. The distinction between the tenses brings us straight to the heart of the Johannine theme of Christian perfection. The apostle affirms that a Christian believer can never be a sinner. He will start to be one, will take the first (aoristic) step by committing this or that sin, but he stops short of the condition of being " a sinner." To be " in Christ " is not to be at once perfect, but whenever such a one disgraces himself, his actions never permanently remove him from that mystical union which is unbreakable. Sin will not have dominion over him. Nothing, as St. Paul also said, can separate him from the love of Christ.

Christian gnosis

There is a right and wrong *gnosis* for the believer. True knowledge is when God is found mirrored in Jesus Christ.

Although the author of the Johannine books, which have the most to say on Christian *gnosis*, has been called the apostle of Love, he might as aptly be named the exponent of Enlightenment. He represents Jesus as knowing God perfectly, revealing him, but not to sinful men, even if they are Jews, for the Truth is acquired only by those who believe in Jesus and follow him to the extent of keeping his commandments. Jesus himself is hidden from all but genuine believers, who have God living in them and themselves live in God. They find *gnosis* in Jesus.

Part of St. John's mysticism is belief in that mutual indwelling which however much he may owe to Hellenistic and Jewish mysticism, he developed into something characteristically Christian. We dwell in God and, in him, find true knowledge. What is this *gnosis* ? St. John frequently used a phrase, " Knowledge is this . . .," or " This is what we know. . . ." The object is Love. Knowledge of God is none other than knowledge of his Love. The idea is practical and experimental.

All that can be said of the situation behind St. John's letters is based on surmise, and because he had much to say about *gnosis* and because there was an early Christian heresy called Gnosticism, concerned with the mode of knowing God, it is often assumed that the Johannine epistles and gospel were directed against this particular attempt to poison the main spring of Christian truth. It is possible to weave one improbable web upon another, out of supposed parallels between St. John's words on the one hand and the aphorisms of the Gnostic Cerinthus and the Dead Sea scrolls on the other. Considering the great interest of commentators in the subject, one is surprised to find how superficially the language is examined. Few of them observe that St. John has two quite different verbs for knowledge, *ginōskō* and *oida*, and that when using *ginōskō* he virtually confined himself to the present and perfect tenses. The facts are absorbing and cry aloud for comment and investigation. *Oida* is used of various knowledge : sometimes of human matters (I John 2[11], III John [12]), but occasionally of a higher kind (" you know all things " 2[20]), even of knowing the Truth (or truth ?) (2[21]), and perceiving that God is righteous (2[29]) and that believers will be like Christ at his *parousia* (3[2]), that Christ came to take away sins (3[5]), that love to other Christians proves rebirth into life (3[14]), that no murderer has eternal life (3[15]), that the true Christian cannot be a sinner (5[18]), that the son of God has become incarnate (5[20]). It is used to describe the certainty with which Christians know they have eternal life (5[13]) and are born of God (5[19]), and their assurance that Christ hears their prayer (5[15]) ; it is cognizance of simple Christian dogmas, credal knowledge. But this verb is not used when God himself is the object of the Christian's personal intuitions.

Ginōskō, on the other hand, has a more mystical connotation, being used for God's own knowledge (3[20]), and often it appears in an absolute sense without stated object (I John 2[3.5] 3[24] 4[13] 5[2]). More often one of the persons of the Trinity is its object : 2[4.13.14] 3[1.6] 4[2.6.6.7.8] 5[20]. Sometimes Truth/truth (as with *oida* in 2[21]) is the object of this kind of knowledge : 3[16] 4[16], II John [1] (probably Truth here refers to Jesus, whom St. John " knew " in his early life). Sometimes *ginōskō* has love as its object (3[16]). Sometimes its meaning appears not to differ from *oida*, as when Christians know that they live in the last hour (2[18]), and that righteous living proves a man to be born of God (2[29]). The world does not have this knowledge which Christians have (3[1]). In 3[19], according to the best authorities, there is a striking change of tense, for it is " we *shall* know that we are of the Truth."

Dr. A. E. Brooke* discussed the difference between *oida* and *ginōskō* no further than to assume that *oida* is intuitive knowledge and *ginōskō* the experience of human life. The distinction is not supported by our evidence, and his explanation of *oidamen* in 3² was scarcely satisfactory if he realized that this is not intuitive, but revealed, knowledge. In spite of the difficulty, he still maintained that *ginōskō* involves progress in knowledge. Classical distinctions no longer hold for the New Testament. St. Paul, St. John and the writer to the Hebrews all used *ginōskō* of our knowledge of God and Christ, and the cognate noun *gnōsis* had become a technical term for an intuitive knowledge of spiritual truth, which is never acquired gradually through human experience. *Oida*, on the hand, had come to be used for awareness and perception ; indeed, " know-how " was already a meaning in classical Greek. Although St. Paul did sometimes use it for knowing God, it applied rather to revealed, than to intuitive or direct, knowledge.

With the lexical data in mind, the grammarian should take a second look at some of the constructions in the first epistle of John. The writer had a strong tendency to the epexegetical construction after a demonstrative pronoun ; it usually took the form of a subordinate clause introduced by *hina*, especially if the explanatory matter (the epexegesis) is theory rather than fact. In the following sentence an epexegesis of theory follows the pronoun " this " : " Life eternal is this, that (*hina*) they know . . . God." Yet when the epexegesis is fact, St. John preferred a subordinate clause introduced by *hoti*, in spite of the preference of other New Testament writers for an infinitive clause (e.g. Acts 15²⁸, I Thess. 4³, Eph. 3⁸, James 1²⁷). An instance is I John 3¹⁶. " Knowledge of Love consists of this : that he laid down his life for us." The application of our principle to 2³ and 5² results in a different translation from the normal. " Knowledge consists of this : that we have gained our knowledge of him if we keep his commandments." In 2³ it makes better sense than the traditional form (" in this we know that we know him, if we keep his commandments ") which is tautologous and makes no allowance whatever for the change in tense from the present (" we know " or " our knowledge ") to the perfect (" we have gained our knowledge "). Again in 5² it is more likely that St. John writes, " Knowledge consists of this : that when we love God and keep his commandments, then we should love his children." This is the very reverse of the traditional version which misses the point : " By this we know that we love the children of God when we love God and keep his commandments." It is not difficult to know whether we love

* *The Johannine Epistles*, International Critical Commentary, T. & T. Clark, 1912, p. 68.

God's children, nor does it follow (in St. John's teaching) that one who thinks himself a lover of God is necessarily a lover of the brethren.

The conclusion is that the verb *ginōskō*, whether it is used absolutely or with divine Love as its object, refers to that kind of *gnōsis* which some of his readers imagined themselves to possess to perfection, and also to genuine Christian *gnōsis*. The latter manifests itself in certain ways : not in credal knowledge (which is *oida*) but in self-sacrifice and love of the brethren. In two additional ways, Christian *gnōsis* is manifest : the life of the Christian in Christ and of Christ in the Christian (2^5 3^{24} 4^{13}). This we found to be very prominent in the teaching of St. Paul.

CHAPTER SIX

OTHER WRITERS

I. St. Luke and the Early Church

The resurrection of Jesus (Acts 4²)

The curious phrase, " proclaiming *in* Jesus the resurrection from the dead," may be the coinage of St. Luke, or he may have cited it verbatim as part of the Jewish Council's charge against the apostles.

The preposition " in " (*en*) was described by J. H. Moulton as a maid-of-all-work. Besides the undisputed meaning of " inside," there are the mystical* and instrumental uses. Neither of them is satisfactory in the present context, unless indeed St. Luke was influenced by St. Paul's teaching on the resurrection of Jesus. " As *in* Adam all die, so also *in* Christ shall all be made alive " (I Cor. 15²²). The solidarity of the race, represented respectively under Adam and Christ, has already been discussed.†

The earliest interpretation may be that which finds expression in the fifth-century Codex Bezae ; both the Greek and Latin sides of the manuscript have a different wording from Vaticanus and the rest, to this effect : " proclaiming Jesus in the resurrection of the dead." A little later we discuss what this means.

The R.V. corrects the A.V. (" through Jesus ") into " in Jesus," but whether anything different is intended is debatable. The Revisers were guided by Dean Alford, who commented that the apostles were using the instance of Jesus's resurrection to prove the general resurrection, " alleging him as an example of that which the Sadducees denied : preaching by implication, inasmuch as one resurrection would imply that of all, the resurrection of the dead."‡ It is therefore " in Jesus " ; which however is like the A.V. : preaching the resurrection of the dead " through Jesus." Moreover, it is even conceivable that such an interpretation lies behind the variant reading of Codex Bezae, but if so, one must supply several words like this : " proclaiming Jesus in (the argument about) the resurrection of the dead." The case is briefly put by Rackham. " In the sermon as recorded no mention had been made in fact of our resurrection : but it was contained implicitly *in* that of Jesus."§

---

* See pp. 118ff.   † See pp. 116ff.

‡ Henry Alford, *The Greek Testament*, vol. II, Rivingtons, 1871, p. 41.

§ R. B. Rackham, *The Acts of the Apostles*, Westminster Commentaries, Methuen, 14th. ed., 1951, in loc.

The weakness is that such a plea makes no assessment of the linguistic support for this usage of *en*. An occasional usage is apparently equivalent to a dative of reference : " concerning " or " with reference to."* St. Paul speaks of " what the Scripture says *in* Elijah " (Rom. 11²). " *In* all things we are more than conquerors " (8³⁷). " Happy is he who has no cause to judge himself *in* what he approves " (14²²). " Be united *in* the same mind and the same opinion " (I Cor. 1¹⁰). " Let no one boast *in* men " (3²¹). " It is required *in* stewards that they be trustworthy " (4²). " I am not writing this in order that it may be so done *in* me " (9⁵). The instances all suggest that it would be correct to substitute the words " with reference to " for the word " in." Indeed, sometimes English and Greek idiom coincide in the use of the words, as when " star differs from star *in* glory " (I Cor. 15⁴¹).

Of all the interpretations of *en* in Acts 4², this is likely to have most appeal to commentators for it seems reasonable enough to refer doubters on resurrection to the precedent of Jesus himself. But the interpretation is not good enough. St. Luke was St. Paul's loyal disciple and he may have been looking at this matter from the same viewpoint. It is not that he is citing the charge brought by the Jewish Council, but he is describing in his own words the message of the apostles, and he is following the characteristically Pauline interpretation of the resurrection which they preached. St. Paul saw mankind's salvation in terms of spiritual unity with Christ : death came by means of Adam and those who partake of his nature will die, but life from the dead comes through Christ and those who are " in " Christ will rise from physical and spiritual death.

St. Luke may have been mistaken in assuming that the early apostles had already reached this theological conclusion, but the evidence at least suggests that he did make the assumption.

If so, he was probably right, for his substitution of " Jesus " for the " Christ " of the Pauline term gives to the whole a ring of historical verisimilitude. Priests, Temple captain and Sadducees were annoyed at the apostolic message, because the apostles preached that all who are " in " Christ shall rise from the dead.

How did they baptize ?

St. Paul taught that Christians are baptized " into " Christ,† as the Israelites were baptized " into " Moses in the cloud and in the sea.‡ The preposition is an interesting choice, since the formula of baptism used by the first Christians had " in " (*en*) and not " into " (*eis*), the

---

* See the discussion in Moulton-Howard-Turner, *Grammar*, vol. III, p. 265. Acts 4² was not included in this category in the *Grammar* ; the other examples are exclusively Pauline.   † Gal. 3²⁷.   ‡ I Cor. 10².

believer being baptized " *in* the Name of Jesus." But St. Matthew's closing words reveal that later the baptism formula did involve " into." " Go then and make disciples of all nations, baptizing them *into* the Name of the Father and the Son and the Holy Spirit."

Most discussions on baptism overlook the difference in the prepositions, perhaps on the assumption that *eis* and *en* are interchangeable. Both are closely connected in origin, and during the Hellenistic period certain writers did sometimes ignore the distinction. Moreover, in the modern language *eis* has absorbed *en* completely. To be precise, we cannot assume that all Hellenistic authors confused them, and some New Testament writers in fact never do. St. Matthew is notable, as C. H. Turner remarked,* and in this gospel at least the student must allow to *eis* the full sense of motion even where, in other writers, one might suspect that it stood for *en*, and he should recognize the pregnant nature of the phrase in 28[19]. The Christian is "in " Christ because he has already made the move " into " Christ. There is a sense in which baptism accompanies a change in relationship and represents a movement towards a goal ; and the believer is conveyed by baptism into realms (" the Name ") where the power of the holy Trinity is operative.

St. Matthew's formula is different from that used by St. Peter and others on the day of Pentecost and later in Jerusalem. Development towards trinitarianism explains one difference, but not the fact that St. Peter, unlike St. Philip in Samaria, baptized " in " the Name. Jesus appears to have proclaimed one instruction and St. Peter to have followed another. The practice of the later Church may represent a compromise : *in nomine Patris et Filii et Spiritus sancti.*

A further complication is that St. Paul at Ephesus baptized Christians " into " the Name of Christ† and some words in his epistles look like a merging of the two formulae : " into Christ's body ", " into Christ's death," " into Christ."‡ St. Paul selected " into," but instead of introducing the Trinity he retained the person of Christ alone.

Our problem has no simple solution. However much one may prefer to accept Eusebius's version of Matt. 28[19] (" Go and make disciples of all nations, *in my Name* "), one is reluctant to decide against all the manuscript evidence. An alternative is to suppose that after all St. Luke did confuse *eis* and *en*, so that the formula in Acts ought to mean " into the Name of." He was not elsewhere averse to making the confusion.§

The spiriting away of Philip the deacon (Acts 8[40])

In every English version, something faintly fantastic becharms the picture of Philip, snatched away by the Spirit in the desert, to appear

* *Journal of Theological Studies*, XXVI, 1925, p. 14. † Acts 19[5].
‡ I Cor. 12[12], Rom. 6[1ff.], Gal. 3[27]. § Luke 9[61] 11[7], Acts 2[5], etc.

later at Azotus. A kind of flight through the lower heavens is presented
to the reader, the deacon finding himself in a faraway place, in Moffatt
and Phillips. The N.E.B. does nothing to demythologize.

Bible translators should have known how prejudicial it is to transfer
idioms literally from one language to another. " He was found " was
an idiom. In the *Acts of Thomas*, the literally construed phrase, " How
were you found here ? " means, " How did you get here ? " The idiom
occurs in the *Acts of Andrew and Matthew*. A striking parallel with
Philip is afforded by the *Acts of Xanthippe*, where " she was found in
the desert " means " she came into the desert " ; the same preposition
(*eis*) is used before Azotus in Acts.* The idiom has survived in modern
Greek, where " he was found to (*eis*) my need " means " he came to me
in my need." It leaves little room for doubt that St. Luke was describing how Philip the deacon was guided by the Spirit each step of
the journey from the time that he disappeared from the eunuch's sight
until the moment that he walked into Azotus.

One day a learned iconoclast among translators will relieve the English Bible of another curio, and we shall read quite sin.ply, " Philip
came to Azotus."

2. THE APOCALYPTIST

St. John's first vision (Rev. 4)

The seer began to write of his vision of heaven in chapter four. The
seven churches of Asia were left behind, and as his thoughts turned
heavenward the first wonder was God the Father and Creator, en-
throned. But this is ineffable, and St. John, like Ezekiel, compared
him to dazzling stones veiled behind a rainbow, surrounded by thrones
of twenty-four glorified men or angels, representing the People of God.
Thunder and flashes of light comprised the background, while in front
was a crystal sea. Immediately around the main throne were the many-
eyed cherubim.

The supreme moment came when these creatures began a hymn of
glory to the Father and Creator, whereupon St. John saw the twenty-
four glorified men rise from their thrones, prostrate themselves in
worship before the great throne of the Father, and allow their crowns
to drop before it as they burst into song.

I have re-told the vision in the past tense, although the Greek reports
it in the future throughout. One has only to examine the R.V. to
experience the weird effect when the tenses are literally rendered, to
the puzzlement of commentators all down the ages. Yet there is no
doubt that the true text has a succession of future verbs ; the manu-

* More evidence is given in Moulton-Howard-Turner, *Grammar*, vol. III, p. 58.

scripts which offer us the past tense are clearly the victims of attempts to wring sense out of the text. In the R.S.V. and N.E.B., " the tense has been correctly changed from the future of R.V., back to that of A.V. The Gr. future is an attempt to render the Heb. imperfect."* The A.V. used the English historic present tense. Even better would have been a straightforward past.

It may be asked how an English past or historic present tense can legitimately render the Greek future. The context demands it ; the scene is not future, but it is the first vision of the seer who then proceeds to describe how a scroll was brought and how the Lamb began to break each seal in turn. The real reason why St. John described the opening scene of praise with verbs in the future is to be sought in the syntax of Hebrew. Future and imperfect forms of the verb look exactly alike in that language, and the accident has caused no little confusion in Greek versions of the Hebrew Bible. A temporal clause, like this in 4⁹ (" when the living creatures gave glory and honour "), might be expressed in Hebrew by means of the imperfect tense, identical in appearance with future, preceded by the strong *vav*, and this would be taken up throughout the sentence by other *vav*-imperfects as often as required, e.g., " *When* Balaam arose he saddled his ass *and* went . . . *and* the anger of God was kindled " (Num. 22²¹ ᶠ).

There is every reason to believe that the author of Revelation was either inexpert in Greek or deliberately provocative in his choice of Semitic constructions ; and although one recoils from the thought that a man who wrote Greek, or translated into Greek, could follow Hebrew syntax as far as to put a future tense where a past tense was required, he so often does this that the instances cannot be explained in any other way. His book abounds in grammatical solecisms which are clearly Hebraic.

After all, some of the translators who contributed to the Septuagint made this very mistake of confusing past and future meanings of the Hebrew imperfect form. An example is Psalm 103 (104)⁷, where the Hebrew author described past events which displayed God's might. " At thy rebuke *they fled* ; at the voice of thy thunder *they hasted away*." The translator rendered the two verbs in the future tense.†

It does not necessarily follow that Revelation was originally written in Hebrew, or that it was compiled from the Hebrew sources. Although

---

* *Peake's Commentary on the Bible*, revised edition, Nelson, 1962, p. 1049.
† Commenting on this feature of Hebrew syntax, A. B. Davidson noted : " In elevated style the usage of impf. is common. The speaker does not bring the past into his own present, he transports himself back into the past, with the events in which he is thus face to face. . . . The Eng. pres. best renders this impf., our historical pres. being a similar usage." *Hebrew Syntax*, 3rd, ed., T. & T. Clark, 1901, §45, rem. 2, p. 69. So also *Gesenius' Hebrew Grammar*, E. Kautzsch, 2nd. English ed., Oxford, 1910, §107, a, pp. 313 f.

for some reason he wrote in Greek, the author believed that Hebrew was the language of inspiration and symbolism, and so he deliberately imitated its thought-forms in every way which came to hand. It is for us to interpret his linguistic symbolism correctly.

Michael and his angels must fight (Rev. 12⁷)

St. Michael and St. George became the patron saints of England. But who are they ?

Christians read of St. Michael in the last two books of the Bible, where he is not a human person, but one of the seven archangels whom Christian theology derived from Jewish. St. George is traditionally considered to be his counterpart on earth, and England's protector, just as St. Michael was venerated by the Jews as the patron or guardian of Israel and the champion of good against evil in all countries. It is under the latter guise that he appears in the book of Revelation and he comes on the stage after the portent of the woman with her child, when the struggle with Antichrist begins.

" And there was war in heaven." At this there follows, in the Greek, one of many solecisms which seem to be a blemish on the seer's language. The interpretation of the A.V. is too facile : " Michael and his angels fought against the dragon." The Greek has no main verb ; there is an infinitive preceded by the definite article in the genitive case. Unfortunately none of the meanings usually conveyed by the construction is suitable in the present context. The best suggestion is that of R. H. Charles,* and it rests on what the diligent student modestly called " some acquaintance with the LXX " (Septuagint), where the construction is found several times literally reproducing a well-known feature of Hebrew syntax, for " Ephraim to bring forth " means " Ephraim *must* bring forth " ; and the brethren " to come in " means " they *must* come in."† On this hypothesis, the seer John is once again employing a phrase in Greek in a way which was previously used in this precise form only by those who literally translated a Hebrew original.‡ Not that he himself necessarily was translating ; his thoughts and the expression of them were steeped in Semitic idiom.

So then, St. Michael *must* fight. But why ? Prophetic destiny was part of the reason, for Michael had been Israel's patron, and the Church became for Christians the new " Israel." Michael therefore inevitably became the inherited guardian angel of all Christians, their protector against evil forces which the seer saw exemplified in his vision of the woman and child. The minions of him who is called Dragon beset the

---

* In his monumental International Critical Commentary on Revelation, T. & T. Clark, 1920, vol. I, p. 322.   † Hos. 9¹³, I Chron. 9²⁵.
     ‡ See previous section, pp. 158–160.

Child even from his birth. Intuitively the seer recognized that all the sorrows which the holy Child endured at the hands of men, from Herod the Great onward, were not the natural wiles of men, but the result of demon-possession. Good angels, led by St. Michael, were never far from the Child and ministered to him at certain critical periods.

It is inevitable that Christ, and those who are " in Christ," when beset by evil agencies immediately receive the succour of the good. For " Michael and his angels *must* fight."

3. CHRISTIANITY ACCORDING TO ST. JAMES

Temptation is not from God (James 1^{13})

Among the most thorny problems of biblical interpretation perplexing the grammarian is the Theology of Prepositions. It must always be a temptation to the enthusiastic translator to over-translate, and particularly to discover in the wealth of prepositional usage in the New Testament a theological significance which is all too often not justified by the context. Although all is not chaos, Hellenistic writers do tend to add prepositions indiscriminately to the simple case. In biblical Greek, therefore, one need not expect that the precedents of classical style will supply all the answers.

Two prepositions, spelt almost alike, were distinct in the classical period. *Apo* meant " from," and *hupo* (with the genitive case) meant " by " in an instrumental or causal sense, but in the papyri of the Imperial period, and in some texts even before this, *apo* quite often seemed to take on the same meaning as *hupo*. It undoubtedly happened in some writings of the New Testament. St. Luke, for example, used phrases in which it is clear that *apo* is instrumental : Eutychus was " sunk down with (not " from ") sleep " (Acts 20^9), they were vexed " by " (not " from ") evil spirits (Luke 6^{18}), with many other instances. Scribes have been busy at work, altering many instances of *apo* into the more traditionally correct *hupo*.*

Not all writers were guilty, and St. James in particular is not among those who used *apo* like this. The point is important in a verse like 1^{13}, which concerns the genesis of a man's temptations. He may be thought to be tempted by God, as crudely as that, or a man's temptation may come from God in an indirect or permissive sense. Had St. James used *hupo* he would have conceived of God as actively involved in the process of tempting, and his use of *apo* is probably a concession to Jewish belief in the omnipotence and over-ruling providence of One from whom all things come, a reaction against a dualism which gave Satan too much independent authority. The view of St. James's readers would be that

* Moulton-Howard-Turner, *Grammar*, vol. III, p. 258.

temptation is really a product of evil, but of evil in a world controlled by God and therefore of evil to some extent permitted. His Greek is too " good " by traditional standards to have countenanced the confusion of *apo* and *hupo* nor would he gratuitously accuse his Jewish readers of holding a view that would permit them to say, " I am tempted by God." He goes further than orthodox Judaism, however, for as a Christian he forbids his readers to shelter behind the permissive nature of man's temptations. God neither tempts nor permits to be tempted. Like St. Paul, St. James re-interprets his Brother's teaching, " Lead us not into temptation," in the model prayer which was given to the disciples during his early life. The Lord's Prayer is not a prayer for Christians, but one which any good Pharisee might use, and is no more consistent with Christian truth about the Father, revealed in Jesus and re-interpreted by the apostles, than the advice of Jesus to the rich young man to win eternal life by means of good works is consistent with St. Paul's exposition of justification by faith alone. The parable of the prodigal son contains no hint of Christian atonement ; it belongs to the old dispensation.

St. James then has re-interpreted his Brother. God neither tempts nor leads into temptation, and as a Christian it was inconsistent to believe that he so much as permits it. Rather it arises from lust, that is, the free misuse of instincts potentially good. " Do not say that your temptation comes from God. He does not deal in evil things nor tempt anyone. Your own lust is the explanation." It represents a break with certain schools of orthodox Judaism which taught that a sinner, although he ought not to plead God's permissive will as an excuse, nevertheless must resign himself to the complementary truth that God orders everything that comes. He had tempted Abraham (Gen. 22), and in some Jewish circles there was the prayer, " Make not thy hand heavy upon us, that we sin by reason of our sore necessity."*

Not a few translators in modern times (Knox, R.S.V., N.E.B.) have missed St. James's point. They render *apo* " by." Only the R.V., especially the margin, Goodspeed, and Moffatt reveal its true signification. Among commentators, however, R. J. Knowling correctly observed that " it signifies the remoter rather than the immediate agent."†

Nevertheless, Knowling failed to go far enough and take *apeirastos*, which follows, as active ; he felt that the passive sense was preferable as it did not make the next words tautologous. The context requires the active. To say, " God cannot be tempted," is irrelevant. So the passive sense is helpful. The active sense of the verbal adjective means " inexperienced in," " having no dealings with." Both voices

---

* Psalms of Solomon 5⁸.
† Westminster Commentaries, Methuen, 1904, p. 19.

are vouched for in early Christian literature.* Assuming that St. James used the active, he produced a play on the stem *-peir-*, when he taught that God neither creates nor manipulates evil and is not responsible for man's temptations.

" *Prayer* " *and prayer* (*James* $4^{2\ f.}$)

Theoretically, the Greek middle voice involved the whole subject in the verb's action, and expressed the subject in some special relationship to himself. It is, then, quite understandable that for practical purposes it mattered very little whether the active or the middle voice was used with verbs of a certain type. " I make a request " is active but is not profoundly different from the middle, " I make a request for myself." It defines the idea more narrowly but in normal conversation either active or middle would do. We may say the same thing about the verb, " I choose," and many others.

It would not be remarkable if the same writer or speaker used a verb in the active voice one moment and in the middle soon afterwards, as his fancy led him, but it has nevertheless provoked much comment in the epistle of St. James when this writer in adjacent sentences ($4^{2\ f.}$) uses first the middle, then the active, then the middle again. It is difficult to believe that the change is simply for variety's sake. " You have not because you *ask* not (middle). You *ask* (active) and receive not, because you *ask* amiss (middle)." Every known attempt to make a distinction is no better than intelligent surmise. None has the support of sound linguistic evidence. Their merit is to avoid a dullness of perception which might do less than justice to St. James's pliant handling of Greek.

The most attractive suggestion, making good sense of the words, is that of Dr. Mayor, accepted by Dr. Moulton in the Prolegomena of the *Grammar*. The active voice implies the mere words of prayer, but the " asking " of the middle voice has the added idea of prayer accompanied by the true spirit of prayer. " If the middle is really the stronger word, we can understand its being brought in just where an effect of contrast can be secured, while in ordinary passages the active would carry as much weight as was needed." (p. 160.) But it is hard to find much solid grammatical evidence for the distinction, and the theory has the appearance of being tailor-made for the passage without suiting other contexts so well and without precedent in other writers. It is true that St. James immediately makes a distinction which supports Mayor's explanation of active and middle voice. His readers are accused of asking things from God in a wrong spirit. The motive force behind their prayer is " that ye may consume it upon your lusts." The fact that they are

* *A Patristic Greek Lexicon*, ed. G. H. Lampe, Oxford, 1961, fasc. 1, s. v.

adulterers and friends of the world does not prevent them from resorting to prayer—at least the outward form of mere words, which Mayor and Moulton understood by *aitein* in the active voice. A man cannot come to God in a true spirit of prayer (i.e. *aiteisthai*, middle) and at the same time live consciously and unrepentant in sin. Commentators have seen the point adequately enough and have instanced the hollow devotions of those who outwardly appear to be saints. Cornish wreckers used to go from church to rocks where they had placed false lights. " Ye kill, in order to gain," wrote St. James. Italian brigands offered prayer to a patron saint before attacking a party of travellers, and there may still be Russian peasants who turn their icons' faces to the wall before they commit adultery. St. Augustine prayed for deliverance from greed and unchastity, adding, " Not yet, O Lord." There is the glib record of John Newton, who thanked God for blessing his cruel trade during the past year.* Such people were not truly praying, however devout the the words may have been.

Here, in so good a cause, the grammarian would like to lend his support to the commentator. The fact remains, however, that the active and middle voices of such verbs are so often used interchangeably, especially in the New Testament, that weighty evidence alone would establish the hypothesis of Mayor and Moulton. It is of course surprising that St. James reverts from one voice to the other and then back again. Perhaps he had before him a letter from his readers complaining, " We ask, and receive not." They had used the active voice, as it happened, and he therefore retained it in quoting their words. He himself preferred to use the middle voice.

The dialogue then resolves itself into disarming simplicity : " You have not, because you ask not." " But we do ask, and still we receive not." " Then you receive not, because you ask selfishly."

The last days (*James* 5[3])

We are living in the " last days."

It was a point made by St. Peter at Pentecost, arising from Joel's prophecy (Acts 2[17]). St. Paul spoke of the " last days " as present, or at least imminent (II Tim. 3[1]). The writer to the Hebrews explicitly referred to " these last days," leaving their present realization in no doubt (Heb. 1[2]). St. Peter too spoke of " these last times " (I Pet. 1[20]). St. John said, " Little children, it is the last time " (I John 2[18]). St. Jude took comfort from the fact that there are to be " mockers in the last time " and he plainly identified them as already present : " These are the ones who separate themselves."

---

* E. H. Plumtre, Cambridge Bible, *in loc.* ; R. J. Knowling, Westminster Commentary, *in loc.*

In view of all this it does not seem reasonable to speak of heaping up treasure " *for* the last days " (James 5³ A.V.). The word " for " is unwarranted in grammar and in the apostolic belief as given above. Greek has, " *in* the last days." In a stylist as conservative as St. James, care must be taken to look at the prepositions in a more traditional way than would be necessary in a writer like St. Mark. St. James does not use *en* when he intends no more than a simple dative, and he does not confuse it with *eis* (" towards "). The N.E.B. has correctly interpreted the sentence : " you have piled up wealth in an age that is near its close."

The same kind of construction occurs two verses later (5⁵) ; *en* precedes the phrase, " day of slaughter." We are not to interpret it, " You have fattened your hearts *for* a day of slaughter "—but the fattening is a process now continuing *in* this day of slaughter. It is an Old Testament phrase, taken from the prophet Jeremiah (12³), and hence originally conceived in a previous dispensation and looking forward to an era to come ; its original form was therefore " *for* a day of slaughter " and that is how it ought to be interpreted in the Septuagint which carefully renders the Hebrew by means of the preposition *eis* (" towards ") ; it is St. James who has, most correctly, revised the quotation by substituting *en* for *eis* in order to adapt it for his own times. He is not thinking of a future judgment, so much as of men who in the present age fatten their hearts merely to perish like beasts.

He has sighed, " What is your life ! A vapour that vanishes away ! " (4¹⁸). His next thought is quite independent, unconnected with the idea of perishing like the brute creation. He passes on to consider the second coming of the Lord, which is for comfort and not for slaughter.

A chain of reasoning binds the verses together. " Do not worry about these rich men who oppress you. They flatter themselves, only to die. Your comfort will come when the Lord comes."

There is nothing here of that savage cry for revenge which seems to mar the apocalyptic visions of Christ's return which come to us from Patmos.

4. St. Peter

The moral Codes of the earliest Christians

Imperatival use of the participle of the verb in a way which is impossible in English, but which was quite acceptable in post-biblical Hebrew and New Testament Greek (perhaps also in the Common Greek) is a puzzling feature of grammar. It occurs with remarkable frequency in the writings of St. Peter and St. Paul.

If at this point the reader is given a literal rendering of this participle in the relevant Petrine and Pauline texts, he will readily appreciate the scope of the problem.

Rom. 12[9-13] : " Love . . .* without hypocrisy. . . .† *haters*‡ of that which is evil, . . .† *adherents* of that which is good. In love of the brethren . . .† *tenderly affectioned* to one another, in honour *preferring* one another," etc.

Rom. 12[16] : ". . .† *of the same mind* towards one another. . . .† *mindful* not of high things, but . . .† *devoted* to things that are lowly."

Col. 2[2] : " They . . .* *knit together* in love."

Col. 3[16] : " In all wisdom . . .† *teachers* and exhorters of yourselves ; in psalms, hymns, and songs, . . .† joyful *choristers*."

II Cor. 8[24] : " They are delegates of our congregations, an honour to Christ (N.E.B.). You . . .* *showing* them a proof of your love " (corrected to imperative in some texts).

II Cor. 9[10 f.] : " He shall increase the fruits of your righteousness. . . .† *enriched* in everything."

II Cor. 9[12 f.] : " The carrying out of this service not only supplies the needs of the saints, but causes them to thank God. . . .§ *praising* God because of this testing of you."

Eph. 3[17] : " That Christ may dwell in your hearts through faith. . . .† *rooted* and *grounded* in love."

Eph. 4[2] : " I beseech you to walk worthily of your vocation, lowly, meek and patient. You . . .* *forgiving* towards one another in love."

In the epistle to the Hebrews : " God will judge fornicators and adulterers. Your manner of life . . .* free from love of money. You . . .* *content* with such things as you have " (13[4 f.]).

The construction is comparatively most frequent in St. Peter's first epistle : " Honour all men, love the brotherhood, fear God, honour the king. Servants, . . .† *subordinate* to your masters with all fear " (2[18]). " Similarly, wives, . . .† *subordinate* to your own husbands " (3[1]). " Similarly, husbands, . . .† *reasonable partners* " (3[7]). " Finally, . . .† all likeminded, compassionate, loving " (3[8]).

When we seek a reason for the unusual construction, an interesting theory about early Christian documents comes to light. Dr. David Daube offered it‖ to counter J. H. Moulton's theory in the Prolegomena

---

* Supply " must be." A series of dots is placed where the imperative of the verb " to be " should be supplied, since this ellipse is quite regular in all periods of Greek ; indeed, the 2nd. person-plural imperative (*este* : " be ye ") never occurs in the New Testament but is frequently to be understood. Moulton-Howard-Turner, *Grammar*, vol. III, p. 303.   † Supply " be ye."

‡ The italics represent participles which, being in the present tense, are substantival rather than verbal expressions. They are best translated as nouns or adjectives.
                  § Supply " they ought to be."

‖ Appended note (" Participle and Imperative in I Peter ") to Essay II in E. G. Selwyn, *The First Epistle of St. Peter*, Macmillan, 2nd. ed., 1947, pp. 467–488.

of the *Grammar*, which had claimed that the imperatival participle was a feature of the Common Greek of the Ptolemaic period. Daube sought to show that Moulton's seven examples are not real parallels to the New Testament usage : six of them may be explained as normal use of the participle. It is doubtful whether many specialists will agree with Daube's attempt to explain them away.* Strangely, he does not once refer to Mayser's indispensable work on the grammar of the Ptolemaic papyrus texts, or claim that Mayser had already declined to accept Moulton's examples of the imperatival participle for Hellenistic Greek, for the same reason that Daube himself tenders, namely, that Moulton failed to notice the presence of a main verb on which the participle adequately depends.† Dr. Daube would have found in the German edition of Moulton's work‡ an eighth example, which runs, "I beg you to give the assurance to Mezakus that I never spoke anything improper against him, and when you have done this, *begging* him to let me come and be freed from custody." No doubt, as Mayser suggested,§ some such phrase as "you would do well" might have been omitted before " begging," but, however one accounts for it, the idiom is there.

The alternative theory to Moulton's, which Daube then supplies, is also open to criticism. With a wealth of examples he shows that Tannaitic rabbinic Judaism fairly regularly expressed communal duties in the form of a participle, rather than an imperative. Some examples bear a likeness to the kind of communal injunction concerning social behaviour expressed likewise with a participle by St. Peter and St. Paul. Dr. Daube suggests that the New Testament imperatival participles arise from direct translation of Tannaitic rabbinical " codes " of moral rules which influenced early Christian writers. The question of dating is crucial, since the Tannaitic examples may well be later than the apostolic period, but Daube's treatment of this difficulty is too slight : he is impressed by the similarity of the Christian rules for social behaviour with many of the Tannaitic " codes ", and he thinks " that there was probably no scarcity of Hebrew rules with imperative participles by which an early Christian writer might let himself be influenced."‖

The suggestion is extremely precarious, for we do not know how much of the Tannaitic material can be dated in the pre-apostolic period. Moreover, Dr. C. L. Mitton has shown conclusively that the author of I Peter is indebted to the epistle to the Ephesians in general ; and in

---

* Thus H. G. Meecham (*Expos. Times*, LVIII, pp. 207 f.) supported Moulton against Daube.

† Edwin Mayser, *Grammatik der griechischen Papyri aus der Ptolemäerzeit*, Berlin and Leipzig, II 1, 1926, p. 340.

‡ J. H. Moulton, *Einleitung in die Sprache des neuen Testaments*, Heidelberg, 1911, p. 353 (virtually a 4th. ed. of the Prolegomena).

§ Edwin Mayser, op. cit., II 1, p. 196, n. 3.   ‖ Op. cit., p. 480.

particular that I Pet. 2¹⁸ (which has the imperative participle) depends
on Eph. 6⁵ (which has the same injunction, but with a straightforward
imperative).* Dr. Mitton acutely observes that, if his own argument
stands, St. Peter felt that the participle was a sense-equivalent to the
imperative in Ephesians, and so " this may be cited as evidence that a
participle could be used to express the meaning of an imperative."†
Dr. Mitton therefore provides a satisfactory alternative to Daube's
suggestion that St. Peter and St. Paul were rendering the Hebrew
participle in moral " codes " in two different ways.

Dr. Daube's theory, moreover, takes no account of Semitic influence
from a wholly different direction, which is at least as likely as supposing
that translation from Tannaitic Hebrew influenced the syntax of a
New Testament writer. Many apparent Semitisms are found in the
secular Common Greek of Egypt, where there was a large Jewish population. The possibility of a spoken Jewish Greek is one which Daube
and many others neglect ; but it is relevant, because the Semitic imperatival participle of St. Peter and St. Paul need not involve a Semitic
document lying behind their work. Biblical Greek may already have
absorbed this construction into its system, as it had absorbed numerous
other Semitisms.‡

" Your faith when tested " (James 1³, I Pet. 1⁷)

There is very strong evidence that *to dokimeion* (or *to dokimion*)
means " something tested,"§ contrary to the generally accepted translations. We give these in italics.

James 1³	I Pet. 1⁷
" The *trying* of your faith worketh patience " (A.V.)	" The *trial* of your faith. . . ." (A.V.)
" The *proof* of your faith worketh patience " (R.V.)	" The *proof* of your faith. . . ." (R.V.)
" The *testing* of your faith produces steadfastness " (R.S.V.)	" The *genuineness* of your faith. . . ." (R.S.V.)
" The *testing* of your faith leads to steadfastness " (Goodspeed)	" Your faith *when tested*. . . ." (Goodspeed)
" The *sterling temper* of your faith produces endurance " (Moffatt)	" Your faith is *sterling* " (Moffatt)
" Such *testing* of your faith breeds fortitude " (N.E.B.)	" Faith *which has stood the test* "

---

* C. Leslie Mitton, *The Epistle to the Ephesians*, Oxford, 1951, chapter XVII, pp.
176–197.   † *Ibid.* p. 193.
‡ The possibility of such a spoken Greek we will consider more fully. See pp. 174ff.
§ The view was dismissed, without reasons, as unusual and improbable by a
reviewer in the *Journal of Theological Studies*, N.S., XV, April, 1964, p. 120.

The important question in James 1³ is whether patience is produced by the tested faith itself or by the actual testing of the faith. St. Paul, at least, taught that " tribulation produces patience " (Rom. 5⁴), but the wider passage in St. James has faith for its theme, rather than trials (James 1²⁻⁸), and in Pet. 1⁶⁻¹² the central theme is that of seeing and trusting him that is invisible. In the latter the point is so obvious that *to dokimeion* is rendered by Goodspeed, Moffatt, and the N.E.B. very much in the way I have suggested : " as much of your faith as has been tested." But unfortunately they failed to do the same for the passage in St. James.

To achieve such a translation grammatically, one must regard *to dokimeion* as an adjective having the same meaning as *to dokimon* (" something tested "). Adolf Deissmann* was the first to insist on this, and R. J. Knowling admitted that his rendering was fresh and illuminative and made excellent sense in both places.† Before Deissmann, there had been a suspicion that the expression was the neuter of an adjective, but he was the first to find the evidence which lies in the Fayyûm papyrus documents in archduke Rainer's collection, where the expression is used closely with gold and the meaning required is " good gold," in the sense of pure or tested.

Oecumenius, a tenth-century bishop in Thessaly, gives further support for Deissmann's view, for he comments : " *Dokimion* means ' judged,' ' that which has been tested,' ' the pure.' "‡

The advantage of taking *to dokimeion* in this way, in the passage in I Peter, " is that it gives a straightforward analogy between the probation of character and the refining of metals."§

The view, therefore, that *to dokimeion* means " something tested " can scarcely be described as improbable, and if it is unusual, all it wants is wider circulation.

" *Persecution is coming. Blessed are ye !* " (I Pet. 3¹⁴·¹⁷)

It has been observed that the first epistle of St. Peter reads more like an address, or two addresses, than a letter. Dedicated to a specified group of people, with a special situation in mind, it may be a sermon for a baptismal service.

Syntax lends support to the suggestion, but not to the further venture of seeking on linguistic grounds to divide the one epistle into two

---

* A. Deissmann, *Bible Studies*, English translation by A. Grieve, T. & T. Clark, 1901, pp. 295 f.

†. R. J. Knowling, *The Epistle of St. James*, Westminster Commentaries, Methuen, 1904, p. 7.

‡ Quoted by Tischendorf on James 1³. See Deissmann, op. cit., p. 260.

§ E. G. Selwyn, op. cit., p. 129.

separate works. The diction is of excellent quality, oratorical in tone, like a sermon, and one feature of syntax in particular is noteworthy. The slightly antique use of the optative mood in a conditional clause occurs in 3[14.17], but elsewhere only once in the New Testament,* and it was sufficiently unnatural at this period to enable us to attribute its use to deliberate imitation of classical style. It is very rare in contemporary secular Greek, outside the stilted jargon of official letters and decrees, and rare in biblical Greek.

The meaning of the two clauses in which it occurs in I Peter must be : " If you should suffer . . ." and, " If the will of God should be that you suffer. . . ." Elsewhere I made the suggestion that " the only way to account for the apparently impeccable Attic of the Petrine optatives is to suppose them to have been abstracted from the archaic periods of a solemn exhortation."† I was not intending to go all the way with the critics who propose a division of the epistle into two sources between 4[11] and 4[12] on the ground that before this line of division persecution is looked upon as something remotely future and that after the division it has already become present. Indeed, syntax points in the opposite direction, in two places.

(1) The observation that the conditional clause is classically phrased applies only to the protasis ; the apodosis fails to keep in line with the classical pattern for it does not give the optative with *an*, required in that form of conditioanl sentence. Like a versatile orator, keeping the element of surprise for the end of his sentence, the author substitutes the present tense. After " If you should suffer," we expect " you *would* be blessed," but instead the author says, " You *are* blessed ! " A probable reason for twisting the conditional sentence like this is tact.‡ St. Peter was reluctant to mention his readers' (or listeners') sufferings except in a tentative way—as if they might not come, after all. Persecution, however, was already present or imminent. This the author deliberately conveys by his own special brand of conditional sentence. The protasis makes the sufferings remotely future by means of a tactful optative, whereas the present tense of the apodosis betrays that they are facing the sufferings now. " If you *should* suffer, blessed *are* ye ! "

(2) There is a statement in the alleged second source of the epistle which is held to prove that persecution is already present : " Beloved, think it not strange concerning the fiery trial which is to try you " (4[12 ff] A.V.). But the Greek describes the fiery trial as " coming " (*ginomenē*), using a present participle of the verb " to be " or " to

---

* Acts 24[19], a speech before governor Felix.
† Moulton-Howard-Turner, *Grammar*, vol. III, pp. 126 f.
‡ Suggested by the Jesuit grammarian, M. Zerwick, *Graecitas Biblica*, 3rd. ed., Rome, 1955, § 228. d. An English translation has just appeared (1964).

become " ; this is a vivid present with a future meaning, such as was as commonly used by the New Testament writers as by any English speaker to-day. The Messiah is frequently described as the One who *is coming* (*ho Erchomenos*), not the One who *will come* (*ho Eleusomenos*) ; and there are scores of futher examples.

So much for the argument that persecution is future in the first half of the epistle and present in the second. Linguistically too there are no grounds for dividing the epistle into two.

Preaching to spirits in Paradise (I Pet. 3[18-20])

St. Peter declared that Christ died as a righteous man, on behalf of unrighteous men, because of their sins and in order to bring them to God. Christ was put to death in a physical sense, but was made alive again *pneumati*. That may be " by means of the Holy Spirit " (Moffatt, Goodspeed), or simply, " in his spirit." The latter is more likely, since it nicely balances " put to death in the flesh." *Pneumati* then would be an adverbial dative with the meaning, " spiritually," as opposed to physically. The suggestion is that the operation refers to the period between his burial and resurrection, when he could be said to be *pneumati* and not yet physically resurrected. At this period (if that is St. Peter's meaning) Christ went and preached to the imprisoned spirits. The phrase *en hō* (" in which "), which follows the word *pneumati*, must refer, in spite of E. G. Selwyn,* to *pneumati* as its antecedent ; Selwyn's submission that an adverbial dative is never in the New Testament taken up by an ensuing relative pronoun, is not really capable of verification since it is not easy to define exactly an adverbial dative. However, it makes little difference to the meaning to accept the alternative and interpret *en hō* in a general sense as " when."

That is the least difficulty in so controversial a passage, for St. Peter writes : " in which (" when " ?) he went and preached to the imprisoned spirits who had been disobedient in the days of Noah " (I Pet. 3[19-20]). The legend that Christ preached in Hades during this period doubtless originated with the text, and perhaps with the promise to the dying robber that he would meet Christ in Paradise immediately after death (Luke 23[43]), or perhaps with the prophecy of Jesus that the dead would hear his preaching (John 5[25]). The obscure cosmogony in Eph. 4[9] has the comparative degree adjective *katōtera* followed by *gēs*, which should be interpreted as " the lower parts *than* the earth " (like the margin of N.E.B.) rather than " the lowest level *of* the earth." All the passages confirm that St. Peter shared the belief of many early Christians that Christ, in spiritual form, visited the abode of departed spirits on Good Friday evening and proclaimed some message there.

* Op. cit., p. 197.

5. To Purchase Joy ?

(*Heb.* 12²)

Readers of the N.E.B., when they come to the epistle to the Hebrews, may wonder what is the exact significance of the footnote to 12². The text has the normal interpretation : " for the sake of the joy " that was set before him Christ endured the cross. The footnote has : " in place of the joy " that was set before him.

The footnote arises from doubt about the true meaning of *anti*, one of those key-words of which the precise connotation is beset by theological difficulties.

In its original and simplest sense this preposition is local, meaning " over against " or " opposite." It has several derived meanings, however, especially substitution and exchange, and these are fairly exemplified in the New Testament, as follows :

(1) " Instead of." This derived directly from the primary meaning, " opposite," since one may readily be said to be a substitute for one's opposite number, as in parliamentary pairing, when the absence of one member from the House cancels the absence of his opponent. This must be the meaning of *anti* in the following contexts : " An eye *anti* an eye and a tooth *anti* a tooth " (Matt. 5³⁸), " Archelaus ruled over Judaea *anti* his father Herod " (Matt. 2²²), " What father whose son asks him for a fish, will give him a serpent *anti* a fish " (Luke 11¹¹), " Her hair is given to her *anti* a covering " (I Cor. 11¹⁵). Here probably belongs the statement in Heb. 12² : " Christ endured the cross *anti* (" instead of ") the joy that was set before him." The interpretation, " for the sake of the joy," seems not to be possible unless one can conceive that Christ's motive in suffering was to enjoy what followed.

(2) " For the price of." This seems to be a possible meaning for the author of Hebrews, since he used it in 12¹⁶ in reference to Esau " who sold his birthright *anti* (" in exchange for ") a meal." The genitive after *anti* represents the desirable object and the previously mentioned noun represents the price to be paid—a meal for a birthright. So in 12², the " joy set before him " may be conceived as the desirable object, and enduring the cross as the price.

That is, Christ purchased the joy at the cost of the cross. But this is open to the same objection as (1). At least, it suffices to explain the gospel usage of *anti* in Jesus's saying that the Son of Man came to give his life as a ransom " in exchange for many," since the price to be paid for them is the laying down of his life (Matt. 20²⁸ = Mark 10⁴⁵). However, there is the objection that when this saying of Jesus is quoted in the Pastoral epistles, *anti* is discarded in favour of *huper*, a preposition

which does not mean " in exchange for," but " for the sake of "
(I Tim. 2⁶).

No doubt, the unusual idiom in John 1¹⁶ (" grace *in place of* grace ")
must be explained under (1). If so, we must understand it as " (new)
grace in place of (old) grace," as Philo did.* The translation of the
R.S.V., " grace upon grace," may be feeling after this, with its hint at
successions of grace poured out one after the other, and the idea goes
back to Bengel, Alford, H. A. W. Meyer, and re-appears with the recent
suggestion, " overflowing divine grace."† But the possibility that the
old grace is the Old Testament and the new grace the New, advocated
by some of the Church fathers must not be dismissed. Dr. Matthew
Black's theory‡ that the phrase means " grace instead of disgrace "
depends upon the unproved hypothesis that this part of St. John's
gospel is based upon an Aramaic original, and if by " disgrace " the
old dispensation was intended, the observation is unexpectedly harsh.§

(3) " In requital of." St. Paul and St. Peter counselled that no
Christian should repay evil in requital of evil (Rom. 12¹⁷, I Thess. 5¹⁵,
I Pet. 3⁹), but perhaps this is barely distinguishable from (1).

(4) " On behalf of." This different meaning of *anti* must lie behind
Matt. 17²⁷ where Simon was sent to obtain a shekel from a fish's mouth
to pay the half-shekel tax to the collectors " on behalf of yourself and
me." Neither the idea of substitution nor that of exchange is relevant
in such a context. *Anti* now has become as colourless as *huper*, but the
weakening may be only apparent. From Exodus 30¹¹ it is clear that
originally the half-shekel tax was a redemption tax, for at a public
census Moses was commanded to exact this amount, so that each man
could give a ransom for himself, and this was understood to be the
purchase money required to buy the subject from a hypothetical
servitude. So " yourself and me " can be conceived as the objects
desired to purchase, preceded as they are by *anti*, and the half-shekel
paid by Simon was the price of purchase. In consequence, we may
safely rule out (4) as a separate category of meaning for *anti* ; the sole
significance of the preposition in each New Testament context is that
of substitution and exchange.

When Christ died on the cross his action was not a conscious purchase
of personal joy, nor was it performed " for the sake of joy." It was a
substitutionary process, not only in the sense that he gave himself
" instead of " others, but that he deliberately chose the way of suffering
" instead of " the joy which might have been his.

---

* De Post. Caini i. 254.
† R. H. Lightfoot, *St. John's Gospel*, Oxford, 1956, p. 87.
‡ *Journal of Theological Studies*, XLII, 1941, pp. 69f.
§ C. K. Barrett, *The Gospel according to St. John*, S.C.P.K., 1955, pp. 140 f.

CHAPTER SEVEN

THE LANGUAGE OF JESUS
AND HIS DISCIPLES

The question of what language Jesus used in his daily life cannot fail to be of interest to Christians. Was it Palestinian Aramaic, the local tongue of his own country, one of the Semitic group of languages known technically as Western Aramaean ? Or did he speak the kind of Greek known as Koine, which was the common language spoken in most countries of the Roman empire at that time ? Although in Jerusalem few Jews may have used Greek it is possible that in " Galilee of the Gentiles " Jesus would find it necessary to converse in the world's language.

There is a third possibility, held by some but not widely, that he spoke in Hebrew.

The question has a wider significance than the satisfaction of devout curiosity. If Jesus spoke Aramaic, rather than the Greek of the New Testament writings, then the earliest records of his teaching and his apostles' teaching were transmitted in Aramaic, and the realization of this must influence our interpretation of them in their Greek dress. The presumption is that when these very early records were put into Greek, mistakes would be made, and at the very least there is the possibility that misunderstandings crept in because reverence would demand that his own language be translated as literally as possible.

As a matter of fact, in the four gospels there are enough traces of Semitic constructions to attract scholars to the conclusion either that the authors of the gospels wrote their original drafts in Aramaic, or that they used Aramaic written sources ; but not enough attention has been paid to the possibility that they wrote in Greek while thinking in Aramaic or, better still, that they spoke and wrote in a dialect of Jewish Greek. Among those who do appreciate the high degree of Semitic influence in the Greek of the New Testament there is a strong feeling that it can be explained on the theory of Aramaic sources,* and they adduce in support several apparently convincing instances of mistranslation, which are mainly within the teaching of Jesus, but not exclusively.

---

* Or Hebrew, in the instance of St. Luke. See the views of various specialists (Harnack, Dibelius, Sahlin, Vielhauer, Winter, Turner, Laurentin, Benoit) conveniently summarized in *New Testament Studies*, X, January, 1964, pp. 202 ff.

To prove translation is sometimes no easy task, although usually the translator betrays his handiwork to the patient researcher. C. C. Torrey* has suggested three methods whereby an apparently original composition may be tested for evidence of translation. (1) The first is the subjective one of testing the Semitic sound of certain phrases—most of the New Testament would react positively. (2) The second is the presence of mistranslations. (3) The third is the cumulative evidence of a great number of Semitic idioms, whether they occur in ordinary Greek or not. It is the second of the tests which is the only really significant one, because the first and third do no more than indicate that the author was thinking in Semitic forms or writing in a dialect of Greek which was influenced by Semitic idiom. It is well to heed Torrey's own warning that each test is applicable only " in the rare cases where it is convincing " ;† if we can find a phrase where a difficulty of exegesis is removed by a literal rendering into a Semitic language, we have the soundest proof that the passage in question is a translation. There are not many of them in the New Testament and a high proportion of those that have been adduced belong to the teaching of Jesus, which indicates, if the mistranslations are admitted, that hardly anything more than the teaching of Jesus was originally written in Aramaic. Contrary to Torrey and Burney, the most that can safely be said is that an Aramaic sayings-source or sayings-tradition lies behind the synoptic gospels. Whatever the problem for the narrative portions of the gospels, there is strong support among Aramaic scholars for the view that Jesus spoke and thought in Aramaic, and that his words were first taken down in that language.

Among the alleged mistranslations is the saying where Jesus uses the verb, " cut in pieces,"‡ which is thought to be too strong a word to be reasonable, and which can be toned down admirably on the theory that Jesus spoke Aramaic. There is an Aramaic verb, *pesaq*, with the double meaning " to cut " and " to apportion." Ignorance of the second meaning may have led an inexpert translator into a misunderstanding of his original. Jesus may have said, " The master of that servant *will apportion* him and put him with the hypocrites." This causes less offence to those who forget that this is after all a parable.

Another misunderstanding, said to have resulted in mistranslation, is the apparent nonsense produced by the aphorism, " Give for alms that which is within " (Luke 11[41]). All is thought to be clear if it is supposed that St. Luke, or someone whose work he used, confused the Aramaic words *dakki* and *zakki* and produced a mistranslation. Jesus

---

* In *C. H. Toy, Studies*, pp. 283 ff., quoted by W. F. Howard in Moulton-Howard, *Grammar*, vol. II, Appendix, p. 478.

† Op. cit., p. 284.

‡ In the parable of the wise servant (Matt. 24[51], Luke 12[46]).

may actually have said, " *Cleanse* that which is within," just as St. Matthew represents him as saying. Not a few scholars are convinced by such examples that Aramaic was the language of Jesus, but I have suggested* an alternative explanation consistent with Greek grammar and excluding the appeal to Aramaic.

The question is unfortunately beset by the difficulty that there are insufficient contemporary sources for the kind of Aramaic which might have been familiar to Jesus, for almost no written records of this language have come down to us from the period 100 B.C. to A.D. 100. However, such translations as *maranatha, cephas, pascha* and *abba*, which have come through into Greek, suggest that the earliest Christian community was Aramaic speaking, and there is little wonder if many scholars—great names like those of J. Wellhausen, G. Dalman, C. C. Torrey, C. F. Burney, M. H. Segal, T. W. Manson and Matthew Black—have been of opinion that Jesus and his disciples used Aramaic at least in Galilee, and although they were probably also acquainted with Hebrew or Greek, they conversed with each other normally in Aramaic and perhaps on solemn occasions, like his arguments with the Pharisees and the Last Supper, Jesus addressed his listeners in Hebrew. Matthew Black sums up the conclusion of Dalman, which he regards as firmly established : " Jesus may have spoken Greek, but he certainly did speak and teach in Aramaic."† Admittedly Aramaic was particularly associated with " the people of the land," and in that class would be Jesus and his disciples. Nevertheless on some occasions at least Jesus may have used Greek, such as his conversations with the Syro-phoenician woman, the Roman centurion and the procurator Pontius Pilate.

Against the extreme view that the whole of Matthew was originally written in Aramaic,‡ we must say that the characteristically Greek phrase, *men . . . de*, occurs twenty times in this gospel, and that is an unusual proportion for translation-Greek, to say the least. Even the reported words of John the Baptist contain this typically Greek phrase (3[11]), and it occurs in the words of Jesus§ and of his disciples.‖ It should be remarked that every occurrence of *men . . . de* is in the words of Jesus, his disciples, or the Baptist—in fact, in that part of the gospel which is commonly thought to be derived from the document Q, about

* P. 57.

† M. Black, *An Aramaic Approach to the Gospels and Acts*, 2nd. ed., Oxford, 1954, p. 14 n.

‡ For the theory of an Aramaic Matthew, see M.-J. Lagrange, *Évangile selon S. Matthieu*, 8th. ed., Paris, 1948, pp. LXXIX ff., especially pp. XC ff. Besides *men . . . de*, see below (pp. 178 f.) the tables for genitive absolute construction, which reveal that it occurs once in twenty verses in Matthew as a whole, making a translation hypothesis the more improbable.

§ Matt. 9[37] 10[13] 13[4.8.23.32] 16[3] 17[11] 20[23] 21[35] 22[5.8] 23[27.28] 25[15.33] 26[24.41].

‖ Matt. 16[14].

as early an account of Jesus's teaching as one could easily conceive. Since such a document bears obvious signs of having been originally composed in Greek, the advocates of the theory of an exclusively Aramaic-speaking Jesus should have reason to be cautious. The *men . . . de* construction occurs hardly at all in translated books.*

Another construction which is rare indeed in the translated books of the Septuagint is the genitive absolute, plentiful enough still in the Common Greek of the period and even in works of biblical Greek authors when they are not translating from Hebrew or Aramaic. It is not very common in St. John's gospel or St. Paul ; opportunities for its use occur in narrative rather than in doctrinal or philosophical works. From the tables which follow, some evidential results appear. St. Matthew apparently is addicted to the construction, and so is St. Luke. Inevitably it occurs less frequently in the Q-sections, as there is a predominance of teaching and sparsity of narrative, but in spite of this the incidence of the genitive absolute is here very marked when compared with the translated books of the Septuagint. For instance, in subject-matter Q is most comparable with Ecclesiasticus and yet even in St. Matthew's version of Q, where it occurs less often than in St. Luke's, the genitive absolute occurs *twenty-eight times as often* as in Ecclesiasticus. If the Q-material was ever in Hebrew or Aramaic—most improbable, in view of these figures—then both versions were very free translations indeed, even paraphrases. Yet that is impossible, for no Christian translator would render the holy sayings of Jesus so freely. Veneration demanded literal treatment, and in this the Septuagint affords a parallel. As reverence for the sacred books increased, so did the degree of literalness in the translation.

Significantly enough, the synoptic tradition is not alone in displaying the influence of Aramaic. The style of St. John, who represents a different and perhaps later tradition, and especially the style of the discourses of Jesus, is that of Semitic speech; indeed, a modern tendency is to see the book as a product of gnosticizing Judaism, with a double influence of Aramaic diction and Gnostic dualism.

Undoubted traces of Aramaic syntax are not an argument against apostolic authorship of the fourth gospel, if the present Greek book is based on the work of the apostle John who, having emigrated to Ephesus, composed a work in Aramaic which was later rendered into Greek. Perhaps he did this himself, for he may have been alive until just before A.D. 100. Alternatively, the Aramaic original of the apostle may have been put into Greek by an Ephesian elder who added the last chapter and perhaps wrote the second and third epistles.

Turning from the Aramaic question we may now ask whether Jesus sometimes at least spoke Hebrew. Although there is little evidence,

* Moulton-Howard-Turner, *Grammar*, vol. III, p. 332.

THE OCCURRENCE OF THE GENITIVE ABSOLUTE

NEW TESTAMENT BOOKS (Gospels)				
Infancy Narrative (Matt.)	5/48	or one in	10	verses*
Non-Q (Matt.)	48/855	„ „	18	„
Matt.'s Special Source (M)	14/251	„ „	18	„ †
Markan sections of Matt.	29/540‡	„ „	19	„
St. Matthew	52/1068	„ „	20	„
St. Mark	30/661	„ „	22	„
St. Luke	43/1149	„ „	26	„
Non-Q (Luke)	34/943	„ „	28	„
Q (in Luke)	9/272§	„ „	30	„ ¶
	6/206‖	„ „	34	„ **
Q (in Matt.)	4/213	„ „	53	„ ††
St. John	12/878	„ „	73	„

NEW TESTAMENT BOOKS (Acts and Epistles)				
Acts 16–28	61/446	or one in	7	verses
III John	1/15	„ „	15	„
I Peter	6/105	„ „	17	„
Acts 1–15	29/560	„ „	19	„
II Peter	3/61	„ „	20	„
Hebrews	13/303	„ „	23	„
St. Paul (exc. Eph., Past.)	21/1609	„ „	77	„
St. Paul (incl. Pastorals)	21/2033	„ „	97	„

* $1^{18.20}$ $2^{1.13.19}$.

† 5^1 6^3 $9^{32.33}$ $17^{24.26}$ $18^{24.25}$ 20^8 $25^{5.10}$ 27^{19} $28^{11.13}$.

‡ Of these, thirteen are copied directly from Mark and sixteen are the original work of the evangelist (From Mark: $8^{16.28}$ 13^{21} $14^{15.23}$ 17^9 24^3 $26^{6.20.21.26.47}$ 27^{57}. Added to Mark: 8^1 $9^{10.18}$ 12^{46} $13^{6.19}$ 14^{32} $17^{14.22}$ 20^{29} $21^{10.23}$ 22^{41} 26^{60} $27^{1.17}$).

§ Based on Streeter's reconstruction in *The Four Gospels*.

‖ Based on Streeter's figures in the original Peake's *Commentary*.

¶ To those in note 7 add 3^{21} 12^{36} 19^{11}.

** 6^{48} $7^{6.24}$ 9^{57} $11^{14.29}$.

†† This includes 17^5 which agrees with Luke, although it is a Markan section. It must be from Q, or else it indicates that St. Luke knew Matthew. Undoubtedly Q are 8^5 11^7 16^2.

Septuagint* (arranged in ascending order of frequency)

(1) TRANSLATED BOOKS					
Ecclesiasticus	1/1406	or one in	1406	verses
Judges-Ruth	1/703	„	„	703	„
Joshua	1/657	„	„	657	„
Ezekiel	2/1273	„	„	636	„
Psalms	4/2534	„	„	633	„
I Chronicles	2/942	„	„	471	„
Isaiah	4/1290	„	„	322	„
II Chronicles	3/822	„	„	274	„
Numbers	5/1285	„	„	257	„
I Maccabees	4/924	„	„	231	„
Ecclesiastes	1/222	„	„	222	„
Minor Prophets	5/1049	„	„	210	„
Genesis	9/1532	„	„	170	„
Jeremiah	8/1343	„	„	168	„
III Kingdoms	6/856	„	„	143	„
Deuteronomy	7/957	„	„	137	„
Exodus	9/1173	„	„	130	„
Leviticus	7/859	„	„	123	„
IV Kingdoms	6/722	„	„	120	„
I Kingdoms	7/806	„	„	115	„
II Kingdoms	6/686	„	„	114	„
Proverbs	8/916	„	„	114	„
Job	13/1074	„	„	83	„

(2) PARAPHRASES					
Tobit	3/241	or one in	80	verses
Epistle of Jeremy	1/72	„	„	72	„
Daniel (LXX)	6/419	„	„	70	„
I Esdras	11/430	„	„	39	„

(3) FREE GREEK BOOKS					
Wisdom	13/439	or one in	34	verses
IV Maccabees	21/484	„	„	23	„
III Maccabees	27/228	„	„	8	„.
II Maccabees	80/555	„	„	7	„

* For the over-all figures I am dependent on Mr. A. W. Argyle's note in *Expos. Times*, LXIX, no. 9, June, 1958, p. 285.

the theory has been advanced and, by the fact that in the synagogue at Nazareth the scroll of Isaiah was handed to him and that he read a passage from it in a manner provoking admiration, one is probably justified in assuming that he was at least well enough versed in biblical Hebrew to read it fluently. All this rests on the probability that in a Galilean synagogue of the period the Law and the Prophets were still read in Hebrew. Even if that is a safe assumption, there was nevertheless an *oral* translation of the Law into Aramaic in Palestine as early as the time of Nehemiah and the written translation which soon followed may very well have been used in the synagogues of Galilee.

Supposing then that Jesus could read Hebrew, I wonder whether he could or did habitually speak it. I would go further. His Bible was not consistently, if at all, the Hebrew scriptures. On the cross he began to quote the twenty-second Psalm in an Aramaic version; the quotation was not originally in Hebrew, for there is no adequate reason why St. Mark or his source should have changed it to Aramaic, and the Aramaic form *Eloi* (no less than the Hebrew *Eli*) could have provoked the taunt of " Elijah " from a scornful crowd. Moreover, there are indications that he knew the scriptures in a Greek version, because Matt. 5[39 f.] (a possible quotation from Isai. 50[6]) appears in a different form from the Hebrew Bible which is known as the Massoretic text. Jesus is reported as saying, " Whosoever shall *smite* thee on the right cheek. . . ." The Septuagint version of Isaiah has, " I gave my cheeks to *smitings*," and Jesus may very well have this text in mind. If so, it was the Greek Bible which came to mind since the Hebrew text has the rather different idea, " I gave my cheeks to *them that plucked off the hair.*" From this evidence one would suppose that Jesus knew the Scriptures in Greek but not in Hebrew.

However, Dr. Birkeland has argued that Jesus regularly spoke in Hebrew ; that the sources of the gospel were written in Hebrew ; and that this was not even the current Mishnaic variety, but a dialect nearer to the classical language of the Bible and less subject to Aramaic influence.* Part of Birkeland's thesis is that a dialect like this was still in use among the lower classes of Palestine in Christian times. He proposed that the upper classes used Aramaic, while the learned classes understood both languages. The argument concerning Hebrew may well be sound as far as isolated country districts or communities, like Qumran, are concerned, but only if it was something rather less refined than classical Hebrew, and probably in Judaea rather than in Galilee.

St. Luke's description of St. Paul speaking to the mob in the Temple " in the Hebrew tongue " is not very significant. Aramaic was the language of the " Hebrew " people and St. Luke, St. John, and Josephus fall into this loose way of speaking ; in fact, some of the words they call

---

* H. Birkeland, *The Language of Jesus*, Oslo, 1954.

" Hebrew " are known to us as exclusively Aramaic. It would be dangerous to argue that the contemporary Hebrew had borrowed these words from Aramaic, since in the case of *Akeldama*, for instance, Hebrew already had a word meaning *blood* (viz. *dam*) and there would be no necessity to borrow the Aramaic *dema*.*

As long ago as 1891 T. K. Abbott argued effectively in favour of Greek as the dominical language, and one of his best submissions was that if Jesus regularly taught in Aramaic it is difficult to explain why St. Mark adopted the curious practice of reproducing only some, and not all, of his sayings in Aramaic. St. Mark gives no more than *talitha coum* 5⁴¹, *qorban* 7¹¹, *ephphatha* 7³⁴, *abba* 14³⁶, *eloi eloi lema sabachthani* 15³⁴. One would think that the evangelist's reason for reproducing this particular selection of transliterations is that, contrary to his usual way, Jesus spoke in Aramaic on these occasions. The reason why is not so clear, but on some of them he may have been addressing individuals whose sole language was Aramaic.

Improbable in the extreme is the contention that St. Mark is giving his readers a selection of Jesus's " words of power " with the aim of letting them hear what the Aramaic sounded like. Another speculation, hardly more worthy of attention, is that St. Mark normally translated all Jesus's Aramaic into corresponding Greek but that once or twice the Aramaic word slipped off the end of his pen by mistake and, thinking it too good to delete, he merely added the Greek equivalent.

Consideration has already been given to the alleged mistranslations, but on the opposite side there is evidence which may establish original Greek composition. In Luke 8¹⁵ Jesus uses a phrase which looks anything but Semitic : " in a beautiful and good heart." It is well known that " beautiful and good " (*kalos kāgathos*) is the traditional Greek phrase for a gentleman ; it has no parallel in either Hebrew or Aramaic. Moreover there is an alliteration (three k's) which is too good to be true if Jesus did not use the words *en kardiā kalē kai agathē*. There are other instances in the reported words of Jesus. There is the vigorous phrase, which seems original, in Matt. 21⁴¹ : *kakous kakōs* (" he will destroy those miserable men miserably "). There is the clever juxtaposition of *limoi* and *loimoi* (famines and pestilences) in Luke 21¹¹ which is less likely to be the creation of a translator than to be original. Again, *Petros* and *petra* are too ingenious for the ordinary translator (Matt. 16¹⁸ : Peter and rock), and we have not yet achieved it in any English version. Besides, it would have been pointless for early translators of the Lord's words to indulge in clever adornments, and interest in language for its own sake could not have been very high on their list of priorities.

* J. A. Emerton, in *The Journal of Theological Studies*, N.S., XII, Oct., 1961, p. 192.

If we may cite the Lord's words in the fourth gospel, there is further evidence against translation from Aramaic in his discourse with Nicodemus. " Except a man be born *again*, he cannot see the kingdom of God " (3³·⁷). The word " again " (*anōthen*) has a double meaning but, as Grotius remarked so very long ago, there is no equivalent in Hebrew and Aramaic which has the double meaning that *anōthen* has ; but Grotius went on from this to conclude that, as Jesus must have spoken to a rabbi in either Hebrew or Aramaic, there can only have been one meaning intended by his use of *anōthen*. This is to spoil the powerful point in the double meaning ; for " again " is the same word (*anōthen*) as is used for " from above." Supposing therefore that Jesus conversed with Nicodemus in Greek we are confronted with the truth that conversion is not only a *new* birth (being born *again*) but also a birth from God (being born *from above*). In spite of general reluctance to believe that Jesus would speak to a rabbi in Greek, it should be remembered that this occurred probably in Galilee and not in Jerusalem (see verse 22) ; and Nicodemus, whose name is thoroughly Greek, may have been a rabbi of a very liberal kind, probably a " Hellenist " like Stephen.

When he is discussing the allegory of the Vine, there is a pun which Bengel called " suavis rhythmus " and which really excludes the possibility of translation : first the verb *airei*, then the verb *kathairei*,* and no English version so much as attempts to reproduce the play on words. If there was such a play in Aramaic, it seems incredible that the evangelist or his sources were lucky enough to achieve the same in Greek. The best we can do in English is : " Every branch that beareth not fruit, he *removeth* ; and every branch that beareth fruit, he *reproveth*." But this has nothing of the brilliance of the Greek and in any case is not quite accurate, which goes to show how difficult it is to transfer paronomasiae from one language to another (John 15²).

It has been pleaded† that if Jesus spoke Greek it would be the Koine and therefore, because the language of the gospels is not actually the Koine but a " hybrid composed of Greek words and Aramaic syntax " (according to Mr. H. M. Draper), Jesus could not possibly have spoken Greek. Such an argument entirely fails to consider the hypothesis that the " hybrid " was a distinct type of Jewish Greek, which I would prefer to call biblical Greek, spoken by Jesus. We need not quarrel in the least with the statement that this Greek is not " good " Koine. But it is wrong to draw the conclusion that because Jesus's words are recorded in such a language he cannot actually have spoken it and so

---

* To read *arei* and *kathariei*, in accordance with the Old Latin and Vulgate versions, is to spoil the play on words.

† E.g. by Mr. H. M. Draper against Mr. A. W. Argyle, in *Expos. Times*, LXVII, no. 10, p. 317, July, 1956.

must have used Aramaic or Hebrew.   The hypothesis of biblical Greek as a spoken language must be seriously considered.

As early as 1949 I put forward my first suspicions that such a language was spoken.   " Even in the matter of possible oral sources in Aramaic the assumption that our Lord and the apostles spoke and wrote in Aramaic must not be too easily made.   Except in exclusively Jewish circles Greek was probably the regular language of Palestine, even though it were a kind of Jewish Greek."*

It is not inconceivable that, whatever the language of Jesus, it was influenced by all those spoken in Galilee at that time, viz. Hebrew, Aramaic, Greek, and perhaps Latin.†   It was biblical Greek, of a kind not very different from the Septuagint—a branch of the Koine, but very different from what we read in the Egyptian rubbish heaps or on the papyrus of more literate people.   Since 1949, intense study of vocabulary and syntax seem to me to establish that there was a distinguishable dialect of spoken and written Jewish Greek.   That is to say, the biblical language was more than a written product of those whose mother tongue was Semitic and who floundered in Greek because they knew so little of it that they must copy Semitic idioms as they penned it.   I am not the first to suggest that the Greek of the Old Testament was a language distinct from the main stream of the Koine, yet fully understood by Jews.‡   Perhaps, as Gehman suggests, those who used this dialect of Greek were bilingual ; it may have been a temporary phase in the history of the language, representing a period of transition for those Jews who were passing from a Semitic speaking to a Greek speaking stage, and coinciding with the New Testament period.   However, as works of a much later date, like the *Testament of Abraham*, exhibit exactly this kind of diction, I do not think it was merely transitional.   Certainly it was not artificial.   Biblical Greek is so powerful and fluent, it is difficult to believe that those who used it did not have at hand a language all ready for use.   This, I submit, was the normal language of Jesus, at least in Galilee—rather a separate dialect of Greek than a form of the Koine, and distinguishable as something parallel to classical, Hellenistic, Koine and Imperial Greek.

Such a view constitutes a reaction against the position of J. H. Moulton in the first two volumes of the grammatical trilogy, and of Deissmann and Thumb.   Some critics are sceptical about Jewish Greek because they observe that the " Semitisms " are also found in the Koine.

---

* *The Evangelical Quarterly*, XXI, no. 1, Jan., 1949, p. 44 : " Were the Gospels written in Greek or Aramaic ? "

† Although there is little evidence that our Lord ever spoke Latin, perhaps there is a slight trace of it in the saying, " Have salt (Latin *salem*) . . . and be at peace (Hebrew *shālôm*) " Mark 9⁵⁰.

‡ Dr. H. S. Gehman, in *Vetus Testamentum*, I, no. 2 ; III, no. 2 : and see my note in V, no. 2, pp. 208 ff., and Peake's *Commentary on the Bible*, Nelson, 1962, 577 c.

Anticipating the objection, C. F. Burney urged that " practically the whole of the new material upon which we base our knowledge of the Koine comes from Egypt, where there existed large colonies of Jews whose knowledge of Greek was undoubtedly influenced by the trans-lation-Greek of the LXX."* Egyptian Koine may in fact have been influenced by Semitic diction. Burney cited others who supported his thesis sixty years ago. " It is precarious to compare a literary docu-ment with a collection of personal and business letters, accounts, and other ephemeral writings ; slips in word-formation or in syntax which are to be expected in the latter, are phenomenal in the former, and if they find a place there, can only be attributed to lifelong habits of thought,"† and Swete raised the further question whether " the quasi-Semitic colloquialisms " of the Koine may not themselves be due to the influence of the many Jews living in the Nile Delta.

The question of Jewish influence on the Koine, raised by scholars like Redpath and Swete, has not yet been met. Dr. Moulton attempted an answer‡ along the lines that the Greek in the papyri does not differ from Greek in the vernacular inscriptions which have been found in widely scattered regions " and we cannot postulate in every quarter an influential Ghetto." Thus, a dozen examples of instrumental *en* came from Tebtunis in 1902, and Tebtunis was not a place which was likely to possess a considerable Jewish population. The point is taken, but there are too many other instances where a Hebrew idiom has obviously popularized and extended one which was already fairly familiar in Greek. The Greek Bible and the synagogues of the Dispersion had a great influence on the world of Hellenism, not solely in Egypt and not on Jews and proselytes exclusively. The Bible has everywhere in-fluenced thought and language, " for from early generations Moses has had in every city those who preach him, for he is read every sabbath in the synagogues."

Again, as one reflects upon those many strongly Semitic phrases in biblical Greek one must comment that there is no secular document known to us that is written consistently in this style. The phrases have come from the Hebrew and Aramaic languages, by some way or other ; Semitic and Greek idioms coincide in too many instances within the pages of one book. Certainly all languages tend to deveolp the same speech-forms, and Koine Greek advanced towards simpler forms of speech on the oriental pattern, but most of the Semitic phrases and idioms in biblical Greek and the Koine have no parallel in the dialects of ancient Greece, which makes it more probable that they have been

---

* C. F. Burney, *The Aramaic Origin of the Fourth Gospel*, Oxford, 1922, p. 4.
† H. B. Swete, *Apocalypse of St. John*, Macmillan, 2nd. ed., 1907, p. CXXIV, note 1.
‡ *Cambridge Biblical Essays*, ed. H. B. Swete, 1909, p. 468.

borrowed than that they developed within the Greek language itself. Such phrases and idioms are : the initial position of the verb in the sentence, the redundance of personal pronouns, prepositional phrases with the word " face," instrumental *en*, resumptive pronouns, " whether " introducing a question. Moreover, we have some fairly definite evidence of borrowing, at least at a later time, for the Hebrew comparison of adjectives by means of a Hebrew word meaning " from " is reproduced in modern Greek by a Greek word meaning " from."

The more important question was bound to follow. Does the phenomenon of biblical Greek arise from Semitic *documents* lying behind the Greek Old and New Testaments ? Are Semitic circumlocutions, like " he answered and said " or " he arose/went and did," deliberate imitations of biblical language by a Greek author who wished to produce a book with a biblical ring about it, or are they indications that a translator was actually rendering a Semitic original which lay before him ? No argument for translation will be convincing until many more examples of dittographs, mistranslations, and paronomasiae, are detected in the New Testament. Indeed, such evidence is very slight. We find no trace whatever of the literalism of the later parts of the Septuagint, much less anything like the barbarism of Aquila. There is not even a trace of the Hebrew infinitive absolute.* The authors are never averse from using *hupo* to express the passive idea, although Hebrew and Aramaic authors, and their translators, prefer to express the idea by means of the impersonal use of the 3rd. person plural in the *active* voice. In the early chapters of Acts there is a large use of Hebrew circumlocutions involving the face, hand, mouth, and name, but in itself the evidence is not strong enough to prove that the chapters are a direct translation and may indicate that their author was acquainted with the branch or dialect of the Koine which was employed by the Hellenistic Jews and proselytes, a dialect which naturally gave a large place within itself to Greek idioms which happened also to be well loved phrases in Hebrew or Aramaic ; it had also absorbed many familiar phrases of the Septuagint and exhibited the Jewish predilection for more concrete expressions and simpler speech.

The more closely I study this fascinating dialect, the more I am convinced that biblical Greek is conspicuously a method of symbolic presentation, like early Christian art within the same and later periods. Literary, no less than artistic, creative effort may be a reflection of an inspiring Spirit making himself articulate, but inability to think conceptually, or even to read, has never hindered the spread of either art or faith. It has often been compensated by a balancing appreciation of visual imagery. Artists use symbols, in words as well as in pictorial art

* Whether the literal rendering in Josh. 17[13]B or the adverbial rendering in Gen. 32[12], IV Kingdoms 5[11], or even the dative of a noun.

and music, for a symbol is the union of a material image with the transcendent supra-sensual—dare we say, " spiritual " ?—message which the image evokes.

The naturalism of contemporary pagan art had no more than a superficial influence on the early Christians, who reverted to the symbol as to the simplest and profoundest form of communication. Pictures of Mary never depicted the beauty of woman or the devotion of motherhood, but were symbols of the Mother of God. The earliest portraits of Christ made no pretence to naturalistic realism but were dogmatic in purpose. No portrait for about four centuries depicts him bearded, and he is endowed with a look of perpetual youthfulness. This may be Art in Chains, screwed down to dogma, and biblical Greek gives the same impression of Greek in chains. But neither form of art loses any vigour because it has shed conventional culture and forged its own primitive medium. Of course, symbols are never created *ex nihilo* and biblical Greek as well as Christian inconography adopted the conventional materials of the time. Biblical Greek is Greek. Having said that, there is so much difference from the contemporary language that we are justified in looking for some special nisus within it.

Recently critics have taken more notice of iconographic art and react against the assumption that the Renaissance liberated Byzantine art from the dominance of Christian dogma, and that the creators of icons, humble servants of the Church, had allowed their technique to be so rigorously circumscribed that it was no more than a handicraft. True, the artists—like biblical Greek writers—were innocent of any ambition to delight the senses and were devoted to inspiring worship and inculcating doctrine. Icons were produced by the hundred, and certainly by the sixth century their subject matter was stereotyped. The technique is described in a very much later Greek document entitled *Explanation of Painting*,* and known as the Painter's Manual of Mount Athos. The collection may go back originally to the eleventh century,† although it was often re-copied, revised, and extended ; a final edition was produced apparently in the early eighteenth century by Dionysius, a monk of Furna, who seems to have been guided by an icon-artist of the monastery, Manuel Panselinos, and who dedicated his work to " Mary Mother of God and ever Virgin." The monks of Mount Athos, being devoted to defending the Faith, preserved the traditional art of the holy icons.

The parallel between iconography and biblical Greek can be studied

---

* Ἑρμηνεία τῆς Ζωγραφικῆς. In 1839 the French savant, M. Didron, obtained the manuscript of this work from Mt. Athos and translated and published it as *Manuel d'Iconographie Chrétienne*, Paris, 1843.

† Not earlier than 16th. century, according to A. Papadopoulos Kerameus, *Denys de Fourna, Manuel d'Iconographie Chrétienne*, St. Petersburg, 1900.

in this treatise which, in each of its several books, deals with aspects of painting, such as the method of applying colour to the wooden panels, the correct kind of ground, and the application of the gilt which still shines through the candle smoke and other defacements of the years. Presentation of the artist's message was governed by elaborate rules concerning the treatment of the nose, eyes, lids and beards, but within these severe limits, Byzantine, Russian, Bulgarian and Serbian artists achieved a mysterious effect of flatness and abstraction which art critics and theologians now discuss with interest. Modern Greeks too* begin to value their heritage of iconography and are ridding their churches of nineteenth-century borrowings from the west.

St. Mark and the author of Revelation give every appearance of having worked in this way, from a text-book, and to have strange aberrations of style which horrify the reader who comes directly from secular Greek, and yet they are faithful to their own severely circum-scribed rules.† The simplicity is often breath-taking, the careless artistry uncannily matching the narrative and the graphic visual imagery of the two books. Even St. Luke's art is not really naturalistic when one examines it carefully, and St. Paul cares as little for this world's canons of literary taste as he does for the rest of its wisdom. We do see a slight departure from symbolical syntax in the more flexible and studied periods of the author to the Hebrews, but the naturalism is more apparent than real.

Scholars like Erasmus endeavoured to mould the Church's taste into a classical tradition, and the study of the New Testament Greek suffered accordingly as men began to look at it with secular eyes ; and yet the old symbolism in painting lived on in El Greco, the Greek who settled in Spain. His earliest pictures—before 1600—show the naturalistic influence in Venice, especially Tintoretto, and Raphael to a less degree, even as late as the Cleansing of the Temple with its Venetian back-ground. Nevertheless with St. Joseph and the Boy Christ iconography creeps in. Each figure is an image of grace, its gestures arranged with inner significance. The boy's upreaching hand speaks of trust which is continued directly into the devoted care of the guardian's hand. Passion in the angelic figures is indicated by their being placed upside

* The austere technique of the Byzantine tradition is well expressed in a recent publication by a modern Greek : C. Cavarnos, *Byzantine Sacred Art : Selected Writings of the Contemporary Greek Icon Painter, Fotius Kontoglous*, New York, 1957. Reference should also be made to Photius Kontoglou, *Explanation of Orthodox Iconography*, text in modern Greek, 2 vols., 1960.

† E.g. " Phrases which occur for the first time without the art. have the art. prefixed on their recurrence " : R. H. Charles, *Revelation*, I.C.C., T. & T. Clark, 1920, vol. I, p. cxx. For St. Mark, see the stimulating work of G. D. Kilpatrick, especially articles in *The Bible Translator*, vol. VII, 1956, " Some Notes on Marcan Usage."

down. The whole symbol is evocative of veneration for the counter-Reformation cult of St. Joseph. Moreover, there is El Greco's unity of colour and texture, which is part of the genius of the *maniera bizantina.*

Every word of this is true of New Testament Greek, if we transfer the underlying image from visual to mental material. There is unity of verbal colour and texture ; there is abstraction, and flagrant disregard of literary virtuosity, breaches of accepted rules of syntax which critics denounce as anacoloutha, and yet the total effect of this barbarism, like barbaric Gothicism, is to evoke a sense of the holy and to point the reader beyond. Especially is this so in that book which closes the canon and which is, I think, the most characteristic example of this kind of Greek,* the chief glory of this hieratic tongue. The Book of Revelation is the sublimest icon of them all.

---

* E.g. *apo* is used with the nominative case (1^4), which is far worse than our saying " From you and I."   There are expressions like, " The he-was " (1^4), and solecistic sense-constructions like, " A reed was given to me, saying " (11^1). There are frequent breaches of concord in gender, number, and case, and participles often take the place of finite verbs. Such characteristics in Revelation distinguish the author only in intensity from other biblical Greek authors, and not in quality. I cannot agree with Dr. Charles that " the linguistic character of the Apocalypse is absolutely unique." Op. cit., vol. I, p. cxliii.

INDEX OF NEW TESTAMENT PASSAGES

INDEX OF AUTHORS AND SUBJECTS

INDEX OF GREEK, LATIN, AND
SEMITIC WORDS